PHANTOM POLITICS

Campaigning in California

MARY ELLEN LEARY

PUBLIC AFFAIRS PRESS • WASHINGTON, D.C.

CONTENTS

ELUSIVE CANDIDATES

When Californians went to the polls on November 5, 1974 and elected Democrat Edmund G. (Jerry) Brown as their governor, they knew remarkably little about him. They did know that he was the son of former Governor Edmund G. Brown, Sr., that he served as Secretary of State and that he was a leader in the so-called political-reform movement. They knew little about the man as a person or about the policies he would promulgate as governor.

In effect, Californians elected a phantom governor in 1974. There were two prime reasons for this. First, Brown started the campaign with a huge lead in the polls, and he schemed to stay ahead by making his contest with Repubican Houston I. Flournoy as dull as possible. Second, the prime communications medium, television, generally neglected to give viewers more than superficial glances at the campaign.

Something is critically wrong with our political system if the nation's largest state can elect its top leader without adequate public exposure of the candidate or discussion of public issues. None of the recent reforms in the conflict-of-interest, public-disclosure and campaign-contribution fields have solved the problem at the heart of the political process—communication between citizens and would-be leaders.

There are various theories for the recent public disaffection with the political system in America. There can be no challenging the statistics that show a substantial drop-off in the number of citizens who go to the polls. Through a close examination of one California election, the study on which this book is based illustrates one of the causes: because of conscious decisions by the broadcasting industry, voters are not given sufficient exposure to the political process to stimulate interest in voting. Yet the disaffection with politics produced by Watergate should make it all the more important that campaigns at all levels of government be given the widest public exposure.

This book examines the communications process during the 1974 gubernatorial election which thrust Jerry Brown into the national spotlight. In studying that election, a great deal was learned about this new star in political space, especially his mastery of the communications media. This book does not focus on Jerry Brown the candidate and man, but rather on the method by which modern elections are won and lost in this era of mass communications.

The California experience may not apply to all states and all elections. But throughout America there has been a decline in old-fashioned, person-to-person elections and a new emphasis on the packaging of candidates through television. In large states it is no longer possible for there to be much direct contact between candidates and voters. Newspapers, radio, and television must act as the intermediaries, and pollsters tell us that about two-thirds of the American people depend on television for most of their news.

Californians have been awarded some sort of special status by the rest of the country. They are supposed to be different, to be the outriders for the nation in lifestyle, politics, communications, just about everything. Whether that reputation is deserved can be debated, but California clearly is different politically. Before other states, it idealized non-partisanship and encouraged the cult of personality. This produced the Progressive Movement of the Hiram Johnson era and a tradition of clean, machine-free government. California introduced professional campaign managers and applied the tricks of the advertising world to politics. More than most states, California has been receptive to television because the motion picture industry, centered in Hollywood, made it susceptible to communication by film—by image rather than by substance.

California is a state of political extremes, and that accounts for its reputation as a forecaster of national trends. Its politicians are not fundamentally different from those elsewhere. They are driven by the same super-ego that drives politicians everywhere. Nonetheless, as Carey McWilliams wrote in his insightful 1949 book, *California—The Great Exception:* "Since California was admitted to the Union, the nation has been vaguely aware of something 'different' and 'peculiar' about the politics of the state."

There are few steadying forces in California, and its population is extraordinarily mobile, moving restlessly from community to community wherever opportunity promises. Above all, Californians are people who seek change and are willing to experiment. Ahead of other states, California exhibited the surge of conservatism that brought Ronald Reagan into the governor's office and made campus protest and welfare mothers the core of political rhetoric. Now, California is in the midst of yet more change, some of it brought on by the climate of the Brown Administration but much of it the product of the media.

California, at the time of this study, had a population of about 21 million, with nearly 14 million of voting age, 59 percent of them living in the four major urbanized areas of Los Angeles, San Francisco, San Diego, and Sacramento.

Reagan's retirement in 1974 brought the state to a political watershed. There was no incumbent in the contest for the governorship, and neither party had developed a consensus candidate. This was the first wide open race for governor since 1958, inviting 29 candidates in the primary. Out of the pack came Jerry Brown, who had built a huge early lead because his name was well known. (His father, Edmund G. Brown, Sr., had defeated U. S. Senator William F. Knowland for the governorship in 1958 and then defeated Richard Nixon in 1962.)

At first the Republican primary looked good for Lt. Gov. Ed Reinecke. But he was indicted on perjury charges stemming from his testimony before a United State Senate committee investigating the ITT controversy, clearing the way for State Controller Houston Flournoy to win the primary with relative ease.

As it turned out, Brown won the election in a close vote. Nevertheless, Californians had little knowledge of what kind of young man they had put in charge of their government. Brown had chosen to be a somewhat invisible candidate. The media, especially television and radio, accommodated him by pronouncing the campaign dull and giving it only perfunctory coverage. Once in office, the media lavished attention on him, saturating newspapers and the air with revelations about his style and personality, delighting in his witticisms, reveling in his idiosyncracies. Invested with power, he became immensely interesting and within 15 months was a candidate for the Democratic nomination for President. His choice of appointees, his fiscal conservatism, his development of a farm-labor compromise, his criticism of university administrators, and above all his Spartan lifestyle have become lively news in California and across the country. What other political figure drives a modest Plymouth, sleeps on a mattress on the floor, and eschews the Governor's mansion for a $250-a-month flat across the street from the Capitol? How can it be that the election events could be considered so dull by the same media that since have found Brown so alluring?

The answer reveals some immense gaps in the communication system, which is the core of the modern election. Why did not the public know what kind of man it was electing? Did the candidates fail to transmit their character and ideologies to the voters? Or did the news media ignore their responsibility to delineate the differences in personality and policy between Brown and his Republican opponent, Houston Flournoy? A detailed examination of the interaction between the media and the candidates in the 1974 campaign provides answers to these questions.

Selected for the study from the four major metropolitan areas were four newspapers, each considered the most influential in its circulation range; six television stations considered strong in their market areas, chosen to represent audience size, a range of broadcast styles, owned-and-operated stations and independents; and five radio stations similarly chosen.

The newspapers were: *The Sacramento Bee, The Los Angeles Times, The San Francisco Chronicle,* and *The San Diego Union.*

The television stations were: Los Angeles: KNBC (Channel 4) and KTLA (Channel 5); San Francisco: KGO-TV (Channel 7); San Diego: KGTV (Channel 10) and KFMB-TV (Channel 8); Sacramento: KCRA-TV (Channel 3).

The radio stations were: Los Angeles: KFWB (Westinghouse affiliate) and KABC (ABC network); San Francisco: KCBS (CBS network) and KSAN (independent); Sacramento: KRAK (independent).

Eight candidates were selected for detailed study, six Democrats and two Republicans:

Democrats: Joseph L. Alioto, 58, successful antitrust lawyer and two-term mayor of San Francisco; Edmund G. Brown Jr., 37, California Secretary of State, son of California's 1958-66 governor, Edmund G. (Pat) Brown Sr.; Bob Moretti, 38, for ten years a legislator from Los Angeles and four years Speaker of the Assembly; William Matson Roth, 57, San Francisco business executive, former trade negotiator in the Kennedy Administration, University of California regent, making his first bid for elective office; Jerome R. Waldie, 48, elected to the Legislature in 1958 five years after law school, elected to Congress in 1966 from a district east of San Francisco, seeking statewide office for the first time; Baxter Ward, 54, for 17 years a Los Angeles television reporter elected in 1972 to the County Board of Supervisors.

Republicans: Houston I. Flournoy, 44, professor of political science, six years a member of the legislature and twice elected State Controller; Ed Reinecke, 49, businessman, three times elected Representative from southern California, appointed Lieutenant Governor by Governor Reagan in 1969 to fill a vacancy, and elected in 1970.

At the outset, it was recognized that television was especially important. It was the most omnipresent and influential of the media and was expected to be a pacesetter, more esteemed by the candidates than either radio or newspapers.

Television dominates political communication, imposes its standards, its expectations, its judgment, and even its commercial price and time patterns on the political process. It influences other media along the way and has a profound effect on the esteem with which self-government is currently regarded. This election happened to illustrate a direction in which the election process is moving all across the country. The "media campaign" raises very serious questions.

Television may not be solely to blame for the significant erosion of the political process. This study indicates clearly, however, that the attitude of broadcasters is a major part of the problem. The 1974 gubernatorial contest, probably the most media-oriented in California history, drew the smallest turnout among recent statewide elections. This book spells out how a campaign involving a candidate as unique as Jerry Brown could be rejected as dull and how he was allowed to run as a phantom candidate.

2

MANIPULATING THE MEDIA

In the spring of 1974 Jerry Brown was the leader among 18 contenders for the Democratic gubernatorial nomination and Bob Moretti was the challenger pressing him the hardest. The scene was the state Capitol press conference room. Both Brown and Moretti had scheduled news conferences, one after the other. Moretti held his session first with five television cameras and 30 reporters. When he finished, reporters egged Moretti into staying for a face-to-face encounter with Brown.

Moretti didn't need much urging. He had been seeking "debates" with the leading candidate for a long time, as any runner-up does with a rival. He had finally achieved one, two days earlier. That encounter, at a college campus in Fresno, far from the major metropolitan regions of California, had been covered by the press, but it had been considered too polite. "A powder puff affair," one television reporter called it. "Dull," another said. "A Forgettable Event," said *The Sacramento Bee* headline. Clearly the Fresno meeting had not conformed to what the media wanted—fireworks. Appetites unsated, reporters now pressed for a better show. It is notable that one newspaper, *The Los Angeles Times,* considered the Fresno discussion a meaningful, if polite, exchange. It had, *The Times'* story said, revealed clear differences in style and in approach to government." Carl Ingram, United Press International bureau chief at the capital, considered it a thoughtful, reasoned discussion, "the highlight of the primary." But such subtleties lacked appeal to most of the media. Television reportage of the Fresno event was sparse. KNBC in Los Angeles carried so brief an excerpt, some 20 seconds, that Moretti's campaign manager, John FitzRandolph, said: "We laughed. It was like it never happened. We tried to make this a decent exchange. We wanted a real comparison between the two men. One TV commentator joked because it was gentlemanly."

The media hankered for an out-and-out confrontation that would stir the emotions. So when paths of the two men crossed only two days after the disappointing initial "debate," reporters fell in with Moretti's effort to create a head-on conflict that would put Brown to the test.

Brown stalled a bit, confounded at finding his opponent still on the scene twenty minutes later, when he had concluded his prepared criticism of lobby spending in the legislature. Moretti's own session had consisted largely of a demand for more debates, and to illustrate his point, an empty chair shared the platform with him, a fragile gold and velvet affair bearing a sign with Brown's name, which Brown, when he took the platform, didn't notice. Reporters listened through Brown's formal remarks with hardly a pencil moving or camera recording. Then the reporters called out their demand.

"Have a debate now," they shouted. "Talk out your differences. Where *do* you differ?" "Talk on the issues." "Let's have your debate."

Trapped, Brown was hesitant and clearly nervous. He could either walk away, ducking a public discussion with Moretti or he could take the challenge. "Come out fighting," he invited Moretti, and the two took the platform to dispute who had experienced poverty in life or which better knew "the real world." Moretti, a family man, jibed at Brown, a bachelor, for never having had "to struggle," and Brown's rejoinder was that he "struggled" as much as anybody and had "identified myself with those people whose struggles are even greater than yours or mine, marching along dusty highways with Cesar Chavez."

At another point, when Brown referred to the "inherently corrupting" influence of lobbyists upon the legislature, Moretti rejoined, "You must be a man of very little security if you think that because somebody buys you dinner he owns you." But Brown had just made the point that lobbyists in California were then spending more than $10 million a year to "influence" lawmakers with drinks, dinners and gifts, "a spending spree that has reached crisis proportions," an "unnecessary political payola." Moretti, far more hot-temperered, charged Brown was "conning" people, trying to persuade them "that you're the only holy man around here." They flailed at each other, Brown red-faced with anger but cooler in his comments. The scene made for lively finger-shaking pictures on television and page one in newspapers throughout the state.

This was virtually the only time during the entire 1974 campaign that the press caught Brown in a situation he did not dominate.

More than that, it was one of the rare occasions when print reporters created the agenda. For what most marked this campaign was the dominance of television as the means of communication between candidate and voter, a dominance that distorted much of the election process, diminished rather than enlarged the extent of political reporting, reduced the access of candidates to the public, and altered the messages they could convey. The campaign illustrated the reliance of the American political system upon television, the limitations of that medium, and its susceptibility to manipulation.

Jerry Brown won the election. Name recognition had made him the clear leader from the start.

In the climate of 1974 there were special bulwarks for Jerry Brown's bid for higher office. As Secretary of State for four years, the sole Democrat to have gained statewide office in 1970 when Republican Governor Ronald Reagan won re-election, Brown had championed purity-of-election laws and had decried the influence of money on politics long before Watergate made these issues significant to the public. In addition, Brown triumphed by adroit accommodation to the broadcast media. This made it possible for him to get elected while remaining an elusive political figure.

He fashioned his campaign around the reality that television and radio are the major news conveyors and that television and radio in California were indifferent to politics. He was able to manage that indifference to his own advantage while other candidates wasted their energies in largely futile efforts to provoke the broadcast media into taking notice.

A curious paradox became evident in Brown's approach to politics. He seemed open with the public, accessible to the media, insistent that government be responsive to under-represented interests such as the poor, the minorities and, indeed, the middle-class taxpayer. But his discussion of specific issues was usually couched in cryptic catchwords or elusive generalities. This paradox was forcefully demonstrated when it came to debates in the fall. Brown expressed an ideal four years earlier in a formal proposal to the Federal Communications Commission advocating the establishment of "free time" in all television stations for major political contests, to guarantee candidates access to the voting public through this medium, so they need not be totally dependent on news programs of the stations' devising, or the stations' public service opportunities, or on advertising. Brown renewed this proposal in 1974, asking for a scattered allotment of free, 2½-minute portions of time for candidates in prime evening time.

Yet when the prospect of debates arose, Brown's conduct was characterized by evasion of rivals in the primary and by unprecedented limits on televising debates in general. A candidate enjoying an advantage normally is reluctant to share the platform with rivals, but this took a new form in the California race. Brown and Republican Houston I. Flournoy came to a most remarkable "agreement" that insured appearances together and put limits on media expenditures but that also insured minimal broadcast attention. It purported to specify exactly how media might be "permitted" to cover their debates. This extraordinary pact was drawn up by the candidates' lawyers and provided a "referee" armed with the power of subpoena, a power obviously derived out of thin air. Unquestionably, such a document presuming to restrict the free exercise of news coverage represents an extreme for candidate dominance of an American campaign. The most astonishing part of the scheme is that it worked.

One hears much criticism about "news management" by the media. This was an exercise in "news management" by candidates. It became a device by which Brown could advantageously reject all unplanned encounters with his opponent. It was designed to prevent any recurrence of such an unseemly confrontation as that with Moretti in the Capitol.

In the Brown-Flournoy plan there were to be six debates, more than had previously been scheduled in a California gubernatorial campaign, but all reproduction of the first was forbidden, and four of the five other encounters might be shown in full by television only within a single area and only on a single designated station. In all cases but the final debate on November 2, immediately before the election, on KNBC in Los Angeles and an earlier one in San Francisco, these showings occurred mostly on public broadcasting stations outside major population centers.

Only one showing was to be statewide and that on the public stations. Radio reproduction was prohibited. Even the duration of the television news coverage itself was defined. News reports, the agreement said, might be no more than "normal news coverage." This meant two minutes or less.

The agreement illustrates the course a campaign can take when standards of news values are tailored to broadcast interests. The remarkable element was not the proscription of coverage by candidates but the willingness of television and radio to abide by the limitations. Broadcasters were not merely docile in complying with the rules but virtually complicit in determining that debates between the two major candidates should be given only the most limited television airing.

The two candidates, each for his own purpose, cut off public access to their joint campaign appearances, and the only protest was raised by a 10-watt university campus FM radio station.

Newspapers duly reported the unusual agreement. They reported its provisions in general, and one or two columnists remarked upon the advantage it gave Brown by limiting the audience before which he might be challenged. Indeed, the indifference of the print media disclosed the myopic self-interest of newspapers as clearly as the agreement disclosed the shortsightedness of television and radio news directors. Despite a frequently voiced lament among California editors and reporters that the public leans more on television for news these days than on the printed word, and despite almost universal concurrence among members of the press that television is the instrument of communication with the most impact on elections, newsmen on California newspapers saw no reason to protest limitations that touched only broadcast freedom, not print freedom. Clearly newspapers still see television as a rival, not a colleague component in a total communication system.

Why did broadcasters obligingly honor the agreement? The telling point is that they welcomed it. Scant news shots, one minute, two minutes excerpted from the encounters, they filmed. Not more. The agreement was an escape hatch for television. It released the stations from devoting time, otherwise needed for game shows, soap operas or situation comedies, to what two men seeking to lead the largest state in the Union had to say when confronting each other.

The maneuver was viewed by many in the media as an amusing and unimportant game between candidates. Nobody, it was assumed, wanted to sit a half hour or an hour listening to the candidates, anyway. Most recognized that it suited Brown's desire to campaign with minimum, not maximum, television coverage, but nobody was exercised. The media had successfully conveyed the idea that politics in 1974 was intolerably dull.

Each of the candidates, Brown and Flournoy, got what he wanted from the bargain they struck. What Brown said he wanted most of all was a ceiling on advertising spending. His campaign strategists, wary of a nonpartisan Flournoy image discovered through polling, feared Republican financial capacity to mount a television advertising campaign that would far exceed what Democratic funding might provide. What Flournoy wanted was all the opportunity he could get to appear before the public on the same stage with Brown. He was confident this would work to his advantage. He wanted the joint appearances not just the week before the election but all through a developing campaign. This had become an accepted mode since the Kennedy-Nixon encounter by which a challenger sought parity with the candidate who was well in the lead. But it is also a situation the print media favor because it encourages lively conflict and interesting political stories. Flournoy desperately wanted to pin Brown to such open encounters. When it turned out that all he could get were six engagements, and these, barring only the last, on minor stations with small audiences, he accepted the agreement but made it clear he would like to see it broken. Several times he urged additional appearances. But having committed himself to the agreement, Flournoy did not—could not—break it himself.

This was in many ways an unusual campaign. It was the first non-incumbent race for governor in California since 1958, when U. S. Senator William F. Knowland and then-Attorney General Edmund G. Brown Sr., battled each other. Of 29 primary candidates, 18 were vying for the Democratic nomination; six for the Republican. Four sought the Peace and Freedom Party designation. One was American Independent.

The field included a number of major state officeholders. Brown was Secretary of State; Moretti was Speaker of the Assembly, the larger house of the Legislature; Flournoy was State Controller. The man initially favored for the Republican nomination was Lieutenant Governor Ed Reinecke, Governor Ronald Reagan's selection. But some novices were also competing. For Republicans, the period of the primary through the spring of 1974 was overshadowed by the catastrophe in Washington that also engulfed Reinecke. On April 3 he was indicted by the Watergate Grand Jury on the allegation he had lied as to when he talked with U. S. Attorney General John Mitchell about Republican National Party convention plans for 1972. The indictment, which he contested until his midsummer trial, led to his conviction and long sparring over the ultimate sentence. It led also to his defeat in the primary and to Flournoy's victory. (Reinecke's conviction was overturned in December, 1975, by the U. S. Court of Appeals, which held that the Senate Judiciary Committee had failed to publish its quorum rules in The Congressional Record and thus was not a "competent tribunal.")

Among Democrats, Brown had the clearest identification although he was closely followed in the early polls by San Francisco's energetic Mayor, Joseph L. Alioto, favored by labor and by many middle-of-the-road Democrats, and by Moretti. Trailing were Jerome Waldie, a Northern California congressman; William Matson Roth, a San Francisco businessman who had held a key foreign trade post in the John F. Kennedy Administration; Herbert Hafif, former head of the California Trial Lawyers Association; Baxter Ward, a former television newsman recently elected Los Angeles county supervisor. The line stretched to lesser-known hopefuls.

The media and most of the candidates wanted debates as a way of putting the contest into focus and injecting excitement into it. The difficulty arose in persuading the front-runner to join the confrontation.

The political air was full of debate about debates. Waldie and Hafif, decided trailers in the polls, staged a debate of their own at a university campus. Brown countered with his own invitation to debate, but it contained a condition dooming it—that all 18 Democrats show up at the same time and that television cover the debate. Television declined to undertake the Armageddon. Television news editors simply had no idea of how to cope with a field of 18 Democrats and six Republicans, let alone the minor party candidates. Television was indifferent to the whole campaign. As to debates, the stations considered the two or three candidates who topped the opinion polls the only ones suitable to air. The only suitable time, broadcast news editors thought, was immediately before Election Day when public interest was at peak. That date, most candidates agreed, was too late to have an effect on the race.

Under Federal Communications Commission rules, debate opportunities must be offered to all seeking the same office. Some stations in major areas tried a catch-all interview program to which they issued blanket invitations to all gubernatorial hopefuls. No major candidates responded, but the two or three such programs drew some of the odd-ball candidates, one of whom appeared on a Los Angeles TV interview program with a paper bag over his head and another who sang her platform. The FCC does permit bona fide news programs to present selected candidates for an office without requiring that all appear, and two television stations, KOVR in Sacramento and KNBC in Los Angeles, had regular interview periods that were suitable for such presentations.

At KNBC a Saturday half-hour news conference was expanded to an hour for June 1, and to this, the station invited Brown, Alioto, and Moretti. Discussion about the program format dragged on though May, with Brown refusing any confrontation and insisting on a side-by-side sequence of interviews with station reporters. The station was not reluctant to accept this formula. Legal problems might arise by proffering any valid "debate." Candidate William Matson Roth protested his omission, and candidate Hafif brought a formal, but futile, complaint to the FCC charging that candidate participation in developing the program format proved this was not a genuine news program. Considerable interest arose out of the Roth protest, as will be shown. But the station went through with its presentation using the Brown format, and this Los Angeles program the Saturday before election constituted the only time in the primary Brown appeared with the two men who ran closest behind him.

The second station willing to air the leading candidates was KOVR in Sacramento, which thought it had a three-way encounter arranged for a regular Sunday public affairs program with a panel of reporter-questioners. It turned out to be very difficult to pin Brown down on a taping time. At one point he insisted his only available time would be Sunday morning. This would mean overtime for camera crews. When the event finally occurred a week before the election, Brown did not appear. The debate took place between Alioto and Moretti.

It was such stalling that drove the news reporters to pursue Brown so hotly, pressing for direct confrontations. And it was this evasiveness through the primary that led Flournoy to demand commitments in writing to joint appearances in the fall campaign and persuaded him to settle for what he could get.

Whatever contribution Brown's tactics of staying out of sight and out of combat made to a diffuse quality in the primary, another equally significant contribution was television's failure to give the campaign coverage in its news shows and its rejection of early debates. Bob Squier, Moretti's media consultant from Washington, D.C., said: "We expected we could count on solid debates. We looked for a substantial confrontation with Brown on television in which Moretti's superior knowledge about state affairs would be evidenced. Beame had debates in New York—six in one week. This format is liked and used elsewhere in the country. We expected it in California. But the fact is the KNBC appearance was the only thing like a valid debate. No other stations would have them."

When television bowed out, the newspapers urged the top Democratic contenders to meet without a programmed debate, and that was how the Fresno encounter between Brown and Moretti occurred. Vic Fazio, Moretti's northern California chairman, explained: "Ken Reich of *The Los Angeles Times* basically forced the debate in Fresno. He told Brown's campaign manager Tom Quinn that he was going to write a story and really blast him. . . . They are caught on the horns of a dilemma. Do they hang tight and refuse to go along with the media, and take the criticism, or do they capitulate and see if they can hold their own?" The decision was to capitulate, but not unconditionally: the debate was set for Fresno, as remote a meeting place as was feasible.

It was common to hear that debates are too dull for commercial television, but after the Brown-Flournoy campaign started there were several instances of stations wanting to air these appearances and being "forbidden" by the agreement. In San Diego, KGTV offered one hour in prime time for the candidates to meet, emphasizing that this, the second largest city in the state, was outside range of any of the scheduled broadcast events, except by public broadcasting. Sorry, said Brown's staff, we are bound by the agreement. We're for it, said Flournoy's staff, if you can get Brown's consent.

One Sacramento station, KXTV, filmed the first engagement at the Sacramento Press Club, toying with the idea of running it in full that night and flouting the restriction. Their request for permission had been refused.

Flournoy's staff fully expected some station would try to break the embargo, and they furtively obtained a copy of the videotape of the first debate, just in case they could figure out how to smuggle it safely to some interested station. No one asked.

"The assumption had been," Quinn said, "that television was passive. And that it is afraid of violating any regulations. We felt they'd be afraid of violating the agreement, if you want to call them 'violations.' "

On one occasion, a debate was scheduled at the University of California campus in Irvine. Students who operated the campus FM radio station asked permission to carry that debate to its modest audience. Peremptory rejection from Brown. Of course not! Forbidden by the agreement. The students were tempted to run it anyway, but a university lawyer clamped down.

"What could we do to them, shoot 'em?" chuckled Brown campaign manager Tom Quinn much later.

But the threat embodied in the otherwise ludicrous episode was political. And it was real. It had implications beyond any campaign spoof. University administrators had to weigh the trifling student bravado against the possibility of irritating a man likely to be the next governor, in a position to blue-pencil university budgets. In California there were no more touchy political relations in 1974 than between university and governor.

The political effect of the debate limitation was felt, too, in public television. Its stations wanted to carry all six debates in full. It seemed appropriate to public television's mission. Through the Association of California Public Broadcasting Stations, they proposed such rebroadcast in letters to Brown. Brown refused permission. The stations pondered running them anyway. They decided against it. The reason: public television was seeking state funding. Approved by the legislature, the budget item had been stricken by Governor Reagan. Should these broadcasters risk ruffling the feelings of a man likely to be asked to sign their bill? The safest decision was not to upset him, so public broadcasting did not run the debates.

Miniscule as this Brown-Flournoy debate issue may seem, there are alarming implications in the influence that candidates have shown can be imposed on the broadcast media, reaching even to a university campus and a public broadcasting system.

The thoughtful observer of government, concerned with making the democratic system work in the context of modern communication technology, will seek ways to enlarge television access to the candidate, ways to provide voters with more opportunities to appraise rivals under as many conditions as possible—debates, interviews, news conferences, public question-and-answer sessions, speeches. Television time will be sought for the candidate to offer his uninterrupted message. This Brown did in his petition to the FCC.

On the other hand, the candidate who enjoys a lead will use the easy access to the broadcast media that his celebrity status provides for frequent, if inconsequential, name reinforcement, will employ crisp, catchy slogans suitable to the fleeting interest span of television; and will avoid specifics that might define a position or alienate a voter bloc. He will answer questions with brevity. He will provide the activity cameras need, and he will endure the media attention to "image" factors such as the style of his attire, the length of his hair, his taste in food, in music or in literature. This was the Brown campaign.

The Brown petition provided the paradox of the campaign. Debate restrictions advanced his cause, primarily because they meshed with the apathy television exhibited toward politics. But Brown's FCC petition argued strongly for more public viewing through commercial television "free time." Although it was given scant attention by the press, the Brown proposal was well received in political circles. Flournoy's campaign manager, Doug Kranwinkle, strongly supported it. Many of the advertising people most involved in 30-second spot creations were insistent upon some access to television time for political candidates outside the limited advertising format, and they cheered Brown's petition. What happened to Brown's petition? Nothing. "Dropped into a vacuum," said his campaign manager, Quinn.

The contradiction between Brown's pragmatism as a candidate and his previous contention to the FCC illustrates some of the complexities that television has interjected into the political process. Media objectives run counter to political objectives and often counter to public interest. They often deflect what the candidate seeks to project and what the public may have an opportunity to receive. Media interests can intrude to such an extent they subvert the public interest.

Even as a one-state situation tempered by the Watergate climate and some peculiarities of party and public mood, the 1974 California election poses national policy questions, especially concerning television licensing and the public interest in political campaigns. It provokes questions on the direction and role of radio and newspapers. Most of all, an examination of this election affords the public a chance for a rigorous evaluation of the modern election system. The California experience proves the need for a far more open process, a more vital and informed media role, and some creative way to bring the voters back into a closer participation in politics.

3

CHASING THE MEDIA

Congressman Jerome Waldie stepped out of his car at the Mexican border in August 1973 and started north on foot in a pledge to "walk the state." His first step signaled the start of the campaign to choose a California governor 15 months later. The energetic Representative from the San Francisco Bay Area, little known in the southern end of the state, set out to cover 1,000 miles of California, his hand reaching out to greet each person he encountered. "My name is Waldie. I hope you'll vote for me for governor." This arduous hike was the most intensive encounter between candidate and voter of the entire campaign.

"I love this," Waldie said. "In all my years of politics, I've done what politicians do—talk to people in the power centers. This is different. I see people who have never seen a politician in their lives. Literally. Most are delighted. . . . This is a more honest and direct communication than the voter ever gets—a more honest communication than the TV screen brings him, with a candidate reading something someone wrote for him and which he rehearsed."

But Waldie didn't make that walk to meet people; he made it to attract the media. In a state with 21 million inhabitants, 13.5 million eligible voters and 9.9 million registered voters in 1974 (6.3 million actually voted), personal contact with 10,000 people is a substantial attainment. Yet, in a state so large, individual encounters are inconsequential. The only useful means of communication is through the mass media. Waldie knew this, and the "walk" was his way of getting television attention, without the cost of setting up formal events. It brought him into successive parts of the state in a deliberately unassuming style. In such a context he could (and did) command attention from local newspapers, radio and television. He left in his wake a ripple of stories and pictures (some of the most engaging showing him rubbing tired feet). The publicity may not have been spectacular, but for the brief passage through town, Waldie was news. To Waldie's campaign it was important that the news presented him as a modest human being, not as a lofty official. Most important, the venture cost very little.

The attention he drew did not happen by chance. Waldie aides were advancemen for each day's journey. "You don't just go out and walk," he explained. "It's a major logistical operation. You have five or six people working full time in preparation." Local newspapers were

notified as to just when and where he would be. Television was alerted
to his arrival at a busy corner where he could be seen chatting with
townspeople. Timing was critical. His appearance had to be scheduled
early enough in the day to allow for a film clip on the local station's
evening broadcast. Local radio talk-shows were also alerted so that
Waldie could telephone at a designated time for a taping or a live
broadcast. To enliven such radio programs, Waldie made a habit of
discussing remarks he picked up en route. The candidate's walk
through town seemed so casual and easy. And it was among the least
contrived and the least stage-managed of all the major gubernatorial
campaign efforts in California that year. But even this event, it should
be noted, was plotted and purposely mounted to attract media attention.

California's election demonstrated with surprising clarity the extent
to which modern elections consist of encounters between candidates
and news media. The critical dynamics of the election process arise
not out of the engagement between a candidate and the voters, nor
out of rivalry between candidates, but between candidates and the press,
radio, and television. Rivals for office are not so much bent upon
besting one another as in battling for command of the media.

The media are bent toward a different goal—news. This often
engenders conflict. The candidate is persuaded that he and his undertaking are newsworthy; the reporter assigned to cover the race, has a
quite different notion of news.

A politician's pursuit of the media rarely gets reported. News
stories maintain the fiction that the heart of a contest is the interaction
between rival candidates, which is attained through exaggerated emphasis
on conflict. This campaign disclosed, however, that each candidate
was far busier projecting himself positively than countering his rival.
The chief rivalry was for publicity through the media. In the primary
election, teeming with candidates, the competition for attention was
so lively and complaints about inadequate coverage so persistent that
media pursuit itself became a news story.

Newspapers, radio and television were courted assiduously. Television chiefly determined the course of the campaign, dictated its
schedule, focused its message and commanded its action. This was not,
of course, immediately visible to campaign observers. Newspaper
reporters constituted the most palpable media presence. Reporters from
the Associated Press, United Press International, and metropolitan and
local dailies clustered about each candidate after the primary—above
all, reporters from *The Los Angeles Times*. At all stages newspaper
reporters were the most numerous witnesses, the most consistently

informed about campaign developments, the most sensitive to nuances in each speech or in small deviations from routine. They shared the campaign with a kind of intimacy, it might seem, almost as partners with the politicians, except for their daily potential to become aggravating pursuers.

Television was rarely part of this traveling company. Its representatives were present only for occasional interludes, burdensome cameras shoulder-braced, the reporter tied by the umbilical cord of the microphone, managing the quick interview, the panoramic shot of the applauded entrance, a few piquant peripheral scenes, then back to the studio with the film.

Houston Flournoy, the Republican nominee, found the difference between the newspaper reporters' informed and constant appraisal of the campaign and television's quick-shot coverage disturbing. "There is no question that television reaches more voters than most print stories can and it has a visual aspect," he said. "People seem to think it is more important what a candidate looks like than what he says. But it seems to me there is a value in the news field from reporters who try and cover the campaign, or have politics or government as their area, to really have some continuity in what they observe, not just a one-shot impression. . . ."

Yet it was evident that what gladdened a candidate, including Flournoy, was to enter a carefully staged news conference and discover the maze of black cables squiggling across the floor to every available electrical outlet, the lights, the ring of half-a-dozen mikes clamped to the rostrum, the obstruction of tripods and cameras filling the central positions in the room. (Press reporters, meanwhile, were settled in front or to the sides, scraping their chairs in annoyance as they sought a position not overshadowed by cameras where they could establish some communication with the candidate.) Such an aggregation of television cameras and reporters was rarer than the public may have realized. Candidates learned to rejoice when only one TV reporter appeared. That one representative, filming 400 feet—a 12-minute total due to be edited down to 20 seconds or 45 seconds or at best a minute and a half—would bring the candidate to the attention of thousands more people than could the writing of a dozen newspaper political reporters. And the effect was judged to be more substantial, persuasive and lasting.

Radio was even less evident. The radio reporter actually covering a political event was a rarity. Radio was reached primarily through wire-service reports or by telephone calls initiated by the candidate. Even the newspaper reporters were hardly aware of these telephone communications, for this is an invisible branch of broadcasting. But radio was considered valuable enough to the candidates that they put themselves to considerable trouble daily to feed the tapes at the end of the telephone lines.

Newspapers were also important because their accounts were permanent in contrast to the fugitive film or sound and because of the greater depth and insight their stories provided. Also, TV assignment editors and radio news directors relied on them for source material.

Nonetheless, Joe Cerrell, an opinionated, professional campaign manager and media consultant, wise with 15 years of Los Angeles political experience, dismissed the importance of the written press to political campaigns as did many others. "There are three key factors in a political campaign these days," he said in his staccato manner. "No. 1 is television, No. 2 is television, No. 3 is television. In all our survey work, we ask people why they voted the way they did, and it always comes up television. This applies to paid and to free. All free media comes ahead of all paid media. Free is the news coverage you get. Paid is the ad. Free is more important to the voter than paid. People do recognize that an ad has bias. It's propaganda. They know. So it is free media—the news stuff—you really want. The lowest form of free media is the newspaper story because it reaches the fewest people. But even it is better than an ad. The highest form—well, that's TV news, of course. Radio is in-between. But don't overlook radio. Not in this commuter paradise, Los Angeles."

Cerrell told of getting his candidate, Joseph Alioto, to Grand Central Market in Los Angeles. "He stopped and commiserated with a grocer about the price of pinto beans, and Richard Bergholz put it on the front page of *The Los Angeles Times*. Now, Alioto didn't have to go to Grand Central Market to learn about the high cost of rice and pinto beans. I could have told him about it. But the point is, that way he got television cameras and the newspaper and all the news guys. You can ring doorbells for three months. It won't have as much impact as one good television news shot." Cerrell stressed the need to keep in mind the opportunity for visuals. "It's a game. You need a gimmick. I had Alioto lunching on a huge sandwich because it made good television."

The candidates shared Cerrell's assessment of television's primacy. "They see your personality in motion, alive," Brown said. "I think it is very important." His campaign manager, Tom Quinn, put it more forcefully. "Let me define news as that which television covers." Jerome Waldie came to his conclusions about the importance of television tardily. "There are some people in the media field who feel that television is the whole ball game. Well, I did not believe it up to this campaign. Now, I'm inclined to think that is correct."

No blanket characterization of all political skirmishes can be drawn from the election that took place in California following the Watergate scandal, including the resignation of President Nixon and his pardon by Gerald Ford. Yet, certain trends are perceivable that appear similar to the political process elsewhere in the country, and these can provide insights into what happens when the appeal candidates make to voters rests upon the mass media. What became apparent in this campaign is that media interests can subvert the public interest. Some of these experiences may be exaggerated, for California is marked by an historic weakness of party organization, by a professionalized approach to campaign management, and by the state's size, population and the diversity of its economy.

This was not a well-reported campaign. Indeed, for television it may have been the least-reported campaign of significance since the 1960's, when television first became a major forum for politics. The national political climate induced by Watergate affected California, diminishing both public and media interest in state political affairs and leaving all politics in disfavor. The scandal so pre-empted attention that there was little space, time or interest left for local affairs. Political appetites were sated, it was widely assumed. The reaction was most negative in television. And yet the almost unanimous view of television editors that "politics is dull" appeared to spring from within broadcasting itself more than from transitory saturation of the public's interest because of national political scandals. The industry's financial self-interest appeared to be the cause of television's disinclination to cover political news and explained its disparagement of politics as news.

Another distracting factor was the extraordinary sequence of sensational crimes that occurred in 1974 in California, such as Patricia Hearst's kidnapping and subsequent adventures with the Symbionese Liberation Army, and the unprovoked series of street killings in San Francisco that came to be known as the Zebra murders after the police code name for the case. Such sensational (and visual) events dominated public interest and, against such lurid fare, the political contestants seemed pallid. The news scales were weighted against the politicians. Yet there were off-setting circumstances—the openness of the race for governor, and the number of bright, experienced, ambitious men seeking the office.

The overwhelming preoccupation with news media could be observed in the structure of all major campaign organizations. The candidates'

pursuit of the media, and particularly of television, shaped almost everything done in each campaign. The post of press secretary or press director was so critical it was, in some cases, akin to that of campaign director.
Looking at the eight most active campaigns, it was discovered that a primary objective in staff selection was inclusion of communications experts. The technical proficiency in getting news releases drafted, written
and circulated, press conferences scheduled and speeches drafted was
a minor part of this specialist's contribution; the chief factor was getting
the media to regard those releases, appearances and speeches as *news*.
So important was the task of penetrating the media that each campaign
found its key internal problem to be a staff capability for creating or
shaping news.

The staff structure pulled together to manage so brief a skirmish as
a political campaign necessarily contradicts many fundamental rules of
organization. The brevity of the campaign, the uncertainty of the outcome, the erratic and unpredictable flow of money all make it difficult
to attract workers of a quality and efficiency that the candidate needs.
Political staffs are also usually new to one another, must work long
hours under great tension, and are riven with internal organizational
problems and personnel strife far beyond those experienced by a business organization.

There are four key posts. Top responsibility rests with the campaign
director—often a committed friend whose political sagacity, common
sense and loyalty the candidate trusts. Comparable in importance is the
finance director. (The close relationship between fund-raising and the
media will be treated later.) The third position is that of professional
manager—an expert highly prized in California in the absence of party
control and partisan organization. The fourth key post is the person
designated as press aide, press secretary or press director (a post separate from that of media consultant or advertising adviser), whose role
becomes more important as the campaign progresses. The campaigns
illustrated a number of press approaches, but all showed that the campaign director (and campaign manager when there was one) was continually alert to the status of media events and continually involved in
judgments on success or failure in terms of media response. By no means
was this responsibility assigned to a press aide alone; it was an area of
constant concern among the key campaign leaders.

In choosing campaign personnel, two qualities are needed: absolute
loyalty and technical capability. It is not an easy combination to
assemble in a hurry and for a short term. In choosing friends to obtain

the first, the candidate risks sacrificing the second. Or he may pit the judgment of friends against that of the experts he has hired and be caught in their contradictions. Several campaigns had difficulty obtaining satisfactory press secretaries. It was extremely hard to find someone with the requisite political understanding, wide acquaintance among the media and ability to perform under pressure. (In two campaigns, when a good choice finally was made the person was hired away to a permanent job.) The following sketches of campaign staffs illustrate the difficulty in recruiting the necessary talents.

Because Joseph Alioto—he was in his second term as mayor of San Francisco in 1974—had sought the governorship in 1970 it might be assumed that he would have laid his plans more carefully than the other contestants. He did have, at 58, a lead in experience, as in years, over most contenders. Born in San Francisco, he was a brilliantly successful anti-trust lawyer who had directed the 1972 California Hubert Humphrey campaign. Since 1970, however, he had endured some severe blows. His bid that year for the governorship was sidetracked by assaults on his reputation, first from a *Look* magazine article alleging he had links with the Mafia, and secondly from a suit filed by the State of Washington and utility districts there alleging improprieties in his legal work.

To clear his name, Alioto twice sued Look magazine for libel, and after the second jury found the article false and defamatory, the U. S. Court of Appeals, 9th District, advised he might press a third trial concerning malice. Because of all this, Alioto had a considerable media problem.

Consequently, Alioto found it difficult to adopt plans to use the media, spending months devising a program. (At least that is how his staff interpreted his tendency to rely on the counsel of relatives rather than on media experts.) The earliest polling in Alioto's behalf revealed widespread skepticism in Southern California where he was least known and the "Mafia" taint lingered most strongly, despite the legal clearance he had won. The central question became how to project him through the media to erase the taint. At least four campaign experts came and went in late 1973 and early 1974. (One staffer said as much as $700,000 was spent in the early months without producing one ad.) The press received confusing and inconsistent indications of who was in charge of Alioto's public relations. At one time it was thought to be Frank Mankiewicz. Another nationally known campaign expert, Joe Napolitan, was identified as the idea man, but the Alioto family hesitated to accept him. Alioto himself had too strong a mind of his own to leave decisions to any professional, as Sanford Weiner, a San Francisco campaign manager, discovered. With Weiner, Napolitan, Mankiewicz all clearly out, and the Mayor's announced campaign director, Charles O'Brien, cold-shouldered, the Alioto drive had a difficult time getting started. It was well into spring before he turned to Joe Cerrell to seek "free" media attention and to capitalize on the mayor's talent before the cameras.

Events kept dealing Alioto more blows. In January, his wife, Angelina, expressed what she later described as exasperation at "being left out" of her husband's absorbing political activity by vanishing for a private tour of California missions. For 15 days, while she was waiting for a public indication that he missed her, Alioto was keeping her absence secret and dispatching investigators to scour the Western states for her. Finally, public disclosure had to be made, and within hours of the announcement Angelina phoned home and came back to rejoin her family and the campaign. In March, some 12,000 San Francisco workers struck for nine days, which diminished the effectiveness of Alioto's boast that he had the backing of labor.

Lacking a consistent media policy and tight campaign command, he did enjoy the services of an experienced press secretary, Tom Flynn, who stepped out of that post at City Hall to work through the campaign. And Flynn found advantages even in woes. "What these other candidates don't have that we have, is that they don't have real problems," he said. "That's what produces television opportunities. I wouldn't say all that helps, but it cuts both ways. The problems get you bad publicity but if you are decisive in moving in on them and strong in solving them, it makes a lasting impression on the public." Alioto's troubles did keep him in the public eye, and peripheral news, rather than his own political aspirations, kept him a familiar figure.

William Matson Roth, 57, heir to the Matson shipping company fortune, 12 years a regent of the University of California, a San Francisco business executive and consistent liberal Democrat, had long been active in politics but always in supporting the candidacy of others. He had been President Kennedy's chief trade negotiator in drafting the "Kennedy Round" of trade treaties with Europe in 1962, then returned to home and business. In the atmosphere of Watergate, at the close of the Reagan Administration with which he had often tangled over university affairs, he decided to run for governor. Discussing his campaign in mid-May, he said: "The key element in a campaign organization I see now is a press secretary. I just couldn't get one, at least one I felt was competent, who was free to go to work for me." (He did find Roy Ringer, who had worked with Governor Edmund G. Brown Sr., but within a few weeks Ringer left for the editorial-writing staff of *The Los Angeles Times*.) "I desperately needed a press-relations man, because I was very little known," Roth said. "It wasn't for speeches. It was to get copy out to the media and be sure it got used. A speech writer is less critical than just a very good newsman, who writes well, cleanly, fast and accurately, and can work closely with your research staff, can help you in taking the daily news that comes along as it relates to your point of view and getting out instant, properly related, punchy statements. I needed somebody who knew everyday what was top news and could plan how to react to it, a professional guy with news orientation." A good press secretary, Roth thought, might have spared him some of the casual dismissals he suffered from newspapers. He was continually lumped into the category of "minor" candidates, reduced to one name in a list.

But even more irritating was the realization that Citizen Roth had a status with the press decidedly inferior to that of fellow office-seekers occupying public posts. "I found that the name of the game is for those in office to use their offices to create news," he said. "It is very difficult for someone to come from outside. I object to the expectation that in politics it is necessary to work your way up the ladder. Yet, I found media automatically discount the candidate who lacks the aura of officialdom." To give his effort better direction, Roth finally added as campaign manager, Don Bradley, a man who had, in the fifties and sixties, been the top Democratic campaign manager in California. Bradley knew perfectly well Roth had wasted the early months enjoying small-group chatter in congenial little meetings when he should have been concentrating on mass media. Roth was able to boast many volunteer groups around the state. He had the nucleus of a real organization. But this grassroots effort was absolutely worthless, compared with a good television advertising campaign. Fortunately, Roth was able to finance the latter from his own fortune. But even in advertising he suffered the amateur's initial bumbling. He had started off with radio ads done by a volunteer, ads so disastrous that when he finally chose the Maxwell Arnold Agency of San Francisco to manage his media approach, the first task was canceling the radio contracts.

Gifted with wit and a philosophical bent, Roth was able to see his own predicament with some objectivity. After the campaign, he wrote an article in *The Times,* largely critical of the media. "The media," he wrote, "has a responsibility to lead . . . not merely to reflect the apathy of the general public . . . Media's responsibility to the creation of political dialogue cannot be relegated to the editorial alone. Intelligent reporting of politics must have some continuing space and time."

One candidate who managed to combine an effective staff, a public office as a base for recognition, and a record of accomplishment was Bob Moretti, Speaker of the Assembly. In that post, often called the second most powerful in the state, he had received a generally laudatory press in Sacramento. He had demonstrated leadership over the Democratic-controlled Assembly and had shown himself able to compromise intelligently with Governor Reagan to get some critical bills enacted. The Sacramento press corps found him more energetic than his two Republican rivals, Reinecke and Flournoy, and they liked him personally better than Secretary of State Brown, who was, in contrast, aloof and enigmatic. But when campaign time arrived, Moretti felt the attention he automatically received from the press as Assembly Speaker was denied him as gubernatorial candidate. He railed at the media during the campaign for failing to cover it adequately.

Moretti, like Roth and Waldie, did considerable organizing at the local level. His strong point was with the minorities, to whom he had given special assistance in the Legislature. It was as futile an effort for him as for others. He undertook the most ambitious get-out-the-vote effort; it made little difference. The media were what he needed.

Moretti's drive was based on an assumption that his intimate grasp of state issues would generate media interest, but his staff found the media unresponsive. Bob Squier of Washington, D. C., who was Moretti's media consultant, said: "The shock of the Moretti campaign was the discovery that TV was giving no coverage at all . . . We simply had not anticipated that." So Moretti, his own organization in control, his press representatives at hand, his name known, his views forceful and often provocative, was nevertheless thwarted by media inattention.

The candidate who fretted most over the lack of a press secretary was Representative Waldie. When he decided to run back in 1971 his Washington staff members occasionally accompanied him to California, getting in touch with newspaper reporters and sending out press releases on his presence, but work in Washington was too demanding to permit separating that staff from the Congressional office for an extended time. Funds were too short to hire someone so early in California. The nucleus of the Waldie campaign was a corps of volunteers who never left him. The difficulty was that they didn't have the slightest sense of the mass-communication needs for waging so extensive a campaign. After the campaign, Marcella Colarich, Waldie's district office coordinator for eight years, said: "Our volunteers did a terrific job. This was a solid asset. You can't buy the kind of devotion they poured out. But a really organized press approach — we never had that. It was our biggest single drawback. If you have somebody who knows radio and television and newspapers, and knows whom to call when, you are halfway to victory."

Waldie was so little programmed toward an effective press that he almost never wrote out his speeches. His staff never knew beforehand what he would say, so there were no advance releases. It was an ad-lib, candidate-managed campaign, strong on warm devotion, weak on structure. John Laird, Waldie's district assistant, illustrated the problem. "I did his scheduling and all the traveling with him from August, 1972 until June, 1973. In that time he gave one prepared speech. Just one. At the Democratic State Conventon, Moscone had a release on his speech, Moretti on his, Alioto on his. Jerry Waldie got up and told what he did on Nixon's inaugural day; he went to visit a Veterans Hospital in Washington instead. It was something spontaneous and from the heart and it was terribly moving. It affected everybody in the auditorium that night, but there was nothing written out from which we could advance a press release. So *The Los Angeles Times* went to press next morning with remarks from the other three speeches. Waldie might as well not have been there."

The central problem with Waldie's campaign was his effort to run it while attending to business in Washington as a member of the House Judiciary Committee. When that committee plunged into Watergate, and especially as it began impeachment hearings, Waldie felt too strongly about the issue to give up his committee responsibility and concentrate on the campaign. Press releases from Washington attracted a large volume of attention from the media in California—but always on impeachment. His "walks" became weary week-end occupations.

Baxter Ward seemed to have one built-in advantage in his try for the governor's post — his many years of experience as a television journalist. He had used this talent to get elected as a Los Angeles county supervisor, which gave him a basic constituency. Herbert Hafif, a Southern California lawyer, headed the state trial lawyers association and sought to build his campaign from that initial base. Ward and Hafif made their individual tours of the major cities, badgered television stations for attention, called press conferences and issued releases but they got scant attention and often none at all. When Ward got so little press and television coverage, his effort collapsed. Hafif, on the other hand, continued a nagging demand for attention by television in the Los Angeles area. He had been aggrieved from the start by media indifference. On Halloween, 1973, Hafif had called a rally in Long Beach to which 7,000 people responded — by all odds the largest single collection of people in the state that year for a campaign purpose, and they gave him $60,000 that night in contributions. The program included Ray Charles and other entertainers, and news accounts treated it more as a circus than as the opening of a campaign. Hafif never forgave the interpretation, and he never recovered from it.

Reinecke's problem was a cruel reversal of the Moretti frustration. He got abundant media attention; he could scarcely walk to the street without a parade of reporters on his heels, and his press conferences were thronged, television as eager as newspapers. The irony of it was that none of the press concerned themselves with his candidacy. They were absorbed in his April 3 indictment for perjury in testimony before the Senate Judiciary Committee concerning Watergate details; they hounded him for explanations and justification while his attorneys were admonishing him against saying anything in public, lest he hazard his position in court.

Reinecke started with a marked advantage in his position as lieutenant governor. He had substantial Republican backing and an organization that came, so to speak, with his office. Don Anderson, his campaign administrator, said that the staff was deliberately seeking free media because the campaign was so short of money. "It is amazing how readily radio will take what Ed has to say, and TV talk shows — all that sort of thing. But then you come to what they want to talk about and that is the heartbreaking thing. The indictment is the newsworthy part of it. The implications, the significance, the impact of it, how it has affected the campaign, how it has affected your people, things of that nature are newsworthy to them. You can't say the media won't let him talk about the issues because this issue is overriding. . ."

The two remaining candidates. Flournoy and Brown, differed in their staff experience and in their approaches to the final stage of the election compared to the primary. Flournoy's primary race was marked more by luck than by acumen. When he won his party's approval, his staff and resources greatly expanded, even though he was pressed for money. Brown began far in the lead, and his campaign was tightly commanded and thoroughly programmed. Once given his party's nomination, he expanded staff in peripheral roles, but the management control over the campaign became, if anything, tighter.

In the spring, Flournoy, Reinecke's rival with two other little-known Republicans, encountered much the same media indifference that outraged Moretti and Roth and frustrated Waldie. Flournoy stood low in the polls. He was not widely known among Republican groups that were enthusiastic about Reinecke, and only 3 percent of the Republicans indicated that they favored him.

The clue to Flournoy's impending importance was the fact that as early as January key Republican financial sources recognized Reinecke's political liabilities. The same Republican business people who had funded Reagan's campaigns (augmented by David Packard, a major California industrialist who had been Nixon's Under Secretary of Defense but had left before Watergate) met with Flournoy. Flournoy insisted that he had made only one promise: Not to "undo" Reagan's general politics. At any rate, he received enough campaign money to bring into his camp the most seasoned Republican professional political manager in the state, Stuart Spencer. Eight years before his company, Spencer-Roberts, had shepherded actor Ronald Reagan through his gubernatorial race and had managed almost every major Republican campaign in the state for several decades. Flournoy's campaign director, C. Douglas Kranwinkle, a Southern California lawyer, was so committed a friend that he set aside plans for a year-long trip to Europe to devote 18 months as a volunteer in the Flournoy drive. Kranwinkle had been a law clerk for Chief Justice Earl Warren. He was, therefore, grounded in the "independent Republican" tradition of California politics. He and Spencer worked together as a strong team. But despite early help, campaign money was scarce. Organization in the primary was spare. As press aide they drew in a young but energetic and thoughtful reporter from *The Santa Monica Evening Outlook*, Kenneth Drake. Drake had the good sense to recognize his limitations and worked hard to learn who was who in the media world related to politics and to cut his teeth on some difficult press conference situations.

It was Spencer who was pivotal to the media development, but through the primary the three of them — Kranwinkle, Spencer and Drake — worked as a unit on press problems. Raising money and getting acquainted in Republican circles were other demanding necessities, but news and advertising came first. Once the primary was past and Flournoy selected, a new approach was in order. It was signaled by a major enlargement of staff, a move to handsome offices on Wilshire Boulevard in Los Angeles and, most of all, by the addition of a television-trained media expert, Peter Kaye, who had been with Public Broadcasting System in Washington after years of California experience as a television and newspaper political reporter. Kaye introduced to Flournoy's later drive the pungent phrases and the specific attack that generated a marked increase in the candidate's press attention. Often, he managed a television advantage by opening strongly in debates. Kaye's forthrightness and candor were sometimes criticized, but he moved the campaign into broadcast adeptness.

Two striking differences were immediately observable about the Brown approach to the campaign. First, it did not suffer the inadequacies of staff or uncertainties of direction that marred so many of the rival campaigns. It did not have to bring in pivotal new decision-makers or turn to temporary talent. (There was one exception: In the primary Brown hired an advertising firm as media consultant. By the general election, however, he had dispensed with it.) Second, the Brown crew did not pursue the media so obviously. In this respect his organization seemed remarkably modest, even retiring. Press, radio and television were advised, invited, given courteous welcome, but they were not beseeched.

This was not a contradiction of the rule that campaign success lies in luring the media. The secret was that media impact had been calculated four years in advance. During this period, when Brown was Secretary of State, a consistent, carefully programmed media campaign had been built, preparatory to the few months of the campaign itself. Brown's team worked on the premise that winning depends on what filters through the media to the public far in advance of the formal campaign. Tom Quinn, Brown's adviser during his first race and chief assistant in the Secretary of State's office, and another colleague, Richard Maullin, a political scientist and public-opinion analyst from Rand Corporation in Santa Monica, began polling with a view to the 1974 race as early as 1971. Nine out of ten Democrats then knew who young Brown was, and had a favorable feeling about him in a ratio of at least 6 to 1, higher than any other Democratic personality in the state except United States Senator Alan Cranston.

The cohesive and seasoned team that Brown developed may have been — next to his name — his most important asset. This is a rare advantage in politics. The three-man team—Quinn, Maullin and Douglas Faigin, the press director—had been formed to advance Brown's political career during the 1970 Secretary of State race. The years together had generated an understanding among them, a capacity for quick communication under crisis and a trust that eliminated the bickering over territorial rights and responsibilities so troublesome in many campaign organizations. They all knew the candidate thoroughly. They had learned what it was like to work with him. All shared a common attitude about the importance of media, particularly the broadcast media. They spent the intervening years capturing media.

It was widely assumed that the creator of this adroit media approach was Quinn, a cherubic, curly-haired young strategist with political acumen and news savvy in his blood, inherited from his father, the canny Los Angeles political insider, Joseph M. Quinn. Joe Quinn was for 12 years deputy mayor of that city as well as founder and owner of a major newsgathering and news distributing organization, the Los Angeles City News Service. Tom, out of college, went to work with his father, and then created an adjunct to CNS, Radio News West, a supplementary service for radio stations. It virtually blanketed Southern California. Tom Quinn, 29 during the campaign, first encountered Brown in his initial political try, a campaign in 1969 for the Los Angeles Community College Board of Trustees. Then he joined Brown's drive for Secretary of State and became the chief assistant. Douglas Faigin, who came to the team a bit later, had succeeded Quinn in running Radio News West. The assistant press representative who dealt most closely with the press, Llewellyn Werner, similarly had a broadcast background, some of it at Radio News West. During the final campaign, Brown plucked a man out of the United Press International's Sacramento bureau, David Jensen, who remained with the Brown press operation after the election.

But pivotal as Quinn was to the smooth running of the gubernatorial race, it became clear through the campaign that it was Brown, not Quinn, who directed affairs. Maullin made clear how much the impetus lay with Brown: "Jerry knows that the communication of ideas and the communication of personalities are a very tricky business and constrained by many factors of the market place, and just public psychology at any given moment. He's tried to get people to work for him who just naturally take an analytical approach to the problem of communication. That is the basic strategy of the campaign. Take what we know to be certain assets that he has, find the communication medium, either free or paid, which best gets them out to these multimillions of Democratic voters. Therefore, we've got to have a very good set of former newspeople who understand that business very well. We do a lot of unpublicized, dispassionate questioning of the public as to what is on their mind. Our advertising people are also very analytical in their approach. We can all make criticisms of the business of communications, but we also have, in the short run, an election to win so we have to work within the constraints that we recognize. The first job is to understand what the constraints are, then to weave a path through them . . ."

Brown was surrounded by press aides. The upper echelon of his campaign structure came from the deadline-driven media world, attuned to its pace and, most important of all, to its priorities. But there is a subtle fact distinguishing these people from the skilled staff that others had, or from press staffs in previous political campaigns: Every one of Brown's key command persons had been trained in broadcasting, not newspapers. Each understood communication in its most modern aspects. How strongly they were attuned to television and radio was indicated by a remark Quinn made after the campaign, when he was describing the staff's effort to seed Brown's public image through advance news: "We always felt it was radio and television in those years that helped identify Jerry as someone apart from his father, gave him some legitimacy as a human being in the public eye . . . All through those years, the media were not indifferent — that is, with the exception of the print media. I don't know about the print media. We hadn't paid much attention to it. That wasn't my background."

What brought Brown publicity was a long sequence of tough enforcement activities in controversial areas within his department which some of his critics called contrived publicity but which Brown said closed "loopholes" in the campaign-contribution laws under the jurisdiction of his office. He enforced existing campaign-disclosure laws ignored for decades. He went into court with successful suits against big oil companies and other special interests for failing to disclose campaign contributions. Before Watergate, Brown had made himself a recognized state champion of campaign reform. As Secretary of State, Brown operated in a sphere considerably removed from the Legislature and, since he is not gregarious by nature, he was not personally well known to legislators, the Capitol press corps or party politicians. He kept himself somewhat aloof. Brown was viewed with outright hostility by the lobbyists for special interests, who generally considered him to be a brash youngster too unsophisticated to rise in politics. But his success in the courts, his rigorous follow-up on campaign pledges, his willingness to enforce previously disregarded laws, commanded news attention. So did his name. He could not be overlooked, even by a press corps not particularly enchanted with him personally, or even interested in him.

The calculation in the Brown camp was that his battles against the symbols of power would create a kind of hero-image that would stay alive in the public's subconscious while all the new Democratic hopefuls struggled to win name identification. Brown's staff understood that the better known the name, the higher the degree of public interest; the "celebrity" rule reinforced the candidate with the headstart. The aim through those years was to create news events with enough excitement and drama to provoke attention to the person and name of Brown.

For the primary, the Brown team was confident that the less that happened, the less news that was generated, the better off Brown would be. They wanted a campaign in which Brown would ride in on his established reputation. They got precisely what they wanted. They had calculated that broadcast media would not respond to candidates' efforts to win their interest. They had calculated that the throng of newspaper reporters would not stir up enough solid news to invest the campaign with drama. The gamble paid off.

When it came to the general election, and the contest with one man as personally and politically attractive as Flournoy, they knew they were in a far more difficult contest. "If there was a strategy in the campaign," Quinn said·when it was all over, "it was to try to keep out of trouble and not get involved with issues like the death penalty or victimless crimes or marijuana — the things where Jerry's views didn't coincide very well with those of the general electorate. We didn't want those to become prime issues . . . We were very careful . . . We stayed away from those issues as much as possible, and the issues we picked were obscure and boring and dull . . . The press coverage never bothered us. It was as adequate as we wanted it to be. It was our feeling that the less coverage the better . . . The duller the race the better. We wanted this dull, dull campaign. I think we succeeded."

4

CULT OF THE CAMERA

"This is probably the quietest political race in state history. You'd think it was a secret. Nobody sees anything or hears anything about it on the streets. There aren't any billboards or placards. Nothing around town reminds you it's going on." John Henning, state leader of the California Federation of Labor, thus summed up the character of the 1974 California gubernatorial contest with particular aptness, for the race departed sharply from tradition and had a distinctly different approach to the voting public. By the extraordinary degree of its reliance on the media—especially television—it established new patterns in political communication.

What was unusual in 1974 was the cutting away of so much of the conventional linkage to voters—the old-fashioned, highly visible, mid-city campaign headquarters teeming with volunteers; placards and pamphlets; buttons, balloons, and bumper-strips. Political endorsements greatly diminished in importance; the structure of campaign communication around recognized social bases—such as labor unions, professional groups, businessmen, and citizen committees—was sharply curtailed. The candidates did meet with party blocs and interest groups, but the importance of these sessions lay much less in the events themselves than in their usefulness as settings for film sequences. The media had formerly been one of many links between candidates and voters. Now they dominated.

Houston Flournoy and Edmund G. Brown Jr. chose to focus on media for different reasons: Brown, deliberately, because television represented the most efficient communication medium for mass appeal; Flournoy, because the manner of his political rise had left him outside most Republican Party organizations.

Nothing more symbolized the change television brought than a virtual demise of local political initiatives. Brown, based in Los Angeles, had few local headquarters. After the primary he let it be known that local organization was "the lowest item" on his priority list, a view that astonished and alienated some local party leaders.

Flournoy's campaign staff made a more systematic effort to muster local support, but the lines were based not on political boundaries but on the state's 12 significant media markets. California had a total of 7,057,000 households with 95.3 percent of them owning television sets. The largest market was Los Angeles. Within reach of its television stations were 3,415,000 households representing 48 per cent of the population. In San Francisco television reached 22 percent; Sacramento 7.9 percent; and San Diego 6.5 percent. In the eight remaining media markets only 757,000 households were counted; the most important of these smaller zones, Fresno, had a quarter million television households, Salinas-Monterey 161,000, and Bakersfield 88,000.

It took a while for rank-and-file Democrats to realize that their customary campaign role had been eliminated. Unlike Republicans, they were available, and, anticipating victory, they were eager. After the primary both Roth and Moretti pledged support for Brown and urged their backers to work for him. A number of energetic party workers stood by waiting to respond. The call never came.

To the Brown team, the involvement of numerous local committees, the effort to spread fund-raising down to the $5 and $10 range, the strenuous work needed to muster masses of people was just not worth the time and money it would have required. One estimate was made by Brown's staff that a substantial statewide get-out-the-vote drive would have cost as much as $750,000. Toying with possibilities of a future need, Brown hired some experts at grassroots-organizing, but no such drive materialized. Instead, available money was used to increase television advertising. As Quinn assessed the situation: "Maybe in the old days, when there were fewer people around, you walked precincts or rang doorbells and handed people a brochure. I don't think it is less valuable or any insult to the electorate to say they should get their information from television rather than a little piece of paper someone hands them at the door. How does one argue that a brochure is more substantive than what one sees on television? I think this traditional organizational politics is an anachronism. There is a better way of communicating with people. I think a more honest way. You get a better feel for a candidate from television than you do from a little piece of paper."

This concept had a profound effect on campaign activities, the choice of places visited, and the type of events favored. California's most influential political pollster, Mervin Field, was exasperated by the attention to media. "The candidates worried constantly over how many reporters showed up for a press conference or what appeared in the third paragraph," Field said. "This year, concern over every little move by the media became a cult."

Television is a parochial institution. Network shows suggest that television is omnipresent, but local news programs are tethered to the local market. This begets an enormous emphasis on immediacy and localization of news that is closely related to the stations' aim of drawing advertising viewers within their signals' reach. Furthermore, there is very little statewide exchange of news on television even between network-linked stations. No television reporter or news editor or station manager suggested that political events outside his own market area would justify the cost of paying for network transmissions apart from election night itself. And they included any statewide presentation of the Flournoy-Brown debates.

Localism is a political impediment of major proportions in a state as large as California. Only one television station, KNBC in Los Angeles, attempted to provide continuing coverage of the campaign on a sustained and regular basis. KGO in San Francisco, an ABC outlet, undertook the next large share of coverage, including travel for four days with each of the two candidates in the general election. This effort produced extensive reportage in the news programs during the following two weeks. But apart from these two stations, and some coverage by television crews at kick-off Labor Day events within 100 miles or so of their stations, television did not travel in the campaign.

To appear before a major station's audience, the candidates were obliged to keep returning to that station's market area. Obviously, Los Angeles, the largest market, received the most visits. The rare trips to rural areas were usually confined to weekends that otherwise constituted "dead time," since the majority of television news audiences turn to other interests on weekends. No previous California campaign had to schedule such extensive travel. On some days the candidates appeared in the four major market areas in one day, a trip of at least 600 miles.

Wire-service and newspaper reporters traveled daily with the candidates. To insure telephone accessibility, each candidate made elaborate provisions at key stop-over points to accommodate the press. Appropriate pauses were scheduled in the day to meet filing deadlines. Radio, too, was within telephone reach. Radio stations all over California were constantly fed news comments or interview responses from the candidates, wherever they might be. Half-hour or hour breaks in the day were often used to get the candidate's voice on shows over a dozen or so radio stations.

Television, however, required the physical presence of the candidate, and this necessity became a basic guideline for campaign scheduling. The schedules showed, by market area:

Los Angeles: During the 64-day fall period in which he campaigned 55 days, Brown visited this area on 34 occasions. Flournoy visited Los Angeles on 22 occasions during the 46 days he campaigned. (A fund-raising trip to the east cut into Flournoy's fall campaigning.)

San Francisco Bay Area: Brown visited 18 times, Flournoy 16.

Sacramento: Brown 11, Flournoy 6.

San Diego: Brown 7, Flournoy 6.

Fresno: Brown 3, Flournoy 4.

Other: Brown visited other areas on 12 occasions, Flournoy on 9.

In short the candidates had to spend a good share of an average campaign day in travel. Brown's scheduled campaign time totaled 382 hours, of which travel accounted for about 25 percent. Flournoy's schedule showed 404 hours of which 144, or 36 percent, were spent in travel. (Flournoy tried to fly home to his family in Sacramento whenever possible.)

Preparation for meetings continued to be a principal activity for the campaign staffs, but the meetings had a new imperative. They must be keyed, as far as possible, to television's convenience. Their value became their likelihood for luring television cameras. Thus, breakfast meetings took precedence over night meetings. Work hours, by old-style political standards, represented a fairly light burden. Brown's campaign day averaged seven hours, Flournoy's nine. It was possible to classify the "events" on the two candidates' schedules from September 4 to November 5 as listed in the table on the next page.

Some settings had so much tradition that they were almost ritual. Among these were appearances before the Commonwealth Club of San Francisco, Town Hall in Los Angeles, and the Century Club of Santa Barbara. Tradition also decided the scenes appropriate for a candidate's mingling with crowds. Some of these had symbolic value because of identifiable ethnic connotations, but fully as important was the color that they provided as photographic background. These political settings, established many years ago for the benefit of newspaper photography, served the same advantage for television.

Olvera Street in Los Angeles, the Mexican tourist market where the city had its start, used to be toured until Chicano centers more

Type of Meeting	Brown	Flournoy
Labor	12	1
Republican or Democratic Party organizations	7	5
Public gatherings	10	20
Newspaper or studio	8	3
Special functions staged by Flournoy/ Brown committees including fund-raisers	46	42
Speeches before clubs (not normally political)	33	49
News conferences	3	11
Debate	6	6
Media taping	9	9

appropriately suggestive of the 1970's were chosen, such as English-language schools or job-training centers. Riding in the San Francisco Columbus Day parade in mid-October had been a custom for at least three generations of politicians, and they sometimes set out from the very heart of the Italian district and wound their way to Fisherman's Wharf. Chinatown was another mandatory San Francisco political setting, and Union Square at noontime, where a crowd could easily be assembled. Santa Barbara, after the oil spills, became the appropriate photographic site where ecology might aptly be emphasized. Candidates invariably toured Los Angeles' Grand Central Market because the narrow aisles crowded with a great range of interesting, work-worn faces, the mounds of produce, the press of people, and sense of activity all created a visually alive scene. Watts, Los Angeles' bleak black neighborhood engulfed in riots in the 1960's, had become the accepted place to express political concern for minorities. Campuses have long been political speech centers. All of these were visited by the gubernatorial candidates. But in 1974 custom-laden settings were augmented by some new backgrounds meaningful to the ordinary television audience: supermarkets and shopping centers; child-care centers; and "senior citizen" clubs.

What the candidates chose to say at these varied appearances is revealing. Flournoy and Brown are men of high intellectual caliber. Each had a lively concern with government and delighted in talking about it. Both were refreshing and thoughtful in private conversation and on the platform, although in public Flournoy tended to overelaborate his point and Brown to reduce it to a quip or a question. The absorbing pursuit of television coverage, however, tended to convert appearances into "media events" more than occasions for thoughtful communication. The preoccupation was excessively with the photographic possibility. As Chuck Rossi, assignment editor for KNBC, emphasized, "The film is the key in this business." This led to an extraordinary hunt for "action," which is not easy to contrive in a political campaign. Frequently, it was reduced merely to arrivals or departures, and hence there was great emphasis upon that moment of expectation and excitement when the candidate came onto the scene. That moment was more action-filled than the candidate's subsequent words.

There was a new aspect to television news during the campaign—an emphasis on "involvement" requiring that the reporter be put in the picture. This arose in part from the stations' efforts to build an audience around "talent," projecting reporters as "personalities." Saul Halpert of KNBC noted on one occasion: "We did the obligatory airplane interview. If the station sends you to fly in an airplane with a candidate, you must interview him in a way to show him inside the airplane. You've got to show people that you were really there."

Campaign staffs put a premium on concocting events for the cameras. This was particularly evident in the primary, when television was indifferent. For instance, Wallace McGuire, Roth's Northern California director, said: "You end up having to create something to draw cameras. I wish it was as easy as just having a press conference and getting media to cover what you say. But you have to create a fascinating event, or they won't turn out." Roth's three-plane junket into the northern countryside was undertaken because, as his press aide said, "All the press seems interested in is the activity of the campaign, so we decided to provide them with some activity."

It was easy to discover what television liked to record. The incessant demand for confrontations made it clear. Fights. Action. Attacks. In short, excitement. Such photographic requirements shaped the election process. A trip to Ukiah by Brown in mid-October was a particularly appropriate framework for observing this point. Ukiah, a lumber town in northern California, was one stop in a circuit of woodlands and agricultural regions that Brown visited with a press entourage in five airplanes small enough to land at the area's modest airports. It afforded television some of its most satisfactory photography.

Cameraman Fred Paladini of San Francisco's KGO-TV had chosen to come in on the first plane at one stop so that he could film the candidate's arrival. (This was the only television crew traveling with the candidate.) It was a flawless, golden Saturday morning. For Ukiah at 10:30 A.M., the airport scene amounted to a good crowd, perhaps 250 people, many of them ardent party loyalists who had driven an hour or more over mountain roads and had brought children to see the young man likely to put a Democrat back in power after eight Republican years. There were hand-drawn signs: "California Needs Brown," or "Brown for California." There were barefooted young people with clusters of barefooted, unkempt-looking children tagging onto mother's long skirts or father's jeans. There were hippies, long hair clubbed behind in a rubber band, and beside them, sturdy, square-built, scowling, bare-armed loggers. There were the more conventionally clad local officer-seekers. A platform had been erected on a grassy square beside the airport office, and a small band played, loudspeakers tossing the sound thinly across the airport to the pine forests. The succession of small planes rolled up, unloaded the reporters; then Brown's plane came, and the small crowd surged to the edge of the field.

Paladini paused, camera riding his shoulder, his free hand waving over the sunspattered crowd. "This is what I love to catch," he said. "This is excitement, movement. Look at those kids! Look at those faces! Look at the hands trying to touch him! That's part of it, that need to touch. You can photograph that. It all makes a campaign come alive. Oh, my God, look at that!"

He interrupted and was off; he had spotted a Pomo Indian leaning against a tree at the crowd's edge, headband knotted around his tobacco-colored forehead, deep impressive lines in his face—a Central Casting Indian. Over the people's heads one could see the candidate take off the suit coat and vest, which were never removed in urban scenes, however warm, roll up his white shirtsleeves and lean pleasantly into the mike with his first joke.

Later, talking with press aide Llew Werner and others, Paladini expanded on his work. "He did a two-block walk down in Los Angeles the other day through a shopping center. I just loved that. I was walking backwards in front of him, and I'd do his feet and his hands. That's always exciting, the movement in a crowd of people—real people—their hands instinctively reaching out. And then Jerry would begin to gesture as he's talking to them and I'd zoom in on his hands. The texture of the thing, the crowds, the sense of motion. That makes good film."

But news situations did not always lend themselves to interesting "action" pictures, or to factual reporting. Dick Duncan of *Time* magazine's Los Angeles bureau described how Flournoy had squatted at the edge of the platform in Chula Vista after addressing 500 Rohr Industries employees, and two San Diego television stations caught him there, as the workers urged him to learn about the employment problems they sought to air at the meeting. Duncan, who had covered the meeting, said that he saw the film on a newscast and that what came through was a marvelously engaging presentation of Flournoy encircled by workers as he listened to them. It appeared to be an attractive Flournoy.

The reporter made a point of discussing the film because that day, October 10, had in fact seemed to many reporters to be one of the most *un*satisfactory on Flournoy's schedule. Richard Bergholz's account in *The Times* was headlined, "Flournoy Has Uneasy Time With Democrats." It recounted three successive incidents in which his replies had been so vague or contradictory as to leave questioners disappointed and the candidate flustered. One concerned the Rohr workers' complaints that their company subcontracted part of its construction work across the Mexican border with cheap labor while local unemployment stood at 10 percent. Flournoy clearly had not been briefed on this issue and floundered. He had sought to recover through his impromptu discussion with the men and did convey his sincerity, reporters thought, but television viewers would not have gathered all that, even though Harold Keen, reporter for KFMB-TV in San Diego, explained that "Flournoy was unacquainted with the problem." Television time was insufficient to explain any complexities, the newspaper reporters felt. Reporters frequently discussed the differences in the film's evocation of a candidate's candor and charm and their own efforts to show his attempts to cope with challenges. Television, they argued, simply failed to capture the essence of what happened when ideas were exchanged. When the campaign was centered on the objective of providing good film sequences, the candidate was no longer intent upon challenging a rival or clarifying a position; he was staging events.

If volunteers were unnecessary for most of the campaign, there came a point, nonetheless, when the Brown camp felt a supporting cast could help. That was election eve. Brown benefited on that day from many conventional Democratic efforts on behalf of the entire ticket, but his campaign staff indicated that the crowds they sought to muster were for the television cameras on the concluding day of the campaign and on election night. On Monday both candidates staged plane hops to the airports of the principal media markets accompanied by a large number of traveling press and timed for maximum media attention on arrival at San Diego, Los Angeles, San Francisco, Fresno, and Sacramento.

News interest was at its peak. Halpert of KNBC accompanied Brown, and his colleague, Heidi Schulman, was with Flournoy.

"We may have gotten the best film of the campaign," Halpert said. "It brought out all the excitement of politics, the atmosphere of a rally at every stop. Balloons. Signs. People yelling and pushing. This was the sort of excitement people go to the movies to get—all the tumult and hurrah. Jerry had big crowds, a real fever aroused in the people. It was clear that the whole thing was set up. He wouldn't pretend otherwise. You don't get about 300 of the faithful down to Burbank Airport at dawn without a lot of work. I think when they got to the San Francisco Airport it was the biggest crowd I saw all through the campaign. But Flournoy—they just hadn't put the same effort into getting crowds out. He had the press all right. He got plenty of local TV. Both of them, they drew every television station along the way, not like other trips when Heidi and I would be the only television reporters around. But when we got the film in, and ran both reports back to back, Brown with his crowds, the capability and the sense to get 'em there for pictures, and Flournoy with his little knot of staff and maybe four supporters talking earnestly to reporters, well, it told you a lot about the two men's styles."

Halpert emphasized how many local television stations had met both candidates. "Those trips were designed to draw media. It was worth the money. The candidates got a terrific amount of coverage."

Quinn subsequently pointed out that Brown had been able to mount his show because he did have a modicum of local organizing capacity. The Brown campaign had the ability to stage media events and to get the candidate away from the need to address substance, he said. "Local organization helps to put those things together. I mean, how do you get a rally at Union Square, how do you put together the airport rallies we had? Well, local organization." He was asked: "Are you saying that the people were there to serve your media needs?" His reply: "Right!"

In years past, the announcement of organizational support was significant political news. Some were self-appointed blocs. Some were the conventional special interests, such as business, labor, contractors, bankers, truckers, fishermen, teachers. Support from community leaders in various fields was recruited by candidates, so recognized names could serve as a token of favor. Newspapers near election time were jammed with advertisements announcing a committee of pharmacists who favored so-and-so or a committee of lawyers or physicians endorsing his rival, and the ads would consist primarily of a list of locally recognizable names whose judgment was expected to be persuasive to voters. Such ads in

1974 were almost totally missing, and none appeared in the governor's race except for one or two in rural communities where they resulted from local initiative, paid for by local funds. Changes in social structures and community relationships have dimmed the value of authority figures, but it would seem that television contributed by shifting political decision-making away from strong group identification to the one-to-one relationship television fosters.

In the campaign, the 145,000-member California Teachers Association made the first endorsement in a gubernatorial race in its 100-year history, and the metropolitan papers carried only two or three paragraphs, most merely picking up the wire story.

Even the endorsement of labor, usually so critical to Democratic rivals in a primary, and so important for the financial backing it represents, was reduced almost to a farce. It had only negligible media impact, although union contributions were important to Brown. Alioto was expected in the primary to have the inside track with the California Federation of Labor. His mayoralty in San Francisco had rested upon a close alliance with labor. He had bestowed numerous top city commission assignments on union officials. But other Democrats had served labor well, too, and the influence of Brown Sr. was a factor. The big news that finally emerged from the AFL-CIO endorsement discussions was an agreement to share the blessing among four Democrats—Alioto, Brown, Moretti, and Waldie. It was a blow to Alioto. But the book was not closed. Labor was extremely uncomfortable over the "political reform" initiative (Proposition 9) that was on the June ballot largely as a result of Brown's persistent support and his staff's aid in writing the proposal. The measure limited campaign and lobbyist spending. The maximum allowable gratuity any lobbyist could bestow upon any legislator was $10 a month, a sum Brown liked to joke would curb lobbyist entertainment to "two hamburgers and a coke." But the plan also imposed severe limitations on lobbying, requiring a separation between executive decision-making in any organization and its lobbying activity. Labor viewed this measure as a serious blow to its lobbying power, but sidetracked this concern when first persuaded to support Brown. When he continued to emphasize his support of Proposition 9, however, the AFL-CIO executive committee reconsidered its Democratic endorsements and rescinded support of both Brown and Waldie, who also continued to advocate passage of the reform measure.

Brown's people knew that the disclosure of such a rebuke would have more news value than the initial endorsement, and they moved rapidly to exploit media attention. Uninvited, Brown himself went to the scene of the labor executive committee discussion, and when the blow fell, it was he, before the cameras, who had the chance to justify his stand and to capitalize on the political independence he exhibited. By excoriating labor's position at its very threshold, he turned an event intended to hurt him into a propitious moment. And he stole the show from the two Democrats who had retained labor's support. Because Waldie hadn't been present for television coverage, his independence hardly registered.

This was the most newsworthy incident related to endorsements in the campaign, apart from President Ford's appearance on Flournoy's behalf in the fall. Flournoy did have the support, as well, of Governor Reagan. This was a blanket the candidate kept trying to keep from smothering him. Brown kept referring to Flournoy as the candidate of "recycled Reaganism," a description the media did not accept, considering it a political exaggeration. It was proof of the dexterity with which Flournoy's team kept Reagan at bay that the identification of Flournoy with ultraconservative Republicans, which Brown kept asserting, never convinced the media.

Newspaper endorsements, once earnestly pursued, had so diminished in significance that they were fading from the scene. Candidates in 1974 maintained the old-style practice of paying formal calls on editors, publishers, or editorial boards of most major dailies and many smaller papers, even weeklies, and having lunch with *The Los Angeles Times* editorial board. Despite the change in media patterns, these visits were still held in some esteem. Through 50 years of state history, from 1910 to the late 1960's, newspaper endorsements mattered more than anything else, except money. With the dismembering of party power by Gov. Hiram Johnson in 1910, newspapers came to wield major political influence. In 1974 Brown and Flournoy made many of their courtesy calls on editors, especially at small papers, during the summer. Flournoy made a greater effort, having been warned by the late Earl Warren that this was vital especially for Republicans. Yet, there were relatively few formal calls on television station managers. There were some, and in a few cases, television or radio stations made endorsements. (KNXT-TV in Los Angeles endorsed Brown; KCBS radio in San Francisco endorsed Flournoy.) These endorsements were followed necessarily by opportunities for editorial reply extended to the unendorsed, which somewhat dissipated their value. The impression was conveyed, however, both by campaign personnel and station managers that relations between top broadcast officials and politicians were strained or distant or lacking in common interests, whereas candidates and newspaper editors seemed to share a great many common concerns that brought them, whether endorsed or not, into a more congenial rapport. Visits with broadcast managers were usually timed conveniently for taping or filming. Visits to newspapers were similarly intended to produce concrete results, a story, a photograph, possibly an endorsement. But the hurried exchanges in broadcast were totally different from the traditional, long, probing, private interrogations conducted by newspaper editors.

It was a matter of dismay to Republicans, and especially to Flournoy, that *The Los Angeles Times,* historically a Republican pillar, decided for the first time in 1974 to abandon endorsements in Presidential, gubernatorial, and senatorial races. The reasons: "The great public exposure given to candidates for the . . . highest partisan offices renders our judgment dispensable. The voters have more than sufficient information on which to arrive at their own choices." Unmistakably this was a decision based on the changes occasioned by the immense public attention to radio and television.

Although *The Times* had announced its nonendorsement plan well in advance, the Flournoy team kept hoping it would be abandoned, for *The Times* was credited with a magic rallying influence among staunch Republicans. Flournoy suffered a severe blow when the newspaper said in an editorial October 29: "Whether it is Democrat Edmund G. Brown Jr. . . . or Republican Houston I. Flournoy, we believe the state will be in able hands for the next four years . . . On issues that matter most, Brown and Flournoy are in agreement . . ." A second reason *The Times* gave for not making any endorsements was to end "possible suspicion" that support could in any way influence the handling of political news.

But other papers did endorse. Among the four papers on which this study focused, *The Sacramento Bee* retained more measurable indication of respect among its subscribers for its political endorsement than others. This was proved by public reaction after it endorsed Roth in the primary. Roth's vote, in the counties where *The Bee* circulated, was second only to Brown's, whereas he ran fourth statewide. In the final election, *The Bee* backed Brown, noting that both candidates were "qualified and honorable." It said both "have integrity and intelligence" but deemed Brown more independent and vigorous. *The San Francisco Chronicle* and *The San Diego Union* endorsed Flournoy, as did *The Oakland Tribune,* another historic Republican spokesman, but it became known in media circles that it very nearly favored Brown.

In tallying campaign coverage, it was discovered that endorsements were among the least frequent news references. Among all topics, endorsements were mentioned for Brown in only 2 percent of the press headlines, 4 percent of television, and 7 percent of radio; for Flournoy in 2 percent of the press, 3 percent of television, and 3 percent of radio. Going beyond headlines to story content, endorsements of any kind were deemed of little news interest. The press made 42 total references to endorsements for Brown and 37 for Flournoy out of 535 "campaign functions" references. Television made 23 concerning Brown and 26 concerning Flournoy of 204 references. Radio was more attentive to the news of endorsements; it made 28 references to Brown's support out of 180 total references, 15 to Flournoy's.

In earlier elections a candidate's principal concern was meeting people. A communication process was set in motion by which people passed on their reactions to candidates, and word spread from circle to circle. Such peer exchanges have not evaporated entirely due to television because, as an election nears, people seek reinforcement of their opinions among family and friends. But in 1974 the candidate's involvement with people markedly diminished.

This may well have been the year when California, with the largest electorate of any state in the nation, had the smallest ratio of people participating in a state contest. And those few were largely media people.

5

THE MAGID MANIA

"I haven't seen any candidates for office do or say anything worth putting on the air—not when I have big stories on cab drivers being arrested for transporting illegal aliens, drug busts on local Navy bases, large buildings being burned down in major blazes, and many other stories like that, all interesting to people right here locally."

Ray Wilson, news director of San Diego's CBS television affiliate, KFMB-TV, was speaking just five weeks before election day. Similar sentiments were uttered by almost every executive interviewed in California's television world. Political news was not merely competing with other news, but it was also somehow inferior to other news. What did interest the public, television news executives believed, was photographic excitement and action—fires, accidents, crowds, picket lines, lively social conflict, human interest stories, and even animal stories. Bob Moretti complained that during the primary one television station interviewed him and ran one minute of his interview and four minutes on the same newscast about "togs for dogs." At another point he said, a different station ran six minutes on a frog-jumping contest and a few seconds on his campaign remarks.

Moretti epitomized the candidates' predicament: Television, one medium through which they could present their case most directly, was shutting them out. Even in the general election television gave only snippits of time, and then, only occasionally. One press conference after another was ignored; one solemn announcement after another was released into a void. Television executives voiced respect for the electoral process, but they felt annoyed when politicians did not make their campaigns conform to television's news standards.

One television producer likely to be well disposed toward politicians was Agar Jaicks, producer of an early-morning talk show at KGO-TV in San Francisco. Jaicks also happened to be the San Francisco Democratic Party chairman. He had showcased a number of the primary election gubernatorial candidates on his program. The experience left him, as a producer, thoroughly exasperated. The candidates were just not interesting. "You rarely see politicians who will commit themselves frankly on any position at all, unless they are extremely courageous or extremely intelligent," he said. "The people who are exciting to listen to are vehement young advocates for causes today, the NOW women, or the Black Panthers, or the prison-reform crusaders, or the Mexican-Americans, those who consider themselves part of a revolution. They articulate their positions with passion and conviction. Compared to them, most politicians seem to be mouthing a lot of cliches to which they have no commitment."

Between the conflicting expectations of candidate and television, the campaign process fell into a chasm, with no one alert to the need for insuring the vitality of communication between voter and candidate, no one concerned to fit television into the democratic electoral system.

Candidates magnified criticism of their rivals because television liked conflict. They designed their campaigns around scenes and activities aimed at attracting television cameras. Not only did television fail to cooperate, it actively resisted.

The television industry was intent on goals of its own. It was engaged in competition for "ratings" through so-called happy-talk or action-news programs. This format stressed brevity, fast pace, and lively visuals—inhospitable to political news. The preferred material taxed the viewers least, was simplest to tell photographically, and was least in need of explanation. It laid great emphasis on the anchorman's visual attractiveness, chatty manner, and light pleasantries. It aimed at the broadest audience appeal.

Television executives voiced many justifications for their reluctance to cover politics: The personalities were "dull." Talk did not suit television. News staffs were too short-handed. Camera crews were too expensive to send with the candidates. There was more photogenic news at hand. The constant complaint from assignment editors was: "The candidates aren't *doing* anything!" The candidates were talking—and television abhorred talk. However, extensive interviews made it clear that the underlying reason was the advertising sandwiched into the evening news.

In the general election six dominant California television stations were monitored, disclosing significant differences among them in their response to political news. Taken together, these stations in Los Angeles, San Francisco, San Diego, and Sacramento provided 257 hours 23 minutes of news time in newscasts that were systematically monitored. Out of that total news time, the six stations gave six hours,

2.3 percent of the available time to reporting on the gubernatorial campaign. One station alone accounted for a third of that coverage.

There was a fundamental acceptance among newspapers that politics is important news, and this election, with results likely to reshape party leadership in the state and affect it in the nation, was assumed to be of exceptional interest. This view was shared by national and international magazines and eastern newspapers, which sent reporters to California to cover the race, among them *The Economist of London, The Washington Post, The Christian Science Monitor, The New Republic, Fortune, The Wall Street Journal, Rolling Stone, Time,* and *Newsweek.* In its estimation of this story's news value, television was in a class by itself. Squier, Moretti's consultant, was amazed. "I've done two recent campaigns in New York," he said, "and I think Los Angeles television is far, far less responsive to political stories. Here you have the largest state in the nation—a government so big it is actually the sixth largest governmental unit in the world. It's like a nation. And the outcome of this contest was of great importance. Yet television summed it up as nonsense. 'It won't sell—it's dull,' television news editors said to us."

There were, however, two exceptions. Two stations, as disengaged as any other television stations in the primary, undertook a substantial effort to maintain a serious flow of news about the candidates in the run-off for governor. KNBC in Los Angeles, whose news executives, backed up by station management, made an initial determination that the gubernatorial race was important and should be reported on a continuing basis, committed money, staff, and air time to the campaign.

Often, KNBC was the only television station represented at a campaign event; and in almost every instance when the candidates were traveling outside Los Angeles, it would be the only nonlocal station present. One striking example of this was the Flournoy speech on October 25 before the San Francisco Commonwealth Club, one of the most prominent California platforms afforded major political candidates, presidential as well as gubernatorial. That event was a KNBC exclusive; no San Francisco station attended. Bob Eaton, news director of KNBC, expressed his station's attitude: "Politics can be interesting. I think that people are interested in the candidates and in what they are saying. Maybe in the upsurge of 'happy news' other stations thought otherwise. But if you believe all the studies that say television is one of the major factors in helping people make up their minds, even if that isn't a role we sought for ourselves, then it has been put upon us. And we do have a responsibility to do as much as we can to cover an election." Chuck Rossi, KNBC news assignment manager, confirmed the front-office support: "I didn't want to leave 'The Making of the Governor' to some Teddy White. I wanted to report it as it went along. Bob Eaton told us early to go ahead and cover the race. That's all."

The other station to make a significant commitment of staff, funds, and air-time was KGO-TV, the ABC-owned and operated station in San Francisco. It sent two news teams to cover Flournoy and Brown for three days in mid-October. They produced four-to-five-minute segments that were run, two to each program, over six successive newscasts. In addition, KGO carried lengthy interviews with each candidate and undertook considerable local coverage, using the same reporters who did the traveling. The interviews were designed to deal with issues, the travel reports with the candidates' style and personality.

Apart from these two, a few stations from Los Angeles and San Francisco made occasional forays to camps of either candidate to spend a day on the trail to film "profiles." Most major television stations, and many smaller ones as well, invited the candidates to their studios for interviews. These ran anywhere from two minutes to ten and in rare instances longer. As a general rule, the candidates were given television news attention only when they were in the individual station's immediate range, and not always then. But, apart from KNBC, the concept of reporting the campaign as a continuing, unfolding process intended to inform the public about the men seeking office and their positions as expressed over a period of time was clearly not what television considered its responsibility.

One surprising discovery was that television newsrooms had discarded specialists (apart from sports and weather reporters.) Reporters were discouraged from becoming expert in any field. In all California broadcast, only one person, Rollin Post of public television station KQED, San Francisco, was designated as a political reporter. And a strike at the station during the campaign period kept him off camera.

Contrast the paucity of political coverage with intense interest in politics during the 1960's. In 1961, KNXT, Los Angeles, started "60 Minutes" of what it termed "Big News," staffing stories well and using generous film on local events. By 1965 this station offered one of the most attractive news opportunities for broadcast journalists, and other stations were emulating it. The concept of airing hour-long news spread, and political news became an important part of it. A symbol of the growing attention to political reporting was the establishment of news bureaus in the capital. KNXT opened its bureau in 1963, and shortly thereafter, KNBC and Sacramento's KCRA-TV followed suit. By 1965, Governor Edmund G. Brown Sr. responded to television's interest by installing a news conference room designed to accommodate cameras in the Capitol. When Ronald Reagan succeeded Brown in January, 1967, the arrival of a movie actor and television personality, whose "talking head" was quick with a quip, attracted unprecedented television attention to Sacramento.

John Jervis, who opened KCRA's bureau and later quit television to work in politics, looked back on that period as a time when news editors and assignment editors were excited about the story quality of politics. "I'd get two, three, even more days to develop a story," Jervis recalled. "Nobody pressured me to produce one or two a day. There wasn't such pressure as they get today."

Three developments tarnished the "golden age"—Vietnam, the recession and "action news."

The Vietnam War and the national turmoil and urban riots suddenly made sensational and highly visual news available in abundance. But it was also deadly serious. News managers began seeking lighter subject matter as relief. On top of that came a financial pinch following the 1967 recession. To California television, Sacramento bureaus began to seem extravagant. Stations began tightening up on news costs. Business offices were no longer satisfied with the production of news at a loss. Attention was turned to local-advertising revenue possibilities from news segments. As this money began to pour in, stations decided to increase the length of their newscasts and go after the larger audiences that trigger higher ad revenue through higher ratings. A station that climbs six or seven rating points, *The New York Times* television writer Les Brown wrote in April, 1974, can boost its advertising charges and "improve its profits by millions of dollars." The quest for ratings brought the phenomenon known variously as "action news," "eye-witness news," and "happy talk." A wave of program change swept the country in imitation of the ABC station in New York City, which had dramatically increased its audience with a breezy, fast-paced news style. By 1972, this format was being encouraged by the consulting firms that had sprung up as a result of the news-time ad bonanza. The consultants moved in on the television world to advise stations how to shape their news programs for still broader audience appeal.

For years the industry used the resources of research firms to determine audience size, most prominently A. C. Nielsen Company and American Research Bureau (ARB). They counted television viewers and rated stations within an area according to audience size. Data about the sex, age, and buying potential of the viewers were useful to advertising purchasers. But the new consultants undertook a more sophisticated task, "qualitative research." They sought such details as audience admiration for a sportscaster's smile or an anchorman's hair style, and they dealt with the visual attractiveness of the set and the "action" in the news. Consequently, television programming became extraordinarily sensitive to what the viewer was thought to want.

The two most successful firms in this field were Frank Magid & Associates, and McHugh & Hoffman, Inc. By 1974, both of them, along with other consultants, were working with a number of California stations all in the midst of fiercely competitive efforts to enlarge the audience appeal of their news programs. The first impact of the consultants was felt in San Francisco, when KGO-TV, which had been trailing in audience size, hired McHugh & Hoffman and then undertook an energetic thrust to "action news." The station promoted its news "team" on billboards, in newspapers, on buses. It dressed newscasters in costumes. It presented them as "good guys," as "happy people" whom everybody liked. KRON resisted "happy talk," but top-rated KPIX went through successive waves of shock as KGO-TV's audience grew. KPIX also began revamping, and political reporter Rollin Post, discovering that politics was no longer taken seriously at KPIX, moved to public broadcasting station KQED. KPIX retained its top rating for the evening news, but KGO-TV was on the rise.

Similar repercussions from efforts to entice larger audiences were being registered in other market areas. KCRA-TV in Sacramento, although dominant in its field, hired Magid to advise it about increasing news-time audiences, an effort coincident with the election period. A rival, KOVR, hired TelCon & Associates of New York. The two stations in San Diego had gone through major shake-ups just before the campaign. Local staff had been replaced in several instances with out-of-town talent. There were new faces on the screen, new top direction in the studios.

Los Angeles resisted "happy talk" more than most market areas, but KNXT, the CBS-owned and operated station, after KNBC passed it in ratings, began to drop many of its solid news reports and quicken its news format. "KNXT," said KNBC's Sacramento reporter Vic Biondi, "went silly." The consultants turned television news into mere entertainment, Biondi said. "They eliminated specialists. Television today does not offer background stories on politics or anything else. These require more than 90 seconds air time to explain, and 90 seconds has become an optimum for a news item. When you limit news to breaking news, spot events, the time required to get the story is short, and any general reporters can pick up enough facts to accompany the brief film. This format does not require specialists. It is a function of cost and of the commitment by station management."

This, then, is how it happened that by 1974 the movement toward "generalists" had gone so far that Rollin Post with public broadcasting was the only television reporter in the state specializing in politics. Even those reporters assigned to the campaign were not exclusively reserved for politics. Only one television person, KNBC interviewer Bob Abernethy, emphasized the "problem" represented by the candidate's difficulty in getting access to television. The medium, he said, has not resolved how to give candidates time before the voters and square this with its own economic priorities.

Although news directors emphasized the "dullness" of the campaign in explaining their reluctance to cover it, many of their reporters maintained that the campaign—and politics in general—could be made interesting and informative to viewers. The brevity to which most television news had been reduced, and the use of reporters who are unfamiliar with politics, are the principal reasons why political news seems dull, reporters contended. "It is very difficult to do a 20-second or a 30-second story that tells anything," said Rollin Post. "It's just got to be superficial." KNXT's bureau chief at Sacramento, Howard Gingold, said, "The emphasis these days is on visuals. We can't get into anything that takes a lot of explaining."

Many reporters kept struggling to get greater campaign coverage. Some assignment editors told of "constant arguments" over the subject; other editors said they didn't concern themselves about the campaign because they trusted the interested reporters to "push" them into adequate coverage. But assignment and news desks remained the decision centers.

On the whole, news directors did not concede the decline in news quality so many reporters dwelt upon. They usually insisted that ratings had no impact on news selection. (Yet, at one Los Angeles station, just as a news executive was explaining during an interview that ratings had no meaning to the news department, a television reporter was overheard in the hallway calling out to a buddy, "Have you seen the ratings yet?") Some newscasters said that they were never shown the ratings. At KNBC, assignment editor Rossi said, "We don't have to worry about ratings because we are presently Number One. When you have to worry is when you are slipping." But Paul Thompson, news director of Sacramento's KCRA-TV, acknowledged that consultants' studies affected the design of news shows because they indicate the public's interest and public interest guides news selection. "Does political news rate lowest?" he was asked. "Well, I don't know whether it is lowest of all, but it is near the bottom" he replied.

The stresses within the television world affected the news "package" and explained the underlying reluctance to cover political news. This reluctance was measurable. It could be tallied in the time devoted to political stories through the two months before the general election. Seven different newscasts were monitored on the six stations selected as representative of the different news programming available in the state's metropolitan regions. A monitoring system also was employed for radio newscasts over the same period. No San Diego radio station was sampled because most Los Angeles stations reach southward into that community and serve it.

It should be noted here the ratio of time devoted to the election by radio was almost identical with that accorded it by television.

Each station's most popular newscast was monitored every weekday from September 2 to November 4, and all segments dealing with the governor's race were taped and transcribed.

The time factor shown in tables on pages 183-84 is revealing not only as a total, but also in terms of how much time was allotted within each news report and how this was distributed over the length of the campaign.

Timing of television's attention is crucial in its relation to the campaign.

There were, among the six television stations observed, a total of 204 television stories about the election between September 4 and November 4. As might be expected, the greater proportion, 53 percent, ran after October 15. The first point that emerges is the small amount of time afforded this continuing story over the two months; a total of 6 hours in these seven programs, with 251 hours devoted to other local stories.

Even more startling is the fact that one-third of that total was the product of one station alone, KNBC; and more than half of it—3 hours 48 minutes—came from only two stations, KNBC and KGO-TV. Also, KNBC carried stories on 21 days; KGO on 20; and both ran their longest stories and used reports most consistently near the end of the campaign, after October 8. The most noteworthy feature they shared was the duration of their individual news reports, compared with the other stations. Unlike other stations, which had many very brief political accounts, KNBC's two briefest news reports actually exceeded 90 seconds each, the so-called optimum "action news" length. KGO was not quite so generous with time, but it had four days of newscasts exceeding 9 minutes and only four days on which the reports were less than 1 minute.

The remaining stations observed—KTLA-Los Angeles, and the Sacramento and San Diego stations—more clearly typify coverage than either KNBC or KGO. It is notable that the smallest ratio of campaign news among all the stations monitored was in KGO's 11:00-11:30 P.M. program—an exceptionally competitive newscast that KGO claims dominates its own area more powerfully than any news program in any metropolitan region in the country at any time of day. (This refers to the share of available audience it commands, not total number of viewers.) This program mentioned the election on only nine days, with only three of those news reports running as long as 60 seconds. Second in brevity was the 10:00-11:00 P.M. newscast monitored at KTLA. It referred to the campaign on only 11 days over the two months but carried two candidate interviews exceeding 4 minutes. Other KTLA segments were brief.

In a tally of merely how many times the governor's race became the subject of a story, San Diego station KGTV turned up very high. It had 43 distinct stories, 2 percent of the total count, compared to 42 stories on the 5:00-7:00 P.M. news time of station KGO-TV and 49 on the 5:00-7:00 P.M. of station KNBC. KGTV gave 2.1 percent of its time to the campaign and reported it on 30 days—more than any other monitored station. But those 30 days of news reports added up to only 39 minutes.

The comparative length of newscasts is shown on the next page.

The proportion of attention to this race provided by KCRA-TV was a major surprise. Out of its daily one hour of monitored news, 6:30-7:30 P.M. with a total of 32 news hours over the campaign period, it accorded the campaign 35 minutes 27 seconds, 1.8 percent of the total time available. This appeared out of proportion with its

San Diego

KGTV. Total number of stories:
43. Total days story used: 30. Length
of daily campaign news time: longest,
3 minutes, (1 day); 2 minutes (9
days); 1 or 1½ minutes (5 days);
30-59 seconds (3 days); less than 30
seconds (12 days).

KFMB-TV. Total number of
stories: 20. Total days story used:
14. Length of daily campaign news-
time: longest, 3½ minutes (1 day);
3 minutes (3 days); 2 minutes (2
days); 1 minute (3 days); less than
1 minute (5 days).

San Francisco

KGO-TV, 5:00-7:00 P.M. Total
number of stories: 42. Total days
story used; 20. Length of daily campaign news time: longest, 9 minutes
(4 days); 8 minutes (3 days); 7
minutes (3 days); 6 minutes (2
days); 2 minutes (1 day); 1 minute
3 days); less than 1 minute (4 days).

KGO-TV, 11:00-11:30 P.M. Total
number of stories: 9. Total days
story used: 9. Length of daily campaign news time: longest, 1 minute
10 seconds (1 day); 1 minute, 2 sec-

onds (1 day); 1 minute (1 day); 30-
59 seconds (1 day); 30 seconds (2
days); less than 30 seconds (3 days).

Los Angeles

KTLA. Total number of stories:
12. Total days story used 11. Length
of daily campaign news time: longest, 4½ minutes (2 days); 3 minutes
(1 day); 2 minutes (2 days); 1
minute (1 day); less than 1 minute (5
days).

KNBC. Total number of stories:
49. Total days story used: 21. Length
of daily campaign news time: longest, 15 minutes (1 day); 11 minutes
(1 day); 10 minutes (2 days); 6
minutes (2 days); 5 minutes (5 days);
4 minutes (2 days); 3 minutes (5
days); 2 minutes (1 day); 1 minute
52 seconds (1 day); 1 minute 32
seconds (1 day).

Sacramento

KCRA-TV. Total number of
stories: 29. Total days story used:
19. Length of daily campaign news
time: longest, 4 minutes (3 days);
3 minutes (1 day); 2 minutes (6
days); 1 minute 3 days); less than
1 minute (6 days).

reputation for concern about political affairs in the capital, but may
have reflected the station's effort to concentrate on local news events
rather than on state affairs. It may also reflect the advice of program-
design consultants. Its distribution of reports over the campaign
period was unusual, too. It ran stories on 13 days before October 15,
on only seven after that date.

Variations among the three media in quantity of coverage over the
two-month campaign are worth noting. Radio ran one quarter of its
coverage in the last week of the election, and if the Monday immediately
before election day is added, almost one-third in that final period.
Its next heaviest coverage, 17 percent, came opening week. Curiously,
both television and newspapers gave about the same proportion of
their attention in opening week (12 percent for the press; 11 percent

for television). Television's interest slumped in mid-October. Newspaper attention lagged midway also, but not as much.

In considering how the timing of election news serves the campaign process, nothing is more revealing about television's role than the point chosen for its maximum attention. For thère does come a time when television's news interest is whetted—election night. Suddenly the opportunity is at hand for what television considers "real" news. This is the time of maximum public interest, and so it becomes the time of maximum television interest. An astonishing amount of effort and expense is poured into preparing for election night — especially when compared to the attention devoted to the campaign.

Election night is recognized by the television industry as an acutely competitive situation. All station executives emphasized how television outdoes the written press when it comes to reporting returns considered the single most important function they serve in the election reports. Several conceded that newspapers may have done a better job on reporting the campaign than television had, but election night, they said, belonged to television.

Newspapers also devote exceptional time, staff, and planning to election-night operations. But the publication of vote results is not considered the single important function they serve in the election process. The press conscientiously (some with greater dedication or resources than others) tried to present the candidates to the public over an extended period of time. For this, television demonstrated minimal response. Indeed, in some cases television executives scoffed at any implication that a voter-preparation responsibility rested on them. As Russ Coughlan, manager of KGO-TV, remarked, "We never see politicians until they are running for office and then they want to use us."

6

THE MEDIA MIX

"Thank God, media is plural! We don't have to rely on just one. The public should not be choosing between television and newspapers. To be well informed, you need both." Jess Marlow, KNBC five o'clock anchorman, sizing up television's responsibilities in the campaign, said he couldn't discuss broadcast without including the press. He accepted the prevailing wisdom, reinforced by opinion polls, that most people get their political information from television. "But," he said, "I must confess I don't think that is entirely healthy. There are too many races we haven't covered at all, and some of our coverage is shallow. On many issues, we just don't have time for an explanation. If I were going to choose the single best source of political news, I would have to go for newspapers. But television gives the viewer something personal. He can make his own assessment. It lets him watch the candidate actually saying it. If he declines to answer a question, or evades, the viewer can spot that. Nonanswers are revealing." Marlow acknowledged his dependence on newspapers, especially *The Los Angeles Times.*

Broadcast news people relied heavily on newspapers for backgrounding and often extracted material directly from them for newscasts. One late-night programmer in Los Angeles at times read items openly from the first edition of *The Times.* Candidate Herb Hafif, to satisfy his own curiosity, checked late-night newscasts in the Los Angeles market for three weeks against the first edition of *The Times* and picked almost perfectly *The Times* stories that would be aired. "I was never wrong," he said. "The assignment editors obviously use *The Los Angeles Times* as a checksheet for their assignments."

Radio reporters were just as explicit as their television counterparts about debt to the written press. They spoke repeatedly of leaning on *The Times, The San Francisco Chronicle,* and *The Sacramento Bee* as resources for news judgment. In their frank appraisal of their own role, radio and television reporters would say, "We trigger interest," or "We get viewers started thinking about the campaign." More than one added: "Our hope is they'll go to the newspapers for more information." Broadcast reliance on printed news, so openly conceded, was wholly apart from the ordinary use of wire services, which represents the core of any broadcast news operation. Some stations did little more than make an occasional telephone interview on a local story but read the news items as they came over the wires—so-called rip-and-read journalism.

One bit of broadcast response to print of particular significance was disclosed by a KGO-TV reporter in San Francisco. An article in *The Los Angeles Times* critical of California broadcast coverage of the primary hit home so painfully among the KGO-TV staff that reporters, already upset at their station's inadequate performance, used this to push management into providing more political news in the general election.

Candidates were aware of *The Times'* status as Ultimate Source. William Matson Roth said, for example, "It's not that *The Times* coverage does you that much good in a campaign, but it affects the attitude of television." Roth's media consultant, Bud Arnold, said "There is a kind of interaction among the media, so the TV news editor suddenly sees a guy picking up ink in the paper and he's going to start taking him more seriously and cover him. . . ."

Broadcasters could be quite aware of their own short-comings and yet critical of the press for not carrying enough politics. Apart from *The Times* and *The Bee,* uniformly praised, other papers sometimes took lumps for not probing enough, explaining, or giving enough space to politics. At KCBS, newscaster Al Hart and associate news director Mike Beeson both stressed, "People are simply not getting enough news about politics. We should have more political reporting. That's true of every medium in the state, except *The Times* and *The Bee.*"

Times political reporter Bill Boyarsky, speculating gloomily one day on how few people read political stories, acknowledged that TV "makes its assignments on the basis of *Times* coverage. That alone makes us tremendously powerful." His colleague, Kenneth Reich, guessed that no more than 5 percent of his newspaper's readers turned to political news but considered that 5 percent to be an influential segment of readership. He speculated that the most direct effect of political reporting was on people involved in the campaigns, working in them or financially supporting them. The next level to whom written news matters most, he thought, was broadcasters. As for the masses of voters, Reich's polling experience convinced him that they turned very little to newspapers for political information. "They vote viscerally, from impressions," he commented. But those televised impressions, he added, grew from groundwork first laid in the press. Said Mark Murphy, *The Times* metropolitan editor: "It infuriates me when I sit down and listen to TV and I hear a story of ours rehashed. It isn't for failure to credit *The Times;* it's because TV people ought to be out there getting their own stories and developing their own approach to news. In effect, we're creating news and I don't think that's good for the public."

Times reporters following the candidates did sometimes glean from the broadcast harvest. Reich recalled an interview he sat through in San Francisco where a KSFO radio reporter taped Houston Flournoy in a hotel room while a cluster of other reporters sat around. "For some reason, this guy was able to draw Flournoy out as none of us ever had. What he said was thoughtful and philosophic. I've never heard him articulate his views so well. It was beautiful, the best argument against Brown he ever gave. I wrote my whole story that day around what he said, and it was the radio guy who made it happen." Then Reich pondered: "I wonder how many seconds of it he was able to use."

But such occasions when broadcast journalists helped "make" news were rare, although they may be straws that show shifting winds. Art Berman, *The Times* assistant metropolitan editor for political coverage, conceded that television "affects us in a lot of little ways," usually by dictating the setting for an event. On the other hand, William Thomas, editor of *The Times,* said that television had absolutely no effect on his paper's political coverage. "I never consider TV a competitor, except for the advertising dollar, and that isn't my affair," he commented.

Newspaper editors generally concurred with the sentiment expressed by Mark Murphy, *The Times* metropolitan editor, when asked if TV had any reverse influence on print: "Hell no! News staged for television makes for the worst kind of newspaper coverage."

Nevertheless, when the content of campaign news in each medium was examined, and the topics most frequently featured in headlines and leads were tallied and compared among press, radio and television, in an effort to identify just what each considered significant political news, it became evident that television's primary concern with the photographic scene, and with movement and action, so dominated the campaign that press reporters also gave setting and the day's activity their major attention.

Content analysis of all the campaign reports from the selected newspapers and stations revealed a high degree of similarity, with strong suggestions that television had an influence in shaping news that appeared in press accounts beyond the reporters' awareness. One of the most persuasive indices was that all three media gave "campaign activities" more frequent mention than any other story factor and all three gave the second highest proportion of attention to "attack" (either one candidate against the other or the candidate against some supporter of his rival).

What the comparisons showed was that dominant news attention was on relatively meaningless repetition of where the candidate flew, walked, spoke, or ate rather than on what he said. Here is a typical 20-second morning news report on KCBS radio: "Flournoy will be passing through town later today as part of a week-long campaign tour, and Brown will be speaking to a group of his supporters here in Sacramento later this morning." Even television stories, despite the illustrative film with quotes from the candidates, devoted much time to such descriptive settings. KGO-TV on October 9: "Both candidates for governor, Jerry Brown and Houston Flournoy, were here in San Francisco today to pick up what political support they could get. The Republican candidate's most influential backer, Governor Reagan, joined him at a luncheon at the Fairmont Hotel today, which was a fund-raiser. The main topic, as you can imagine, was the economy. . . ." Then came a 15-second quote from Flournoy and a five-second summary of his views by a reporter. The next item began: "The elderly of San Francisco are here every day, in the basement of the First Congregational Church—one of the few places where they can afford lunch. It is only 50 cents. They don't have much money, but they do have a vote. And the elderly are a powerful voting bloc in this city. Edmund G. Brown Jr. knows it, and he came here today. . . . He promised more aid for the elderly, and compared the philosophies of Republicans and Democrats." There followed three sentences from Brown's remarks.

The 160 newspaper references to "campaign activity" for Brown and the 168 references for Flournoy went well beyond such scene-setting phrases. The election catered so openly to television's interests that print reporters were swept along. Television's appetite for "media events" seemed to rob the campaign of policy discussion. It played directly to each candidate's wary vagueness and desire to avoid commitment, and it turned attention away from basic public problems. Television's dominance, largely unnoticed by the "boys on the bus," transformed the campaign into an entertainment played on different stage sets.

The three media also shared the next most-frequent emphasis: "Attack." In both primary and general campaigns, they viewed the campaign in combat terms, their stories strongly focused upon criticisms, slurs, bitter words, exchanged recriminations. The uncomplimentary phrase, the sharp jibe, was picked up more than the substance of the criticism. "Attack" references or rejoinders were reported with such journalistic zest that in a third of the broadcast stories dealing with this subject, it occupied half or all the story, and in the press almost half the references to "attack" took up the bulk of the story. Dick Rodda, political editor of *The Bee*, said in one of his columns during this campaign: "there is a tendency among newsmen these days to lean on that word 'attack.' They want a good strong verb in the lead." And Lee Fremstad, *The Bee* Capitol bureau chief, remarked on the astonishing speed with which "instant rebuttal" erupted after a candidate attack, almost as though the mimeographed press release had been prepared in advance. "It was a new phenomenon," he said.

One might expect that the multiplication of news outlets—television and radio added to print—would have enlarged the variety of news available. The opposite seems to have occurred. The increase in the media has brought conformity among them. It appears clear that the three news outlets affect each other, often without recognizing it, and rely one upon another with broadcasting relying on the press to provide greater substance in political stories.

Recognition of this interrelationship was far more evident among broadcast reporters than among newspaper reporters. Television and radio people spoke often of this reality, newspaper reporters rarely. But, if newspaper reporters were not much given to discussing it, candidates were. The office-seekers were keenly aware that three avenues had to be approached, each with its own technological problems, requirements, advantages, and shortcomings, and that all three were needed in their campaign. Although Brown's approach was more consciously designed toward broadcast and Flournoy's toward newspapers, each sought all the coverage he could get from all three. Only Quinn discounted the importance of newspapers; everyone else referred to them as the essential underpinning for the political-communication process.

The reality of the media interrelationship was demonstrated with special clarity in Brown's initial reach for public awareness when he made his mark as a newsworthy figure on radio. In fact, the genius of Tom Quinn, Brown's campaign director and chief assistant through four previous years, had been in thoroughly understanding radio in California and the size of the commuter audience. In the Los Angeles area, Quinn contrived to project Brown through his years as Secretary of State by continual newsbreaks with such persistence and impact that eventually the other media fell into line and gave similarly heavy coverage. Through all those years Brown was, as Ken Minyard of KABC Radio in Los Angeles put it, "terribly accessible." ("Candidates should bear in mind," said Minyard, "that early accessibleness counts. News people have long memories.")

If the three media are interrelated, they are also in the midst of rapid change. And the handling of news in political campaigns is a particularly sensitive field in which to observe these changes. This is partly because newspapers have been radically altering their approach to the coverage of politics over the last generation. Having struggled to achieve objectivity and "balance," they now confront the intrusion of television. The extent of change has been remarked upon in every newspaper office and by every television reporter. Not many station managers have lingered over the large question of political coverage, but one has, Robert Kelly, partner-owner and manager of KCRA in Sacramento, who said:

"In the last ten years, there has been a bona fide revolution in this country, and television is at the core of it. You can grasp this if you draw a diamond and at the top of the diamond you assume all the wealthy, educated, decision-making people, the traditional consumers of news. They read. In the bottom of the diamond are the very poor and uneducated. In the middle, the traditional consumers, the bulk of us. When all news transmission depended on reading, only the top half of that diamond was interested. But now you don't have to read. The news-consuming public now involves practically everyone. This represents a tremendous change in society which people tend to overlook. And this has sent the print media into various traumas, trying to find the way to go."

In this shifting picture, the era of mutual disparagement among the media appears to have nearly ended. (Only once did a newspaper editor seriously discount broadcasting.) Most of the press had come to accept television as an alternative mode of reporting. Rubbing shoulders and swapping repartee in the lulls before events, print and broadcast reporters had come to an accommodation. For instance, through the first few minutes of Brown's press conference the morning after his election, the newspaper reporters sat silent, permitting the broadcast reporters to ask the earliest questions. A newspaper reporter remarked in an understanding aside, "They've got to get their film out in a hurry, and every one of them has to get his own damn voice recorded. That's what their editors expect."

What most distinguished newspaper from broadcast journalism were the differences in the assignment of specially trained staff, the expenditure of money to allow close observation of the campaign, the initiative displayed in seeking out the news, and the assumption of responsibility for playing a part in the political process. In all areas, the commitment to coverage was far greater by newspapers. Although station managers spoke eloquently about the sanctity of the political process and equal-time obligations under the law, they also disclosed their need to hold the interest of their audiences, to keep ratings high. Thus, the most fundamental difference between press and broadcast in political coverage lay in management's attitude. But the distinction that reporters most discussed was that economic measurement, time, represented partly in staff time, partly in news time. Unlike broadcast reporters, most newspaper journalists covering the race had years of political specialization behind them. The press accorded the campaign some attention as much as 15 months before the primary, reporting on it through the summer. During the last two months most California newspapers carried stories about the campaign with considerable consistency. Moreover, the major papers were footing the bill for reporters to travel with the candidates virtually full-time. Most television editors agreed with the Los Angeles broadcast news editor who said, "When it comes to providing information people need on which to base a vote, my feeling is voters don't make up their minds until the last minute. They aren't much interested until the last week. That's when we give the election attention."

Statistics verified this last-minute broadcast deluge: radio ran one third of all its campaign stories in the final week; television, one quarter. The press in that same last week ran only 14 percent of its stories, although the final week's newspaper stories did run notably longer than before and occupied a greater proportion of news space than in any previous single week. However, these four newspapers had covered the campaign so industriously during the summer that they ran one-third of all their stories, 260, from June 5 to September 2, when broadcast virtually ignored the contest.

Sheer quantity of time versus space was the difference between the two media forms that most concerned reporters. Television newsmen, harried by the 90-second span which consultants considered the appropriate maximum for any news item, contrasted their news capability with that of the press. They openly envied print's chance for explanatory detail.

Yet there were many similarities among the three media. One that content study and interviews brought into view was the effort to achieve "balance." An even-handed presentation of all candidates, free of editorial slant, has been a goal of newspaper journalism since the 1930's, when schools of journalism first began having an effect in city rooms. No one pretends that editorial influence has been totally eliminated from news columns; the effort to achieve "fairness" has been notable only in the last generation, and it is one that must be pursued. But it would be unfair to suggest that newspapers needed the example of broadcasting under the FCC threat regarding "fairness."

In California the freeing of political reporting from the will of publishers has been so recent that city editors and political editors still speak, defensively, about their "independence," and the reporting style in some papers still reflects the effort with a certain stiffness. The decision by *The Los Angeles Times* in the 1974 election not to endorse candidates in major contests was related to such freedom. *The Times* said, explaining its new non-endorsement policy: "It is difficult for many readers to believe that our endorsements of political candidates on this page would not incline us to favor them on the news pages. We don't; our editorial preferences have no influence on our news judgment. But to put to rest possible suspicion that this might occur, particularly in the important races that arouse the greatest passions, we best preserve the credibility of our news by not endorsing for President, governor or senator unless there are exceptional circumstances."

It was nevertheless astonishing to discover how much "fairness" was sought by newspapers in this election. The degree of "balance" bore a strong resemblance to broadcast equality of access carried on under the mandate of the FCC. This standard of objectivity set reporters to puzzling whether benefits outweighed distortions, and whether a measured equilibrium was the proper norm. Some reporters came to feel, near the end of the race, that "equal time" ruled newspapers as autocratically—and in the closing days of the election as inhibitingly— as it did broadcasting news. On television news, on monitored stations in the fall, Brown spoke for a total of 57 minutes 44 seconds; Flournoy for 55 minutes 14 seconds. On radio, Flournoy worked the field harder than Brown and spoke 7 minutes 31 seconds, while Brown had 4 minutes 46 seconds. In the newspapers monitored, Brown's name appeared 3,993 times, Flournoy's 3,621 times. Had newspapers become engulfed in broadcast restraints not intended for news? The phenomenon of "balance" became visually apparent to any newspaper reader. To a degree never before approached in California, campaign stories were presented in all four papers in tandem under a common head or in companion columns under separate heads with identical headline styles, sometimes even deliberately alike in word choice. For instance (*Chronicle,* September 6): "Flournoy Assails Brown Plan" and "Brown Attacks Flournoy Idea." Almost one-third of all the newspaper stories were laid out in this fashion, either "twinned" under a common head or paired in careful parallel (twinned stories—53—10 percent of all; paired stories—100—19 percent of all).

Comparisons of headlines and lead photographs provided another indication that newspapers were operating as if they were under the same "fairness" restrictions as apply to airwave access. In all three media, the leads and headlines were coded "positive," "negative," or "neutral," a judgment *not* related to the political advantage in the news event or the propriety of a candidate's action, but to the favorable or unfavorable impression conveyed by the choice of words. Evenness in treatment was shown by comparison of newspaper headlines directly involving Brown or Flournoy from September 2 to November 4 and by television reporter-leads and radio anchorman-leads in that period. All media gave far more positive headlines or leads than negative, but the two men received notable parity in television and in the press, radio being slightly more divergent. A noticeable difference in television was the blandness of most of its lead statements. In the press and in radio over one-third of all headlines or leads were neutral, but in television more than two-thirds of its reporter-leads were neutral. It was parity in the handling of the two candidates that stood out, though, as much in press as in broadcast.

LEADS AND HEADLINES
September to November 1974

Press (Headlines)	Positive	Neutral	Negative
Brown	43%	44%	14%
Flournoy	38%	44%	16%
Television (Reporter-Leads)			
Brown	29%	61%	10%
Flournoy	22%	67%	11%
Radio (Anchorman-Leads)			
Brown	39%	35%	26%
Flournoy	39%	45%	16%

The parity effort in the newspaper stories increased as Election Day neared. Reporters began voicing indignation near the end of the campaign that their editors were ordering them to write to precisely the same length as their colleagues on the rival's trail and even advising a lead framed around the same concept. In *The Chronicle* city room, for example, reporter Michael Harris was summoned by phone one day near the end of the race to add a couple of paragraphs to his story on Flournoy to match the length of a story on Brown. "I guess it's good to have that balance," shrugged Harris, "but there is a kind of mindlessness about it." City editor Abe Mellinkoff added: "Equal space sounds fair, but I don't know that it is, when you consider that our obligation is to the voter, not to the candidate." At *The Bee,* editor C. K. McClatchy reported that efforts had been made to police balance more carefully. "The goal," he said, "is to have our coverage so equal for the two candidates that the reader can't tell who we are going to endorse." Such a policy "builds credibility of the newspaper and, in the long run, makes editorial endorsements more effective."

Nevertheless, the goal of equal handling rankled reporters. In the closing days of the campaign, *Bee* reporter Steve Duscha exploded in outrage over the "twin" treatment being accorded the campaign news. "I expressed my horror about this to the city desk," he said. "I felt I had to complain at the way the stories are being run exactly alike, irrespective of news value. Just because it is near the end, they are putting stories on page one which they wouldn't even have put in the paper a week ago; they are so lacking in news value—dull, old rehash of earlier news, reused statements. They shouldn't be carrying that stuff as news."

Times editors insisted that they kept no "balance sheets." Said Art Berman, who rode herd on all political stories: "We didn't take out a ruler, but we tried to give equal treatment to equal candidates—to look at each fairly." He and other editors stressed that use of such a large staff enhanced even-handedness and that rotating four or five reporters among the candidates insured a variety of viewpoints to improve objectivity.

Pollster Mervin Field observed that the press effort to achieve balanced reporting blunted journalistic perceptions so that reporters missed the significance of his final poll showing a Flournoy surge. He detected a new "style" in political reporting: "They achieved 'balance' and, in doing so, the result of their campaign coverage was sterile."

Equal space allocation to rival candidates is custom with the wire services. Associated Press and United Press International supply between them most radio stations and small newspapers with the bulk of their news content, while backstopping the major papers. At the Capitol, the bureau head of each service in 1974—Bill Stall for AP and Carl Ingram for UPI—were intensely competitive and proud of the service they were providing. For this election AP had inaugurated a more elaborate reporting approach, undertaking more interpretive and "color" coverage. Ingram, conscious of the newsprint shortage, felt that his "round-up" packages and weekly summaries provided plenty of analysis and interpretive reporting in addition to two daily news reports. Despite the AP venture, Ingram maintained UPI's economic writing style and felt that his rivals had overwritten the campaign and at times exceeded its news value. (The four major newspapers studied relied on AP and UPI mainly to backstop their own reporters. In the primary, AP accounted for 9 percent of all the stories and UPI 4 percent. In the general, the proportion was 10.3 percent for AP and 6.6 percent for UPI.)

The question of "fairness" in the press cannot be considered without taking into account the evolution of political reporting since editors and publishers gave up dictation of political coverage after World War II. The effort to invest political news with unassailable objectivity had been a dramatic change in recent years, but change again pervaded the the city rooms in response to television. The previous goal of political reporting—clear, uninterpreted reports of what candidates said— no longer sufficed since a broadcast technician holding a microphone can get that much to the public. This election was marked by city-room consideration of how to make political coverage more informed, more investigative, or more interpretive.

At *The Chronicle,* the long-expected retirement of Earl (Squire) Behrens, who had been a political correspondent for 51 years and the paper's political editor for most of that time, represented the closing of an era. Behrens was the last of the old-style, powerful political editors in California, a final symbol of the day when political editors wielded immense influence because they wrote for both publisher and party objectives. Behrens' counterpart in Los Angeles in that era was Kyle Palmer, political editor of *The Times* from 1936 into the the 1950's. Palmer, too, enjoyed "absolute trust" among the paper's owners and immense power with the state's politicians. The three strong family-owned, Republican-oriented newspapers—*The Times, The Chronicle,* and Joseph Knowland's *Oakland Tribune*—operated in conjunction on many political questions at that time; and Palmer, as dominant political editor, had an influence extending beyond *The Times* circulation area. There was little attempt at impartiality or "fairness." But by the late 1950's, *Times* publisher Norman Chandler, grandson of founder Harrison Gray Otis, began to curb Palmer's power—a move strongly supported by the paper's editor, now retired, Nick Williams. When Otis Chandler succeeded his father in 1960, he made a clean break from the partisanship and centralized power of the past and set about recasting *The Times* in a quite different image. After the 1960 election, James Bassett became "political analyst," not "political editor." "They were determined no longer to have kingmakers," Bassett said. By 1962, *The Times* had two others covering politics, Richard Bergholz who had moved over from the *Times*-owned (and folded) *Mirror;* and Carl Greenberg, formerly *Los Angeles Examiner* political editor. They, with Bassett, established a style of objectivity so successful that at *The Times* it is credited with being the real cause of Richard Nixon's outrage against the California press, which was expressed in his famous "you won't have me to kick around any more" outburst. (Greenberg's impartiality was so patent, however, that even Nixon lauded it on that occasion.) By 1971, all political reporting was coordinated under one assistant metropolitan editor, Art Berman, and staffing greatly increased. The possibility that someday *The Times* would decide against editorial endorsement was discussed, Bassett recalled, as early as the Nick Williams era as a means of erasing the paper's stigma of Republican Party dominance and further freeing news columns to criticize and interpret.

If the heritage of manipulated political reporting has been erased at *The Times,* interest in politics has remained. The paper is more dedicated to the reporting of public affairs and government than any other California newspaper, except the capital-based *Sacramento Bee.* "State government is extremely important," said metropolitan editor Mark Murphy. "It involves a lot of people's lives and a lot of money. In covering politics, we are fulfilling an extremely important role in the political process."

Typically, planning for coverage at all the newspapers was done well in advance, with informal discussion between editors and reporters. "We don't map it like a battle," Murphy said with a laugh. "We talk. We sort of size up what to expect and then we work out assignments."

The Times' three main political reporters were assigned to the governor's race, but they also had supplementary responsibilities. During most of the campaign, *The Times* had six reporters on politics: Bergholz, the senior political reporter whose rank is marked by an office on the same floor with editorial writers; Los Angeles-based Kenneth Reich and Bill Boyarsky; and from Sacramento, Capitol bureau chief Tom Goff and reporters George Skelton and William Endicott. By the final two weeks of October, however, six more reporters had been assigned; and two from the San Francisco bureau were involved in political stories—a total of 16. "It gets to the point," said Berman, "where I'm on the phone with them literally all day and haven't time to read their copy." Peter Kaye, Flournoy's aide, told about encountering seven *Times* reporters in one day, each pursuing a different campaign assignment.

Because of concern for politics, *The Times* was known in the trade as "a reporter's paper." Those assigned to politics were assumed to have top talent, initiative, imagination, and persistence. Their professional "field sense" was respected by the editors. The rapport between editors and reporters was open, friendly, collaborative, and constant. This was totally unlike the carefully structured atmosphere in most broadcast news operations, where some experienced reporters may have suggested stories and worked to get politics extra time, but none enjoyed leeway to define what was or was not a story.

At *The San Francisco Chronicle,* a reporter called the paper "less serious than any other California paper about covering political news," a view not shared by city editor Abe Mellinkoff, who was thoughtful about his responsibility for steering coverage. But in 1974, the staff was alive with subsurface dissatisfaction over the way politics was being handled. Candidates sometimes referred to San Francisco as "a political wasteland" because of *The Chronicle's* disinterest. But this, too, needs historical perspective. *The Chronicle,* like *The Times,* had its "rebellion" against political reporting designed to advance the publisher's objectives. Some 30 years ago, a "young Turk" upheaval swept the San Francisco bastion of conservative Republicanism. Brash, bright, and adventurous reporters, with a succession of creative editors, rejuvenated a waning newspaper so emphatically that the publisher's family was hemmed in by economic success. The paper was compromised in its political coverage, for a major ingredient in the metamorphosis was overt rejection of all politics and even hostility to politicians. An uneasy balance was achieved between the liberalism of the "new era"—by 1974 grown gray— and the continuing con-

servatism of the paper's ownership. Two talented reporters, George
Murphy and Michael Harris, were assigned to most political stories,
but there was little enthusiasm at the editor level. Planning campaign coverage was done by city editor Mellinkoff, who relied largely
on Murphy and Harris, for whom he had respect and with whom
he work easily. Both enjoyed as much freedom as *Times* reporters,
they felt, but far less editor-level support.

"Our primary duty with the paper is to make the democratic government work," Mellinkoff said. "It can work only if people know what
is going on. I'm square that way. I believe the press has a duty
in relation to politics." But the paper was so charged with its wary
internal struggle over power, and too divided in aim between publisher
and lower-echelon talent to project this view as recognizable policy.
The quiet retirement of Behrens during the campaign only personalized
the political vacuum reporters sensed. It was recognized that never
again would there be political coverage designed to express publisher
preference, but what kind of political reporting might replace it remained unsettled. In that indecision, *Chronicle* coverage settled largely into a careful "balance" which one editor described as "a meaningless middle."

For all that, *The Chronicle* staff was alert to the significance of
Flournoy's changing position in the final Field poll (which is based in
San Francisco). An observer at *The Chronicle* city room on October
30, while the paper was being made up, witnessed the discussion among
editors about how best to convey the poll's significance, along with the
report on President Ford's appearance in Los Angeles on Flournoy's
behalf, and still maintain "balance." They wound up using the four-
column President Ford-Flournoy picture on page one, the poll story
under a two-column head beneath it, with a Brown-and-Flournoy
story balanced on either side. On the Flournoy bus that day, noting
this prominence, coupled with the paper's editorial endorsement of
Flournoy, a *Times* reporter mockingly derided the page-one play as
"old-fashioned journalism" with editorial bias guiding news display.
Flournoy jokingly praised "old-fashioned journalism."

It would hardly surprise reporters on *The Bee* that the total number
of stories about the campaign in their paper was the largest among the
four. *The Bee* has always put politics at the top of its priorities, often
with a "cover-like-a-blanket" thoroughness. (Richard Maullin of
Brown's staff called *The Bee* "the poor man's *Washington Post*.") For
more than a generation it considered itself a "paper of record" in

state affairs and gave space accordingly for virtually all political news, depending largely on editorial-page columns by political editor Richard Rodda for interpretation. But the passage of time was affecting its approach to politics, too. Shortly after the primary election in 1974, Walter Jones, editor of McClatchy Newspapers since 1936, died; and C. K. McClatchy, grandson of the founder, took command. Thus, the primary was covered in traditional *Bee* style, with voluminous reporting on the whole array of candidates, interpretive pieces by Rodda but relatively little travel outside *The Bee's* circulation area, which covers most of northern California and, through sister papers in Modesto and Fresno, much of the Central Valley. In the fall, however, coverage was more closely run by managing editor Martin Smith than had been possible under Walter Jones, who liked to call the shots through his political editor. Two reporters traveled with the candidates at all times: Lee Fremstad, Capitol bureau chief; and a young city-side reporter, Steve Duscha, who alternated with Fremstad on the governor's race. *The Bee* had eight reporters in its Capitol bureau and gave similarly extensive coverage to all races and issues. With a new editor, *The Bee* was abuzz with ideas about how to improve political reporting, with more interpretive writing, more "color," livelier attempts to interest readers in political stories, and a strong thrust to so-called investigative reporting. Its editors spoke frankly about a shift toward providing more interpretation of political events, rather than the massive accumulations of undigested data, which had been characteristic. This change, dramatic as it was for *The Bee,* nonetheless was in line with the direction already perceived in *The Times'* reporting and which *Chronicle* news editor William German expected would eventually replace that paper's treadmill evenness.

Athough *The Times* had the resources to make lavish coverage possible, some reporters thought San Diego better served than Los Angeles because its two Copley papers, the morning *Union* and evening *Tribune,* had such differing styles of coverage and shared so strong a commitment to political news. Despite their common ownership, they offered an interesting rivalry and range of information. *The Union* was generally regarded as the more influential. This had once been the voice and virtually the spirit of the ultraconservative Republican establishment in San Diego, but a succession of changes since 1959 had produced a rigorously objective reportorial style that deleted editorializing from news columns at the expense, however, of interpretive writing.

As issues dissolved into vaporous rhetoric in this campaign and personality emerged as the campaign focus, reporters Otto Kreisher and Mike Davis grew irritated that *The Union's* standards of "objectivity" prevented development of this aspect of the race. Kreisher came to feel that *The Union's* style prevented his capturing the essence of the Brown-Flournoy tussle, since reporters were not allowed to describe their impressions. *The Union* probably exhibited the most self-conscious monitoring of reportorial style observed in 1974. The move toward objectivity was signalled by Herbert Klein's appointment as editor in 1959 after he returned to the paper from duty as Vice President Nixon's press secretary. Klein remained editor, with leaves of absence to help direct Nixon's 1960 and 1962 campaigns, until 1968 when he served Nixon at The White House.

James Copley, who inherited the newspapers from his father, Colonel Ira C. Copley, had decided to differentiate the political style of the two papers. In 1974, this distinction was carried on more explicitly than before. While *The Union* held Kreisher and Davis to rigidly objective standards, *The Tribune* adopted a plan deliberately designed to encourage reporters George Dissinger and John Kern to present the campaign through interpretive pieces that would convey its meaning, not the mere sequence of events. On *The Union,* political editor Charles Ross said, "we don't try to put things into perspective. We aren't interested in color. We don't use adjectives." When Kreisher reported, for example, that Brown "addressed San Francisco's Commonwealth Club yesterday, and left its members laughing and impressed," everything after the comma was omitted. On *The Tribune,* the wire services were used to cover the daily developments, and reporters Dissinger and Kern, alternating between the candidates, concentrated on two weekly stories, one appearing on Mondays, the other on Fridays. These were aimed at summing up the campaign and giving readers some glimpse below the surface. They were played prominently on the front page, whereas most of Kreisher's and Davis' pieces ran unobtrusively inside *The Union.* "Months after Brown was in office people were writing in a 'gee whiz' way about the strong degree of conservatism mixed with his liberal tendencies," Dissinger said, "but we had discovered that in the campaign. Because Kern and I had the chance to sit through a press conference or a speech evaluating what the man said, not scrambling for tomorrow's lead, we picked up nuances that amounted to the real news."

The perceptible move towards interpretive reporting of politics, couched still in a certain wariness about past partisan bias, was the most notable innovation discovered in newspaper reporting, and it was clearly a response to television. *The Times'* managing editor, Frank Haven, called television "the biggest competition we have," adding: "As a result, we want stories that do more than tell what a guy says; we want background, interpretation, something to tell the reader the significance of it all. Reporters, of course, have to try hard to be honest and fair while doing this."

In the long run, this may be the most profound impact that television is having on the press. "Television," said C. K. McClatchy, "is forcing newspapers to go one step further in journalism. Any paper that hasn't moved that step yet is going to have to right soon."

7

THE 30-SECOND PITCH

The one real surprise of the campaign was not that Brown won, but that he came so close to losing. The narrowness of his victory—2.9 percent of the vote—was unprecedented among governors in 20th-century California. Brown's strong early lead in public opinion, rooted in his well-known name and nurtured by publicity about his performance as Secretary of State, had virtually disappeared by the final weeks of the campaign. Brown had been polled as a favorite over Flournoy by 8 percent just after the June primary, recorded a 14 percent lead over him in August, and held at 11 percent in September. In late October the gap narrowed. The key point emphasized by pollster Mervin Field was the rapidity of the shift, which showed that a new current was moving through the electorate and altering the balance of popularity between the two men. Brown's own polling detected the phenomenon. "Things got kind of scary," one aide said.

What caused the shift is not known. Field, who was doing the only large-scale opinion testing in this period, did not consider media a critical influence. He thought that other factors—such as party allegiance, friends, association, family tradition, the state of the economy, and personal impressions—played key roles. A resurgence of Republican Party pride was probably the most significant element, according to Field. Flournoy became a new rallying figure once the California Republican Party shook off its shock. He was, after all, totally untouched by Watergate.

The only observable difference in the campaign process in October was that Flournoy's television advertising had commenced. Brown had initiated a strong broadcast advertising drive at the start of September and maintained it until the election but Flournoy's television spots did not begin until October 15. This was precisely when public sentiment began to change. Not until Flournoy's television appeared was he able to make an impression on his party, let alone the rest of the electorate. The Brown camp considered Flournoy's ads to be a serious threat and attempted to put together a counter-advertising marathon during the final ten days, but it was thwarted by the FCC requirements that advertising opportunities be balanced between candidates.

Flournoy's campaign used some newspaper ads on the assumption that Republicans are readers who pick up political information from the printed word. In all, Flournoy devoted $187,245 of his ad budget to newspapers, but he spent four times that—$874,454—on television. Brown put $1,392,962 into television ads and only $8,000 into newspapers. Money spent for television ads was deemed worthwhile, because a single ad was presented to millions of voters. For example it cost $3,200 for a 30-second spot in Los Angeles during the popular "Waltons" show; the ad had a potential audience of 1,045,000 viewers.

Several interesting aspects of political advertising emerged in this race. How much advertising bears upon public awareness of a candidate and how this relates to poll standing were traced and verified. A subtle relationship between advertising and news was discovered. For example, reporters and editors discounted the viability of a candidate who could not buy considerable television time. Moreover, campaign managers designed ads to produce news, respond to news, or in anticipation of what a rival might do by way of news. There were also ads to answer ads. The urgent need to pursue money was a first obligation with which everyone had to grapple, especially the candidate. And the need was to buy television time.

In the primary alone $2,946,302 was spent on media advertising (Flournoy spent $322,350; Brown, $656,356); and another $1,416,497 was spent in the general election, a combined total of $4,362,799. In the general election Flournoy spent $679,891 and Brown, $736,606. This represented 45 percent of Flournoy's officially reported costs ($1,526,683) and 54 percent of Brown's ($1,349,709). In other words, 49 percent of what the two candidates spent between June 5 and November 5 went to the media—and nearly all of that to purchase access to the airwaves. These figures somewhat understate the total costs since staff salaries were also involved. Tom Quinn estimated after the election that about 90 percent of the Brown budget was involved, one way or another, with the media. The importance of this one communication vehicle so outweighed other campaign efforts and its cost was so high that it seemed to threaten a distortion of the election system. The campaign, supposedly so "dull" that news interest dried up, may have thrown the advertising requirements into stark and possibly unusual relief.

Raising money for television ads became the overriding obligation of the campaign effort—not consideration of state problems and possible solutions. It was an unpleasant task. Brown kept his mendicant role as obscure as possible. He spoke very little with reporters about it, although Quinn said that during the primary 80 percent of Brown's time was "normally allocated" to fund-raising. The remaining 20 percent went to traditional campaigning. After the primary, Quinn reported, "we had no money, and we had absolutely no idea where we were going to raise money, thinking Flournoy had a hell of a lot. . . .We had bled our contributors dry. . . ." Brown's daily schedule for media events omitted some appointments, reporters discovered, and these were mostly dinners with potential donors. Unlike Brown, Flournoy talked openly and often about how difficult he found it to extract campaign funds and how much he needed them. His drive was hobbled by lack of finances far more than previous Republican campaigns. After the primary, Flournoy's posture as a candidate took on more importance; but his disadvantage in the polls, lack of familiarity among Republicans, and the skepticism among some of them as to whether he was conservative enough, along with the growing recession, seriously hurt funding efforts. His finance chairman, John Tretheway, remarked that people who used to buy tables at dinners now bought two seats. Until the end, Flournoy was still wheedling money. His campaign manager, Kranwinkle, lamented that the usual burden of raising political funds was very difficult "because CREEP (The Committee to Re-elect the President) went through this state like a vacuum cleaner in 1972."

So accustomed are political circles to the rude reality that candidates must beg and plead for money that even the presidency gets commercialized, which was apparent when President Ford visited California in the final days of the election. *The Los Angeles Times* headlined the President's appearance: "Ford Due Today To Boost Flournoy But Ticket Sales Lag," and reporter Bill Boyarsky wrote: "In commenting about Mr. Ford to newsmen Wednesday, Flournoy spoke more about financial benefits of the dinner than about the President's own appeal to voters . . ." " 'We'll raise some money,' Flournoy said. 'And in that respect the visit will be a plus.' "

Fund-raising events for both candidates were so conspicuous throughout the fall that they constituted news in 16 percent of the newspaper stories concerning Flournoy and 15 percent about Brown. Television, though alluding to money-raising with more abbreviated remarks, referred to campaign funds in 16 percent of its stories concern-

ing Flournoy and 10 percent of those about Brown. Radio noted
Flournoy's fund-raising efforts in 10 percent of its stories; Brown's
in 8 percent.

Conversations with campaign managers and candidates made it
apparent that customary electioneering, from breakfast meetings to
walks through supermarkets, represented a kind of charade—a spectacle
staged primarily to cheer up contributors and to justify further pleas
for money. Subsequent press stories—clipped, photo-copied, and
circulated among supporters—became a record that could be laid
before potential donors as proof of the candidate's rising popularity.

Television's chief value is that it reaches so many. Although news
programs may reach hundreds of thousands each evening, the two
broadcast media in their entertainment periods through the whole
range of daily programming reach millions. Campaign managers
calculated that 95.3 percent of California households had television
and 85.6 percent of them could be reached by television ads in the
four top market areas. The utility of broadcast ads is that they are
uninvited, unexpected messages dropped into the viewer's or listener's
consciousness when he or she is in a passive and receptive mood. The
political ad is calculated to create the same kind of subliminal, pleasant
awareness as is any commercial message. Name recognition is the first
goal; a favorable impression from the ad "package" is next; reinforcement through repetition is third. The candidates used words like
"character," "philosophy," or "inner self" to describe what they trusted
television to convey. The campaign became a subtle, obscured and almost private experience. The experts charged with responsibility for
political advertising are usually the most inconspicuous of all participants in the campaign. In general, the content, style, timing and
frequency of ads are all developed in the backroom.

Reporters did become alerted to this aspect of the campaign. After
all, since 1960 and the various books about "the making of the President" and especially since 1968 and Nixon's use of "image" in his
advertising appeals to voters, reporters have been aware of the importance of electronic political messages. In California they wrote
stories primarily about the funds raised for ads, the 30-second "spot,"
which was utilized to the virtual exclusion of other time segments, and
the unadorned directness that characterized the ads.

Brown's forces kept an impenetrable veil over the preparation of ads.
Flournoy talked openly about his ad plans and even invited the
press to sit in on the preparation of a final batch (though when the

reporters arrived and were shunted into a side studio to observe via screen, they did not consider this as open as they would have liked). What was remarkable about Brown's conduct was the contradiction between what was said and what was done. Brown himself scoffed openly at the commercialization of politics. He disparaged "packaged" politicians. He advocated "free" television time for candidate appearances. His assumption was that he did not need ads, which seemed reasonable in view of his commanding lead. His campaign staff labeled ads as mere "defense." One staffer said: "Television ads don't do much for you. . . . They kind of keep you from fading into obscurity, that's all." This was consistent with Quinn's view that elections are not won at campaign time but far in advance, through action that creates broadcast news and thereby a favorable public impression. "I tend personally to think that commercials during campaigns are bullshit," Quinn said at one point. Ironically, it was Quinn who prepared Brown's commercials for the final election.

Prior to their agreement to hold media expenditures to $900,000, roughly equivalent to the limit set by the Political Reform Act adopted in the June primary, but not officially in effect until January, Brown invited Flournoy to join him in eliminating ads completely. This was a grandstand gesture from the leading candidate, of course, but it also showed how apprehensive he was about the advertising Flournoy might use. The fear was not only that the Republican might get more money for ads; it was also that his personality might seem more appealing in them. When it was all over, Quinn said Brown would have won the campaign very handily if Flournoy had agreed to ban paid television spots in exchange for a series of debates. Despite his disparagement of political commercials, Brown spent three times as much as Flournoy on advertising in the primary and more than anybody else in his own party. In the general election, where Brown insisted upon a ceiling for such spending, he outspent Flournoy on ads by more than $100,000.

Brown provoked one of the sharpest exchanges between the candidates when he breezily charged during a KNX radio interview in early July that Flournoy was surrounded "by public relations men like [H. R.] Haldemann and [Nixon press secretary Ronald] Ziegler." Brown had been seeking some way to discredit Flournoy by linking him to Nixon, and he used this comparison to warn that the Republican campaign might turn out like "the selling of the President," a reference to Joe McGinnis' unflattering book on Nixon's use of television in his presidential campaigning of 1968. Flournoy's ad men, Brown charged, "want to sell him like a bar of soap."

This was infuriating to a Flournoy camp already outspent on advertising. Peter Kaye, an experienced press and television reporter, who had just been hired by the Flournoy staff, considered Brown's remark to have been triggered by rejection of the "no-ads" proposal. And it irritated Kaye that reporters quoted Brown without questioning what he meant or measuring the charge against the remarkably open and uncontrived campaign Flournoy was running. "This is an example of what can happen if the press isn't challenging," Kaye said later. "You take a charge. You float it out on the airwaves. The interviewer doesn't question it. He doesn't say 'Wait a minute! What are you talking about?' It just goes floating out." *The Times,* Kaye said, carried it without elaboration from Brown, but a reporter did call Flournoy headquarters for comment. Later, Kaye said, Richard Bergholz of *The Times* asked Brown specifically what he had been talking about and was told: "I didn't have anybody in particular in mind. It's just that if he [Flournoy] relies on radio and television commercials, obviously he'll be packaged like soap." Brown's own reliance on radio and television commercials received no such counterconsideration.

Flournoy aides decided to block any future Nixon linkage by confronting the issue head-on. At the July 15 meeting of the Broadcasters' Association of Northern California, to which Brown had also been invited (he declined), Flournoy cited the Democrat's charge as proof that "intellectual honesty for politicians as well as broadcasters" was lacking. He brought his challenge sharply home to the broadcasters by saying: "You have been magnificent on the big things—conventions, assassinations, Watergate hearings. But in the day-in, day-out business of covering politics, covering government, you've too often been lazy, naive or indifferent." He was explicit in denying that any comparison could be made between his advertising tactics and Nixon's, and called the charge "character assassination."

Flournoy's criticism of the broadcasters went out over the air and was picked up by the wire services and many newspapers. There were no more Brown allusions to Watergate-style politics in California, but Flournoy's sharp remarks did not noticeably increase the broadcast industry's concern with political coverage. In fact, in that same speech Flournoy had pleaded with the broadcasters to give full coverage to the forthcoming debates. That proposal was not reported nor heeded.

Through interviews at the various stations studied it was discovered that, in the last days of October, Brown's camp undertook a major effort to buy more television ad time. This was not easy. In a campaign's closing days, air time has been pretty well allocated. As it is, "bumping" commercial advertisers, which stations must do under FCC rules if necessary to accommodate a candidate whose rival has an unfair advantage, causes a frenzy which Brown's people aggravated by their big effort. At KNBC in Los Angeles, for instance, advertising manager Des Phelan said that Linda Manown, Brown's time buyer, telephoned October 31 to order $75,000 worth of spots to run between November 1 and November 4. (Brown had spent $28,100 at KNBC in September and $56,285 through October.) What was proposed was a four-day blitz. The station turned it down, Phelan said, because it could not permit the air time to be so monopolized by one candidate. State records showed that both candidates bought about $2,000 extra time in the last week on KNBC. Station records showed that from November 1 to November 5 Brown spent $9,282 and Flournoy $5,957.

At KSAN, a modest-sized independent radio station in San Francisco, acting sales manager Jane Oliver was frantic four days before the election. "I'm up the wall," she said. "They [time buyers and ad agencies] call at the last minute with more money. They all want stuff on. Brown's people especially are driving me crazy. . . . His people are really pushy. I'm not taking any more shit from them. I told them to forget it." At all-news radio station KCBS in San Francisco, sales representative Jack Sweeney reported that he turned down $10,000 worth of ads in the last weekend. The demand was so great, he said, that on October 28 the station carried no commercial messages at all, only political ads. On KNBC, 35 political ads were carried on election eve — including nine for Brown, seven for Flournoy. One Los Angeles television station, KNXT, refused to sell Brown more time at the last minute, contending that he was already "equal" in purchases with Flournoy. Brown's people were so irate they initiated an investigation after the campaign.

It was clear from Brown's crash effort that he credited ads with Flournoy's increased popularity near the end of the campaign. From a different source came another indication. John Shinn, a member of the study staff who accompanied *Los Angeles Times* reporter Kenneth Reich while the latter conducted a public-opinion poll for *The Times* in the final weekend, observed that respondents preferring Flournoy repeatedly used phrases identical to language in the Republican's ads.

Campaign managers commonly said that news was the more credible communication medium than advertising. But they would throw in qualifications. Stu Spencer, Flournoy's experienced campaign manager, emphasized: "You can totally control the paid media. You can buy it, you can dictate it. The only leavening factor is dollars. Without dollars, you can't do the job. But advertising is a strategy totally at your command. Press strategy is not controllable." He added a qualification later: "Media—electronic and print—may be more important in news now than in advertising because people are a little tired of political commercials." He attributed this to public skepticism generated by Watergate and Nixon's use of television ads.

Campaign strategists confessed that they did not know whether ads were more effective with voters than news. Nobody suggested that advertising alone could elect a candidate. But ad people tended to concur with Lenny Pearlstein, a partner in the Los Angeles firm that handled Brown's media account in the primary. Pearlstein said that people did not know whether they learned about a candidate from news or from advertising and basically did not care. Ken Sullet, creator of Flournoy's ads, said that political advertising experts "do the same commercial everywhere—the same formula applied to different men in different races. And some win and some lose. And whether they were helped or hindered by the advertising, nobody knows."

But advertising represented an entry to the vast public that is basically uninterested in politics until confronted with election day. "The rationale for paid advertising in an election," Pearlstein said, "is to make up for the inability to reach people through the news media. Not that many people—especially Democrats—pay attention to news. They don't read newspapers or watch television news in sufficient numbers or with sufficient regularity to let you depend on getting your message across to them consistently. Because of the information-gathering habits Americans have, you have to go to paid media. Free media is important, but it is not sufficient." Even if free television time were available, as in Britain, or "voter time" were provided by American television, as advocated by Twentieth Century Fund studies and recommended by Brown, advertising consultants in this campaign and campaign managers uniformly said that they would favor continuance of some paid messages as the only way to reach certain blocs of voters by intruding in entertainment periods.

The 30-second ad segment prevails in television because the networks have found it advantageous. It was the only length they would accept for prime-time commercials. Thus, the time segment found most suitable by the broadcast industry for commercial products was by and large imposed also on political advertisements. Some independent stations accepted occasional full-minute ads, and a few were run on network-owned stations in nonprime periods. Pearlstein explained that advertising research had discovered that the major perception of what was conveyed in a 60-second message occurred in the first half of its delivery. A 30-second spot was considered brief enough to discourage viewers from getting up to change channels. Despite these supposed advantages, however, many campaign managers found the 30-second format frustrating and inadequate for the messages they wanted to put across. "In 30 seconds, there will be no substance, obviously," said Bob Carpenter, co-partner with Sullet in the Flournoy advertising operation. "Thirty seconds—that's a terrible package for politics," said Bob Squier, Moretti's advertising consultant. "There should be a better way of dealing with political communication." Roth's speaking style was not compatible with brief messages. Roth's media adviser, Bud Arnold, felt that at least a minute and preferably five minutes should be the standard time provided candidates who must confront public issues as well as convey personality. Expecting voters to make judgments on 30-second flash impressions was a disservice to democracy, he felt. "I look for the day when speechmaking will be revived. Not everybody would listen, but a lot would—enough to make decisions on the basis of thought." "We would love to have 60-second commercials in prime time," said Pearlstein. "It would give us a chance to do what we have wanted to do. But they are not available."

In the general election the 30-second ad length on television was universal. In the primary, however, some candidates bought longer segments in off-peak times. Alioto used a five-minute Sunday afternoon spot on KNBC April 14 as a device to break through what he considered the inhospitable Los Angeles media market. Certainly the most poignant use of a five-minute segment was Ed Reinecke's. The original Republican front-runner had been indicted by a Washington grand jury April 3. Legal advisers insisted that he make no public statements in defense of the actions that had brought about the perjury charges. Not until May 20, when the Federal court rejected moves for dismissal and set the trial for July 15, was Reinecke free to make a public comment.

Only two weeks remained before the primary. The Lieutenant Governor's friends considered how best to put his case before the

public, and settled for a five-minute spot. Into that time they packed
the essence of an explanation (which they also mailed to about 2,100
key Republicans). This was a restatement of a "Dear Mimi, Mark
and Tom" letter which Reinecke had written his children about the
slips of memory when he had been called to testify before the Senate
Judiciary Committee about what he termed, "the bad dream called
ITT." "The mistakes I made were honest mistakes," he said.

It was Thursday before the June primary when Don Anderson,
Reinecke's campaign chairman, had the filmed presentation ready
and contacted television stations. The broadcasters recognized this
was Reinecke's first chance to claim "equal time." He had only $27,-
000 to spend, but he found time available in as many stations as the
campaign could afford. "It amazed us," said Anderson, "how many
stations juggled their slots and created time for Ed. Some even called
to offer time before we got around to contacting them."

Radio's importance as a political advertising medium must not be
underrated. Its political spots usually were accorded a full minute,
and these cost far less than television's. A package of 18 60-second
and 12 30-second spots purchased for Alioto on KNBC-AM radio
for $1,200, for example, reached an estimated 1,117,000 people.
As a rule, these ads were constructed around the same theme used in
television, often using the same words, but the candidates expanded
their statements. Radio lent itself better to the testimonial ad. For
instance, several candidates in the primary bought ads in which endorsing newspaper editorials were cited, thus reinforcing and spread-
ing their effect, something not easily managed on television. Usually
political advertising plans for a market area called for the television
thrust to be accompanied by substantial radio ads. This was especially true in the Los Angeles area, where commuters tune in for an
especially long "drive time."

Federal communication law and FCC regulations impose a number
of restraints on advertising to insure the same kind of "equal opportunity" that the law requires in nonexempt time proffered by a station. A licensee has the option of determining whether it will accept
advertising for any particular campaign: It makes its own choice as
to which races may be represented by ads—a barrier to those campaigns
not accepted—and it can prevent air time from being inundated by
politicians. The large stations, under the law's assumption that a
broadcaster works in the public interest, are unlikely to bar such a
major race as that for governor. But once a station opens its air-

waves to ads for one candidate in a contest, all candidates for the same post have an opportunity guaranteed them to purchase, if they can, a comparable amount of time. Ensuring that this access is equal becomes a considerable task as election day nears. The licensee can control the maximum amount of time to be accorded a race — a freedom Brown's crew found arbitrary — but within that limit, must keep all rivals aware of their "opportunity" to buy and attempt to equalize air time if a candidate has the funds—even if a commercial account must be bumped.

Most stations refuse to permit political ads during news programs, but next to prime time, when costs are high, candidates favor placing their ads immediately before or after the news. While news is not particularly high in ratings, it draws people motivated toward public affairs and thus likely to vote.

The FCC has also required that any rate discount a station offers its wholesale commercial customers must be made available to candidates within 45 days before a primary election and 60 days before a general election, provided that the candidate is actually seen or heard on the message. This led to subterfuge: A radio ad purporting to present supporters in praise of the candidate without his presence sometimes carried a concluding tag-line. "This message has been brought to you by a Committee for. . . . ," spoken without identification by the candidate himself. Similarly, TV shots that did not include the candidate in person would show a picture of him to insure the bottom rate. A number of stations automatically gave the rate cut to all candidates regardless of how long before election day their ads commenced and regardless of the "voice on" technicality.

The Roth campaign provided a startling example of advertising effectiveness. A rare candor on the part of Roth and his media consultant, Bud Arnold, made it possible to trace the effect of the advertising on the candidate's poll standing and how press interest responded to his improving poll status. Because Roth figured little in the news, it was possible to discern just how much advertising meant. Basic to an advertising drive is the money a candidate can command. Roth was able to use his family money, and this permitted him to shortcircuit the elaborate ritual of financial enticement. Roth spent $1,250,000 on his effort—$860,000 of his own funds: $250,000 from his mother; and $170,000 from outside his family. His statewide media budget was $596,318. (Much of his money went initially into local organization, which he had mistakenly expected to be important). Roth began his drive about a year before the election, but it was early February before he brought Arnold into his campaign. At that point he stood at precisely the same point in the polls as when he commenced his drive. One percent of the Democrats "favored" him. Arnold's thrust was totally to television, with a message keyed largely to Roth's "independence," the experience he had had in the Kennedy Administration and, most of all, in private business.

Advertisers use the term "flight" to describe a package of time purchases distributed over varied markets and stations. Roth's first flight ran February 11 to March 3. He spent $65,000 on seven Los Angeles television stations. The second flight began April 10 and was scheduled to run solidly to May 1. At the time he began, Roth's 1 percent standing in the Field Poll was the lowest of any Democrat. By April's poll, he had moved up to 3 percent and by early May to 6. By the end of May Roth polled 7 percent.

The significant point is that Roth obtained very little news notice until his television advertising became so extensive throughout the state that his poll standing rose. In mid-April, however, Roth suffered what he conceded was "a failure of nerve." The cost of his self-financed adventure bore in on him, and he feared that he would not be able to finance ads in the critical final weeks. So he interrupted his program. (It started up again in May.) As a consequence, two things happened, both related to *The Los Angeles Times*. For one, Roth met with *The Times'* editorial board while in the grip of his despondency and said that he had interrupted his ad program, which was interpreted, he heard from friends, as a loss of heart. For another, *Times* political reporter Kenneth Reich had just become impressed by the public's growing awareness of Roth when the advertising schedule broke off. Reich was certain that the interruption in the ad schedule had broken Roth's momentum just short of the point at which the press might have viewed him as a "comer."

Roth was not the only candidate to become convinced that a relationship existed between command over ads and press coverage. Hafif and Ward were two among the Democrats who operated on modest budgets and expected to campaign through news. But they learned that candidates lacking budgets for ads simply could not make it; reporters assumed that viable candidates had to have money for advertising and looked upon candidates who banked on news alone as amateurs.

Representative Waldie, however, was no amateur. And he had

come to feel by early April that he was not getting adequate coverage from *The Times*. He stopped at the paper to talk about it with Reich, who raised the question of Waldie's advertising budget. The fact that he had drawn considerable television attention with his "walk" was recognized; but if Waldie had no money for television spots, he could hardly be taken seriously as a candidate in a statewide race, Reich said. Waldie was outraged at such an assumption:

"Had I, instead of trying to organize supporters throughout the state, spent nothing on that and put my entire $380,000 into television ads, or most of it, then the newspapers would have considered me a credible candidate and I would have made an impression where it mattered. I don't mean to be cynical, but that's what *The Los Angeles Times* theory seems to be. . . . They were basing their judgment on a candidate exclusively by how much money he had . . . It's incongruous! I say if you are a decent individual and have experience and a platform, ought you not be covered on that basis? But, no, it is television that counts!"

To Waldie, this experience showed that television dictated the outcome of the campaign, even to setting standards for the print media; and those standards sprang, not from news value but from the flow of money into ads.

Waldie had other personal proof of the value of advertising. He did put $21,000 into preparing three 30-second spots, but he was able to raise only $45,000 for television time. So it was a rare opportunity when supporters offered to buy time on his behalf on a television station in Salinas, the heart of California's "salad bowl," about 25 miles east of Monterey. When returns were in, Waldie carried only one county, his home base of Contra Costa, in finishing fifth statewide with about 7 percent of the Democratic vote. But in the three counties within viewing range of the Salinas station, he drew from 10 to 14 percent of the vote. He finished third in one county and a strong fourth in the other two. To Waldie's staff, this showing in the only area with a strong television campaign was incontrovertible proof of the importance of television commercials.

Other incidents showed that news could prompt advertising. Brown's staff, for instance, created an ad carrying the endorsement of a law-enforcement group called COPS (California Organization of Police and Sheriffs). The expression of law-enforcement approval of Brown was intended to forestall Republican attacks on him as "a liberal kook," for Brown had, for example, supported easing criminal sanctions for personal use of marijuana and opposed the death penalty. As it turned out, Flournoy did not attack on a law-and-order front until this ad appeared. Flournoy countered the COPS endorsement with an ad in which the larger California Peace Officers Association called the Brown backing "deceptive" and announced its support of Flournoy. Thus the parry and riposte, which made news. The game got more complicated when an ad endorsing Flournoy became immensely irritating to Brown. A San Diego hotel owner, Larry Lawrence, a wealthy Democrat who supported Bob Moretti in the primary, switched to Flournoy in the fall with some scathing remarks questioning Brown's "judgment and maturity." This ad provoked an anti-Lawrence maneuver that became a campaign issue.

Broadcast ads and news appeared interrelated in yet another manner. In the primary, a number of advertising directors made the point that the paucity of news attention to campaign issues forced them to structure ads more to the candidate's position on issues than to "image" or personality. As an example, Moretti pressed vigorously for more public attention to rape because, as his advertising consultant, Bob Squier, remarked: "The real issues of the campaign did not get talked about in the press. In their news stories, reporters were all involved with the politics of what was happening, who was attacking whom, not the content of what the candidates said. The content was in the advertising. We dealt with solid issues in the spots. The frills were in the news stories."

Brown's approach in the primary focused most on his championship of election reform while Secretary of State, but he was concerned about the allegation that he was a "one-issue candidate." So he purposely asserted concern about oil, air pollution, the environment, transportation, and economic needs. His 30-second spots were capsule speeches. "I'm Edmund G. Brown Jr. I'm running for governor. There are three things a governor can do about air pollution. One. . . ." Later in the primary, Brown developed nine other ads, each around an issue, one of them on education. In it, he said that inability to read at age eight was serious, but inability to read at 18 was tragic. And he mentioned wanting to distribute state money for schools on a "more nearly equal" basis. In a postelection poll, the Brown team discovered the only clearly identified position most voters liked about Brown was his stand on education, and that stand was expressed only in his ad.

The focus on issues dissolved into much fuzzier language in the ads during the general-election campaign. Brown's commercials in the fall were designed to convey such campaign themes as "new spirit" and "new beginnings" more than solid talk on specific state problems. Flournoy's theme was an attack on Brown. One widely used spot for Flournoy, for example, began: "I'm Hugh Flournoy . . . . Jerry Brown seems to be running against Ronald Reagan or Richard Nixon. That kind of Joe McCarthy behavior demonstrates a contempt for voter intelligence. . . ."

Thanks to the openness of Roth and Alioto and their media representatives, time costs could be analyzed in detail. Even with the discount rate for politics, prime time costs plenty. When Alioto wanted time during "The Sonny and Cher Show," which was rated then to have an audience of 1.2 million in Los Angeles, he settled for 10 seconds for $1,200. He paid $1,134 to buy 30 seconds on the 7:30 P.M. Wednesday game show, "Let's Make A Deal," and $1,000 for 30 seconds on "I Love Lucy." On a Sunday night between 7:30 and 10:30 in Los Angeles, he could reach a half-million homes for 30 seconds for $1,500. Time during less widely watched programs came cheaper. A 30-second spot on the "Today" show cost $200 in Los Angeles, and 30 seconds on Sunday's "Issues and Answers" went for $50 (the audience was judged to be 76,000). A 30-second spot on the "Today" show in the smaller San Diego market could be purchased for $18, providing access to an estimated 38,000 people. In Fresno, 2.2 percent of the broadcast market, Alioto was able to buy 32 30-second spots for $1,745; these reached a potential audience of 1,274,000 adults over a week's time.

Alioto's southern California radio budget for the concluding two weeks was $30,000, half the sum committed to television ads in that market for the same period. That bought 1,600 radio spots, most of them 60 seconds long, compared to 300 30-second spots on television for twice as much. (While the television purchase gave access to 50 million adults, the radio ads reached 20 million.)

Roth's television records showed that in the Los Angeles market alone, the candidate bought 283 minutes (4 hours 43 minutes) for $255,220. This represented an enormous amount of access to the public for a candidate scantily covered in the news reports. Roth's 374 30-second spots ranged from $67 for a morning program to $2,750 in prime time.

This kind of factual detail demonstrates just why campaigning is so expensive when a politician is dependent largely on broadcast commercials to communicate with the public.

The enormous advantage advertising gave a candidate in opportunity for a direct approach to the voting public, in contrast to the snippets of time news editors permitted for a candidate's direct remarks, was vividly illustrated when comparisons were made between ad time and direct speaking time on the six monitored television stations. Adding together the measured newscasts on all six of the stations, Brown spoke in newscasts throughout the entire campaign period a total of 57 minutes 44 seconds; Flournoy a total of 55 minutes 14 seconds. The bulk of this was on KNBC, by far the most generous, with 19 occasions when Brown spoke (a total of 23 minutes) and 22 occasions Flournoy was shown speaking (18 minutes). These were in regular newscasts, not the debates or interviews at non-news periods. KGO accorded Brown 14 minutes of speaking time in its newscasts; Flournoy, 15 minutes. But the rest of the stations carried direct remarks from each candidate that totaled in their newscasts through the entire two month period anywhere from two minutes to five minutes. With such abbreviated news exposure, advertising time became the critical avenue for getting a message across to television viewers. As a consequence, the candidates for governor augmented their newscast appearances on these same six stations with $158,678 worth of ads for Brown and $151,817 for Flournoy. Even on relatively generous KNBC each bought more time: Brown more than doubled his exposure with the purchase of 55 minutes; Flournoy, 21 minutes. The ads ran, of course, in 30-second segments.

On radio, the contrast in direct speaking opportunity between news and ads was even sharper. On the two all-news radio stations monitored both morning and night, together with two independent stations and a talk-show station, Brown totaled through the whole campaign 4 minutes, 46 seconds, when his voice was carried in regular news times; Flournoy, 7 minutes, 31 seconds. On KCBS, San Francisco, and KABC, Los Angeles, neither candidate's voice ever was carried on a newscast (though they were interviewed at other times). But their ad purchases on these stations were heavy. On KCBS Brown bought 74 minutes of ad time; Flournoy, 164 minutes.

One would not argue that direct and uninterpreted communication from the candidate is all a citizen needs to know. The value to the public from a reporter's political interpretation, backgrounding, and perspective is enormous. Even if thoughtful reporting had been available across so large a state, however, candidates would still have needed some opportunity to state their views directly.

Political ads provide a substantial source of low-expense income for broadcasting. Stations require that political time be paid in advance, and this money comes to them without sales or production cost. KCBS radio in San Francisco collected $101,921 from political advertising in 1974. At KNBC Los Angeles, ad revenue from the gubernatorial candidates was about $400,000, and that station had the policy of setting candidate rates at half the normal rates. Yet questions about the financial significance of these revenues were usually answered with laughter or expressions of annoyance. Robert Kelly, partner-owner of KCRA-TV in Sacramento, said: "They raise Cain with our legitimate advertisers."

Ad directors delight in divulging their techniques after the campaign ends. Ken Sullet of Sullet & Carpenter, Flournoy's advertising firm, told how artificial the once-effective ads for major campaigns of 1970 and 1972 seemed when reviewed in 1974.

In reaction to Watergate, Sullet said, ad professionals believed that their products must be direct, honest, free of any pretense and focused on issues. "In 1970," said Flournoy, recalling his previous campaign for the state controller's post, "I walked on the beach at sunset, my coat flung casually over my shoulder while someone else talked about my virtues. This year, I look straight into the camera and talk." To achieve naturalness, Sullet brought Flournoy into a studio, seated him on a couch (a board hidden behind the cushions to discourage his usual slouch), and conducted a running bull session, from which the spots were culled. Flournoy was not the malleable politician most agencies would prefer. "No way was he going to change the way he dresses or what he does, just for pictures," Sullet said. . "For instance, we shot lots of pictures of him before it dawned on me that he had the same tie on in every one. I said 'This is crazy. Why are you always showing up in the same tie?' 'It's my tie, I like it,' he said. Turns out he actually has three ties, almost identical, red and blue stripes, and that's all he wears. Narrow ties, too."

The approach to Brown's primary ads had the same emphasis on reality. Said Pearlstein of his firm's ad design: "We wanted to be direct and clear, without being boring. We wanted to avoid tricks." For authenticity, film was shot of Brown speaking at political events, the sort of film news cameras were getting, but more centrally focused. "In ads," Pearlstein said, "the viewer is not intrinsically interested. He doesn't just *want* to see what you are showing. On news, the audience brings itself to the picture. With ads, the camera work has to reach out and bring the audience in. The quality of work is terribly important." As Pearlstein and his camera crew worked out ideas for Brown, Quinn took increasing command of the process, pouring out creative ideas in his usual indefatigable fashion. When the primary was over, the Brown camp was in a financial fret and uncomfortable with its ad agency. In a quiet decision that left no hard feelings (and may have been a relief to both sides), Brown and his aides, Quinn and Maullin, decided to handle television advertising for the fall "in-house." This saved about three quarters of the normal 15 percent ad agency fee, although the campaign still had to hire a camera crew, buy film and editing equipment, and employ a time buyer. Quinn conceived, ordered and edited all the ads used in the general election. Whether those "in-house" ads helped Brown squeak through or whether professionals might have confected a larger victory is anyone's guess, but any agency would have had a job sharing command with the Brown-Quinn-Maullin team.

Flournoy's campaign also was operating "in-house." His team of experienced professionals, Bob Carpenter and Ken Sullet, had stepped out of their firms to establish their own company, for which the Flournoy campaign was the first assignment. "Introducing campaigns into a regular agency is inefficient," Carpenter said. "To get good work done you have to put a lot of high-priced people into the campaign, and that removes them from on-going clients for six months to a year. . . . Political advertising is very personal. You can't do a good job unless you know the candidate and are committed to him."

The Flournoy approach was developed a year before, centering on Flournoy's academic background and legislative experience, which constituted a special set of qualifications for office. As one ad put it: "If there were an academy to train men for high office, it would include the kind of training Hugh Flournoy had. . . ."

In midsummer, the blackboard in Kranwinkle's office disclosed the shaping of the future ads from descriptive comparisons between the two men. One of the terms noted was "integrity." It was written under both names and canceled. A number of other parallels were noted and crossed out similarly, but under Flournoy's name one word remained uncanceled: "Maturity." The Carpenter-Sullet team used this focus to produce a newspaper ad that ran widely in the general campaign. It was a comparison of the two men's records, unusual because it displayed not only the rival's name but also his picture. Down

the center of the ad ran a list of years; on one side Flournoy's activities were listed, and on the other were Brown's. "Elementary school"
on Brown's side matched Flournoy's "B. A. in Government at Cornell";
"High school" for Brown was opposite Flournoy's "Air Force lieutenant." When Flournoy was studying for his doctorate, Brown was
in a seminary studying for the priesthood. When Brown was at
Berkeley and Yale, Flournoy was serving in the Legislature. Across
the top ran the heading: "Compare Carefully. We Can't Afford A
Tragic Mistake." The ad, which infuriated Democrats, was the lone
deviation from the persistent direction of advertising to television and
was the only significant piece of advertising directed to the reading
public.

Brown's research lieutenant, Richard Maullin, illustrated the
exasperation campaign people experience over the high cost of television ads. He was talking at a bar with a potential contributor, and
he had finally wrestled a promise of $3,000. While the two talked,
Brown's education ad flicked on a TV set in the bar and was gone.
"It dawned on me," Maullin said, "that in the 30 seconds that ad took,
the sum I had wheedled out of that fellow had bleeped by. There it
went, another $3,000 for 30 seconds.

8

"FAIRNESS" AND THE UNSEEN DEBATES

A basic purpose of the "fairness doctrine" in broadcasting is the promotion of "robust, wide-open debate." In the context of California's 1974 election, it was almost an amusing phrase. Yet vigorous political exchange on matters of public interest, the U. S. Supreme Court has said (and the Federal Communications Commission has underlined), is essential to the preservation of our form of government.

The FCC has urged broadcasters "to make the maximum possible contribution to the nation's political process. That process is the bedrock of the Republic." In an amplification of the "fairness doctrine," the FCC emphasized "the paramount right of the listening and viewing public to be informed of the competing viewpoints on public issues." The "public interest" in broadcasting, said the Supreme Court, "clearly encompasses the presentation of vigorous debate on controversial issues of importance and concern to the public."

Against these standards, the gubernatorial race occasioned news coverage and broadcast access that were minimal rather than maximal. Candidate self-interest, coupled with station self-interest, produced, if not a news blackout, certainly a gray-out. Candidates obtained access to the airwaves when they bought ads or turned to public television, but on commercial television the decline of interest in political reporting, the pressure for advertising revenue on the stations and the elusiveness of Brown, the leading candidate, all lessened the coverage. No one appeared concerned whether the public interest was adequately and fairly served. The election can hardly be regarded as an experience consistent with the spirit of the Federal Communications Act.

Since broadcasting is so central to mass communication, it is impossible to examine a political campaign without taking into account the standards and regulations of the FCC and its underlying mandate that the air is to be used in the public interest. This is not an easily measured requirement. The concept of licensee responsibility has grown since 1927 through Congressional revisions, court opinions and FCC rules. In this election, broadcasters were particularly aware of recent FCC assertions that "fairness" affected *bona fide* newscasts which must "afford reasonable opportunity for the discussion of conflicting views on issues of public importance." Such deliberate limitations, as witnessed in California, appear to run contrary to the intent of Congress. Although there were numerous efforts to conform to specific FCC requirements, there were developments that appeared to be out of accord with the spirit of the FCC statutes. What took place showed that machinery intended to protect the public interest may protect a self-interested participant in a political struggle, but ignore voter interests.

There were three areas in which the FCC rules figured significantly. The most dramatic was the deliberate restraint on debates and on broadcast media coverage of debates, contrived by the "agreement" struck by the two leading candidates and successfully imposed on the broadcasters. The second area involved a prevelant custom in California broadcasting, especially in television, that tends to apply the "equal time" regulation even in exempt news periods. Such caution about handling political news in the name of "equal time" and "fairness" appeared to impede adequate coverage of the governor's race, especially in the primary.

Station managers, news directors and assignment editors frequently said that they were hampered in coverage by the FCC requirements, especially when confronted by so many candidates. Trailing candidates invariably blamed their inability to get coverage on the FCC equal-time rules. Yet, there kept intruding, through all the wringing of hands over legalisms, hints from experienced broadcast reporters or suggestions from candidates that the equal time and fairness mandates were virtually welcomed by the stations. Some people in politics and broadcasting apparently considered the FCC rules a handy shield that permitted the stations to minimize political news and thus escape responsibility for allowing time to matters they considered "boring."

The third area concerned specific complaints to the FCC that arose in the campaign and events that might have occasioned complaint. Although such complaints can lead to the filing of charges and, eventually, hearings and decisions, none of the protests stemming from the campaign led to such results. But there were complaints, and they suggest areas of public policy in need of reconsideration.

During the primary period, the broadcasters, faced with 29 candidates for governor, virtually abandoned coverage until the last ten days, justifying their inattention on the ground that it was impossible to meet equal time and fairness requirements with such a number of aspirants. The lack of coverage became the single most significant candidate grievance in the primary. Most stations interpreted the requirements so strictly that they reduced campaign reporting to news about candidate poll-standing, to "attacks" one candidate might make on another, and to the last campaign swings around the state. Does this level of coverage come within Congressional intent and FCC concepts of fairness?

The two major-party nominees—Brown and Flournoy—held six joint appearances or debates but no commercial network carried any of them statewide. The upshot of television's reluctance to air a debate until the campaign was that only one debate was aired commercially in prime time, and that was only three nights before the election; only one was carried statewide, and that by the Public Broadcasting stations.

Such restrictions seem to have been a direct result of the pact the candidates entered into with great solemnity—although the real explanation is much closer to broadcaster indifference than to political machinations.

Douglas Kranwinkle, Flournoy's campaign manager, pointed out that television offers of debate opportunities were nearly all proposed on the verge of election.

"We would have liked to have had statewide network television," he said. "None of the networks was at all interested, except maybe in the last four days. None would even consider a debate until about November 2. We felt we needed a series of debates as early and as frequent as we could get. We had to take the best we could get."

"Are you," he was asked, "suggesting it was not just Brown but the television stations themselves that restricted the debates, and wouldn't permit statewide showing?"

"Yes, television. They simply don't have a statewide concept of presenting programs. We even had stations within the same network coming in separately and asking for conflicting times. They don't coordinate on a statewide basis at all."

After the agreement was reached, the four CBS stations did write jointly to suggest something novel for them: a debate all four would air on the Sunday before the election. The KNBC offer had been accepted by that time. Campaign managers did not relish debates one day after the other.

The prohibition on broadcast use except as specified came entirely from the Brown camp, asserted John Tretheway, attorney for the Flournoy campaign. "We wanted all the air time we could get, anywhere. We'd have let 'em sing it or dance it. The more use, the better." But he recognized the conventional belief that leading candidates risk more by frequent appearances and lagging candidates gain, so Flournoy's team accepted the limitations.

The Brown campaign philosophy about debates was summed up by Tom Quinn at a not-for-direct-quotation conference conducted after the election. The Brown campaign felt, he said, that the less coverage that was given the contest, the better off Brown would be. Brown was reluctant to debate, according to Quinn, because a confrontation was the one thing that could make the campaign exciting. Quinn wanted a dull, dull campaign, and he succeeded. The Brown camp was never quite sure what was happening in the dynamics of the campaign but viewed Flournoy as a very strong opponent. As for the agreement, Quinn said he was surprised by the complete success of it although he expected that it would somehow cow the media, who were not viewed as very gutsy.

The meetings were scheduled thus: September 10, at the Sacramento Press Club, no broadcast; September 27, at the Irvine University of California campus, public television; October 8, 90-minutes, public television, shown statewide; October 20, KOVR in Sacramento-Stockton, "State Capitol," a Sunday public-affairs program; October 28, San Francisco KQED public television; November 2, KNBC "News Conference."

The absurdity of the agreement was that the two candidates set limits on what news of the campaign broadcasters could dispense— and threatened legal action should their agreement be violated. So carefully was this specified that the language of the agreement stated, after each television debate was designated by station: "No other television or radio use of all or part of the program may be made by any person, including a candidate or the station, except for regular news coverage."

In a flourish at the conclusion, the agreement warned: "No person other than a signatory hereto shall have any right to seek judicial remedy as a result of the existence of this agreement or any alleged violation thereof." This seemed to demolish the normal constitutional right of any citizen to petition the courts. If it was not nonsense, it was censorship. The only thing more remarkable than the extralegal document itself was the piousness with which broadcasters respected it.

Probably the gravest aspect of the affair was a disclosure by Brown's lawyer, Stephen Reinhardt, that the legal charade was viewed seriously as a model by which future candidates might impose similar restrictions on broadcast responsibility during elections. Looking back on the negotiations with Tretheway, Reinhardt said they had dressed up the pact with such elaborate interdictions in legalese — power of subpoena awarded to the arbitrator, bars against recourse to the courts, and so forth—to "formalize" the obligations on each party. "The stations," he added, "would know that they couldn't really be bound by this, but they would recognize the agreement as a step toward what they would like, so that the wishes of the parties (the candidates) should be respected if the stations wanted other candidates to do similar things in the future." That's how it worked: The prohibitions on airing campaign discussion so neatly coincided with the broadcasters' own preferences for the use of their time that no breach occurred. "I was appalled by their gutlessness," said Tretheway.

The brevity of the coverage given the face-to-face encounters tells more about the broadcast attitude toward the campaign than the analysis of their news programming (2 percent during the principal campaign months). Would coverage have been more extensive had there been no agreement? Here is the record: Of six hours of total debate by the two men, all six monitored television stations carried a total of 32 minutes 16 seconds in total news references; radio carried a total of 6 minutes 4 seconds. Only one radio newscast included actual excerpts from the debates, and KNBC alone accounted for more than one third of the television time, 12 minutes 27 seconds. But the contrast between six hours of candidate discussion and the capsuled news accounts, 32 minutes on six television stations and six minutes on five radio staitons, only partially discloses the shortcomings of broadcast's reporting. The content principally concerned the occurrence, not the substance of what was said. Many individual television accounts ran no more than 20 seconds or 35 seconds, conveying only that the two had met or had "accused each other." Often newscasts simply ignored the debates. KGO-TV, for instance, reported on only two; KCRA-TV carried film of those in their own vicinity but gave less than 30 seconds of attention to those held elsewhere. Station KFMB, the CBS station in San Diego, reported on Sept. 10 "They flipped coins for choice of speaking place; Flournoy won and spoke first" and this 20-second account was the total attention this station gave to the debates through the entire campaign.

By contrast, the four newspapers all carried something about every debate, even though the October 20 Sunday event got wire-service coverage in most instances. All the stories attempted to report what substance was raised, analyzed the impact each candidate seemed to have on the other and on the audience. The press gave lead emphasis to the personal attacks, which became the focus of the encounters for the media as the debates progressed. For the most part, however, newspapers outside Los Angeles carried little about the KNBC debate. A total of 42 newspaper stories were devoted in whole or half to the debates. For the newspapers and wire services, the debates gave the gubernatorial campaign its only continuity and direction, since issues did not arise elsewhere to clarify the candidates' differing approaches to state government. But the only people who saw them all were newspaper reporters.

Stations might have tested the restriction the Brown-Flournoy compact laid on First Amendment freedoms but none did. Chuck Rossi, assignment editor at KNBC voiced the prevailing spirit of acceptance: "Because of the way Brown has insisted these debates be run, we can't use it for live broadcast, but it is open for ordinary news coverage, so that is the only thing we can do." Doug Kriegel, a reporter for the CBS Sacramento outlet, had taped the opening debate, hoping to use it irrespective of authorization. Kriegel telephoned the "arbitrator" named in the pact, Dean Dorothy Nelson of the University of Southern California Law School, to ask what risks they might run should the film be shown.

As Tretheway recalled, Dean Nelson said it was not her responsibility to advise broadcasters on First Amendment rights. "They lacked the nerve to go ahead." Tretheway said. Recalling the same incident, Quinn said that Kriegel called him, and Quinn refused permission to use the film. "So he just told me, 'Look, I don't know what the hell you're going to do with me, have our license revoked?' ". Quinn remembered "I just said to him, 'Doug, we refuse to let you do that, that's all. You can't do it.' And he said, 'Ho! ho!', and with that got his general manager to agree to it." But after the general manager talked with the station's attorney, the station decided that maybe nobody would be interested in viewing the film. It was not shown.

The October 28 debate had been planned for KQED, the San Francisco public television station, but its staff and engineers were out on strike. KPIX was talked into substituting, some said, but KPIX officials claimed to have leaped at the chance. Indeed, Len

Schlosser, KPIX public affairs director, asserted that his station had wanted to produce a debate originally . Once the ambition was realized, however, the station did nothing to promote the program. The taping was conducted on Monday, but was not aired until Wednesday night, when KPIX obtained Westinghouse clearance for prime time airing. Apart from those who tuned in by chance, the public had no way of knowing KPIX was carrying the debate.

What comes through clearly is how few Californians had a chance to know anything about the debates. The principal news aired was that the meetings took place. Beyond that came the exchange of insults. The striking differences in KNBC's coverage was not merely in the amount of total time given the debates—12 minutes 27 seconds, plus the hour-long airing of the last debate November 2—but in KNBC's effort to provide viewers with substance in its reports. Four times, KNBC used film of the two candidates debating, affording each from one to two minutes to state his case, sandwiched between interpretation and comment by a reporter. This was a sharp contrast to the erratic and abbreviated reports aired by other stations.

Of the five other television stations observed, KGTV and KCRA-TV carried two newscasts with direct excerpts (briefer than KNBC's) and KGO-TV's late-night news had included a one-minute excerpt showing the most heated attacks; KTLA had one 2 minute 14 second report of a serious interchange filmed during the 90-minute public television debate. That undertaking, broadcast statewide by public television on October 8, was less than edifying, since questions were posed by an array of people representing minority groups and other symbolic interest groups who were inclined to make speeches. There was no chance to follow up on a reply.

There are contradictory versions of what happened at the second meeting held at the University of California's Irvine campus, where students were refused permission to transmit the public television program over the campus radio. Flournoy, in his remarks, apologized for the student cut-off, which he said was due to Brown's refusal to sign a waiver to their agreement; Brown told the audience that it was the fault of the university lawyer, not himself. Brown reportedly refused to sign the waiver but indicated that the students should look to their legal rights themselves. When Brown made his public disclaimer of responsibility before the campus audience, he was booed.

Besides Doug Kriegel, a few other reporters murmured during the campaign that their stations should have defied the ban and thus created news out of the situation. But the only reporter on monitored stations to speak out on the air about the candidate control over debate broadcasts was Bob Abernethy, Los Angeles interviewer and commentator at KNBC. On his September 3 "Viewpoint," he pointed out that the two candidates for governor and "most broadcasters are joined in an unwitting conspiracy to deny most of us the opportunity we should have to see the leading candidates side by side." He emphasized that Brown was the controlling agent, since the polls gave him the lead. "This relative invisibility," Abernethy said, was somewhat due to the equal-time law, because a station that would carry a Brown-Flournoy debate might feel obliged to offer equivalent time to the American Independent and Peace and Freedom candidates, "and most stations apparently feel that their time is too valuable to justify giving it away for the small audience such a program would attract."

Some stations, notably KNXT in Los Angeles (CBS-owned and operated), had insisted on adhering to the letter as well as the spirit of FCC regulations and wanted the two major party candidates to share any joint appearance with two others in the race representing minor parties. (Edmon V. Kaiser of the American Independent Party and Elizabeth Keathley of the Peace and Freedom Party each drew about 1 percent of the vote.) When it came to determining which station would get the final pre-election debate in Los Angeles, the candidates indicated they favored KNBC's "news interview" style in preference to a KNXT plan to include Kaiser and Keathley in a full-scale presentation.

The spending curb in the agreement absorbed most newspaper reporter attention. Some of the press were beguiled into viewing the pact as Brown had intended: an unusual bit of generosity on his part. *The San Diego Tribune* editorially commended the two for their mutual limits on spending, and said before reading the fine print: "Their agreement to meet each other in debate . . . suggests that voters will have ample opportunity to familiarize themselves with California's problems and the approach each would take to solving them." It didn't turn out that way, of course. One television columnist, Terrence O'Flaherty of *The San Francisco Chronicle* wrote on November 4: "What ever happened to Edmund G. Brown Jr. and Houston Flournoy and their highly touted agreement to debate on television? Here we are, on the eve of an election, and California voters have seen practically nothing of the two men they are being asked to consider for the highest office in the state. . . . What's worse, it appears to have been planned that way. Is this any way to run a campaign? Is it any way to run television?"

These were the only protests encountered on the curtailment of debate transmission. Neither Common Cause nor the American Civil Liberties Union explored the question, nor had it been called to their attention. In summary, the broadcast industry generally gave the debates far less than "robust, wide-open" reporting. The goals stressed in court opinions and agency rulings were different from the performance of licensees. Even Brown's staff, which had helped arrange curtailment of the coverage, was surprised at the dearth of solid television reporting.

The second remarkable response to the FCC regulations was the widespread caution over equal time and fairness on newscasts. Station personnel distinguished clearly, in discussion, between the freedom that regulations afford straight news reports and the limits imposed when stations' facilities are offered for a "public affairs" program, a studio interview, special documentaries or pre-election round-ups. Such "use" of broadcast facilities is covered by Rule 315 (a), which requires that such an "opportunity" offered one candidate in a race must be offered to all candidates in the same race. Yet Rule 315 (a) contains four specific exemptions, all of which concern the reporting of news-related events and, together, give the stations considerable latitude in deciding what constitutes news. In this campaign, however, curious pressures on the news programs turned up as a result of the pervading fearfulness of license challenges that might be raised from many sources should a slip-up occur in handling political news or political ads. In practice, the FCC rules intruded constantly into broadcasting newsrooms.

Wariness may have been especially evident in 1974, because the FCC, from 1972 to 1974, was refining its own statement of how the fairness doctrine should apply in political discussion. Its initial position was that fairness imposed two responsibilities on broadcasters: "Coverage of issues of public importance must be adequate and must fairly reflect differing viewpoints." Various rulings since that 1949 *Report on Editorializing* emphasized that "adequate" could raise the question of "a reasonable percentage of broadcast time," and the rulings brought the interpretation of fairness closer to the situation relating to contests between politicians, rather than just to discussion of issues. In 1970, the case of Nicolas Zapple brought from the FCC a reiteration of its admonition that fairness had to be considered even when equal time did not, and that it applied in "those news-type appearances of the candidates themselves which were exempted from the equal opportunity provisions. . . ." Sensitivity over increasing attention to fairness may explain the exceptional caution of station lawyers in 1974. In fact, the new fairness standards were issued during the campaign, in July 1974. The FCC document acknowledged that "this system is far from perfect," but it left questions of fairness and of serving the public interest "to the licensee's journalistic discretion." The same section stressed an expectation that this leeway would lead to "maximum public enlightenment on issues of significance with a minimum of governmental intrusion into the journalistic process."

There were, however, some comments in the campaign on equal time and fairness either as hampering limits on political coverage or as unenforced and ineffective ideals. Russ Coughlan, station manager of KGO-TV, expressed the prevailing view: "The fairness doctrine prevents us from lending ourselves to the campaign effort." The station would be happy to televise candidates, he said, but their numbers defeated them. KABC radio newscaster and talk-show host Michael Jackson said that he refused telephone calls from Senator Alan Cranston, "because it was hard to draw the line definitely that what he was talking about was really news and not campaigning." He said that he had invited former Representative Helen Gahagan Douglas to appear on his program but "had to ask her to promise not to mention Roth (whom she had endorsed) because, if she did, I'd get into the whole equal-time mess." At KNX radio in Los Angeles, a reporter said that a verbal order had been issued that no member of Congress was to be interviewed during the campaign because of the equal-time doctrine. So cautious was this station's reporting, in its efforts to avoid demands for equal time that another KNX reporter said that a special program prepared on campaign financing purposely made no reference to Proposition 9, the "reform" measure limiting political expenditures because it was before the voters at the election. By talking around the general subject, not directly on this proposition, the station felt that it covered the issue while avoiding the necessity of interviewing "pro" and "con" factions.

A great deal of attention has been paid to the protections offered minor contenders for political office—and the democratic system as a whole—by insistence upon equal opportunity. The election disclosed, however, that in practice this proviso leads broadcasters to steer clear of political stories where possible and drain those that cannot be avoided of any elements that could cause equal-time problems. At Los Angeles radio station KFWB, news director Charles Sergis said, "A station can't do a proper job on candidates who matter because it is constantly under the obligation of providing the same reports on everybody." Bill Fyffe, news director of KABC-TV in Los Angeles, said that equal time, fairness and special-interest-group pressures on a station "present such problems that political coverage on television and radio is being very timidly handled." At KSAN radio in San Francisco, news director David McQueen said, "To avoid trouble, we go into political news in less depth than we do other news."

"Balance" was the word most frequently heard about political news coverage, and radio was especially sensitive to it. Many news rooms kept careful logs on each candidate's appearances to the second, just in case the FCC should query the station. At San Diego's KGTV (NBC), news director Ron Mires said that he kept a log of the time accorded all candidates on news programs and checked weekly "just to see how it stands." At KABC-TV, Fyffe said that he kept a log to apportion political time evenly between rivals. At KABC radio, anchor Randy Roach said during the primary, "I'm laying off Republicans. That's being fair to both of them. I'm leaving them completely alone." Log-keeping often did not benefit the list of primary hopefuls because, as Mires put it, "The governor's race just wasn't important enough in the full run of the news to cover all these candidates." Many stations, in short, avoided equal-time problems with 29 candidates by withdrawing attention from the governor's race and reporting local contests more heavily. Sacramento's KCRA-TV maintained a log on political appearances, although it pegged its coverage to the candidates who rated highest in the opinion polls "because, obviously, we couldn't cover them all," explained Paul Thompson, news manager. He said that his log was kept "so that we are fair and so we don't get caught by the FCC." But equal-time and fairness posed a problem in news coverage, he said, explaining: "Why should we give the 18th guy on the list the same amount of time as we give the Speaker of the Assembly, Moretti? Well, there's no way! That's ridiculous!" He added, however, that "we get a lot of phone calls and letters from people who wonder why we can't cover their candidate."

The extent to which timidity over equal time sometimes shaped the news was most graphically illustrated by an experience Rep. Waldie had with KCBS radio in San Francisco. As a candidate for governor, he had become familiar with the difficulty of getting broadcast time, but knew the stations were eager to use any news he could provide on the Nixon impeachment proceedings of the House Judiciary Committee, on which he served. Logically, he was most likely to communicate with the media in his own congressional district, which was included in KCBS's area. So when he had something to say about the committee's developments, he telephoned the San Francisco all-news station, and he called at one point with what he felt was "a big news break." "I got the station on the phone," he said, "but this night news editor sounded frightened to death. He said, 'Oh, I can't take that. I have to get a Republican comment on it.'" Waldie was dumbfounded. "I said, 'What do you mean, you can't take it. I'm not asking any mention about the governor's race. I am on the impeachment committee. We just voted 33 to 3 to subpoena the President of the United States. That happens to be a national news story. Are you interested?'" The reply: "I just can't take that news item unless I can get a Republican to comment at the same time. I don't want to argue with you but this is too touchy around here. They are putting a lot of pressure on us." The congressman was outraged. "Who is putting pressure on you?" The fellow replied, "Oh, I didn't mean to say that. I don't mean that. Look, I didn't say that, understand?" Waldie shrugged: "So he didn't use the news. I called up some other stations and they took it gladly."

Just having to be answerable for anything that prompts a query tended to make the stations careful. And to be especially careful is to be quiet. Norman Woodruff, for six years with KCBS radio (three of them as news director), told how constantly a news director must refer to legal counsel. The prospect of a "20-day letter" haunts every station manager, he said:

"You have the government thing hanging over, which is a threat whether it actually materializes or not. The fact that any member of the public can send you into a hearing—that really acts as a restraining influence at all times. . . . If any one listener writes a postcard to the Federal Communications Commission saying, 'I am offended by what this station has done,' the FCC sends a mimeographed letter to the station saying, 'Mrs. So-and-so complains about your broadcast on such-and-such date. Explain why you did that.' It's the 20-day letter. You must reply within 20 days or else face fines and penalties and things like that. Now, when you're faced with that kind of pressure by a federal agency . . . , well, it's not exactly pressure, it's just a question. But if you are a giant corporation, how must you respond to that question? First, you call your attorney, right? You can't think of responding to a letter like that when you have a very expensive property with maybe a hundred or more jobs on the line, unless your lawyer helps you draft the reply. You just can't take any postcard or phone call from any listener lightly."

In short, the FCC requirement to extend equal time to all candidates made stations extraordinarily selective in their news coverage and particularly timid in contests drawing a large number of candidates. The fairness warnings became interpreted as an equivalent of equal time because equal time was the easiest standard to apply.

The effect of television's minimal response was discussed by Brown and Flournoy representatives at a Sigma Delta Chi meeting after the election. David Jensen, a Brown press aide, said television coverage was heavy during the Labor Day kickoff and the initial week. "After that it dropped off to almost nothing." Peter Kaye, Flournoy's press aide, spoke with greater sharpness: "Was the coverage fair? Yes, it was fair. Was it adequate? No, it was not. . . . As far as I know the campaign wasn't covered at all on television. . . . KGO was out for a week. . . . they did a pretty good job. KNBC did a fine job, a competent professional job. Other than that, there was nothing."

It was a reflection on the California style of campaign reporting that Kurt Malarstedt, Washington correspondent for a Stockholm television station, followed the campaign for about four days. His 45-minute report was to be aired in Stockholm November 1, paired with a segment on New York's gubernatorial race. That was more time than many California stations devoted in all their newscasts through September and October to the election!

Many of the difficulties in complying with FCC requirements on advertising have been described. Every station had set up strict internal rules to insure equal advertising opportunity after selecting the races for which ads would be accepted. The necessity of policing the even distribution of ad opportunity, of keeping each candidate advised of the rival's purchases, especially in the concluding days when previously underfunded contestants scurried to buy up their equivalent shares, brought bedlam to most broadcast business offices. No station executive considered the revenue worth the trouble, but broadcasters tolerated the inconvenience and warned regular customers that they might be "bumped." Although FCC guidelines are more precise for advertising than for news handling, some variation in interpretation was discovered. For instance, the commission requires that the charge for political ads conform to the lowest rate that a station offers its best customer. One ad specialist said that he could not place political ads under those conditions with one particular station, however, because it always turned out that the station was unable to find lowest-rate time available except at undesirable low-audience times such as mid-afternoon. He was forced to pay top rates for prime time. Another station set a special low rate, one-third of its regular charge, whatever the time of day.

Much about political advertising is dictated by the networks, since they specify what they will accept in prime-time periods. Indirectly, they mandated the 30-second spot as the advertising mode for 1974, since that was the only format acceptable for prime time. When a full minute or, on rare occasions, five minutes were run, the time was at an independent station and during low-rate periods. Amid the many complaints that the 30-second spot was inadequate, Bud Arnold, Roth's campaign media adviser, said he felt that the FCC should require longer spots. John Waugaman, business manager at KFWB, conceded that the station had pared political ad time as far as it felt it could within fairness limits. "We wouldn't take a penny of it, if we could avoid it," he added. For all the difficulty, however, political advertising appeared easier for stations to handle than political coverage in public affairs programs or news when faced with many candidates for one race.

The most obvious area for concern about the effect of FCC rules relates to minor-party candidates. Did they get intended protection? All 11 monitored broadcast stations afforded Elizabeth Keathley, Peace and Freedom candidate, and Edmon V. Kaiser, American Independent candidate, some air time on regular newscasts or on special public affairs programs, although the larger share was on non-exempt public affairs presentations. Radio stations monitored in the study referred to them in the lead of their news stories in 6 percent of the total (10 stories). This attention was disproportionately high compared to the other two media because at least one station, KSAN, felt that airing minor-party challengers was in accord with its audience taste. In television stations monitored, minor party candidates figured in the anchorman's lead in 7 stories, 3.4 percent of the total. The press, of course, was under no legal obligation to report on minor candidates but did so out of professional concern for fairness. In the four newspapers, 12 stories, 2 percent of the total, gave headline emphasis to minor candidates. The brief TV reports afforded minor candidates were in most cases studio shots, requiring minimal commitment of crew time and cost. Composite figures obscure differences between the stations. Some, such as KGO-TV and KCRA-TV, never even mentioned the minor-party candidates on their newscasts. The most extensive single news report was KFMB-TV's account for 2 minutes 25 seconds on Kaiser's appearance at a gathering in San Diego. The station also had a 1-minute 20-second interview with Keathley. Primarily, what stations did was offer minor-party candidates rather frequent invitations to appear on nonexempt programs such as talk-shows, community forums and "community scene" presentations. The minor-party candidates did not buy broadcast time. They relied exclusively on proffered time or the scant news coverage. No protests came from them.

A significant difference cropped up in the way stations airing debates approached their obligations to minor-party candidates. KPIX carried a Keathley-Kaiser discussion in the half-hour following its presentation of Brown-Flournoy. KNXT insisted from the beginning, even in the primary, that FCC "debate" rules required that all contestants for the same office share in one presentation, a situation Brown absolutely refused to be a part of.

KOVR, the Sacramento-Stockton channel owned by the McClatchy interests which also own the *Bee* newspaper chain, had the earliest of the commercially presented debates. Host John Iander offered a choice: an appearance of all gubernatorial candidates together on October 20, or a half-hour each separately. Keathley and Kaiser preferred appearing alone. Brown and Flournoy accepted for October 20, providing that other candidates for governor would *not* be present. To make air time exactly equivalent, the station increased its usual half-hour to a full hour for Brown and Flournoy and the two minor-party candidates enjoyed the unusual advantage of being aired subsequently, nearer election day.

Newspapers shared the problem of how to cope with minor-party candidates. Arthur Berman, assistant metropolitan editor of *The Los Angeles Times,* said, for example, at the Sigma Delta Chi meeting: "We did not give equal coverage to all 29 candidates. Should we have given the Peace and Freedom and the American Independent Party candidates equal treatment? Do you take a candidate from a party with less than 1 percent of the registered voters as seriously as you do somebody chosen by the Democratic or Republican party? People would have thought we were just silly. I think we gave them more coverage than they deserved." Peter Kaye, from Flournoy's staff, worked for public broadcasting immediately before the campaign and might be assumed to have special concern over making time available to minor candidates. But he also concluded: "They would take up needed news time. . . . In fact, I think the equal-time requirement should be dropped so they wouldn't get on at all and then maybe we'd get some debates and some decent dialogue going and people could really find something out."

It was in the primary that serious problems arose. The broadcast world to a large degree took the easy way out and avoided all coverage.

Those who could only be considered fringe candidates got a few invitations to mass "zoo" appearances on the air, some in news time, some in special programs. KTLA presented a parade of these hopefuls and said its effort drew surprisingly large appreciative response from its audience. KSAN, the progressive rock radio station in San Francisco asked all 29 primary candidates two questions on prisons and on utility rates, and aired 60-second answers in sequence for weeks.

The gravest charges of injustice or inequality arose from the middle level of serious candidates in the Democratic list whose bid for news notice could not be dismissed as fringe, whose advance or decline in opinion polls was clearly related to the share of media attention they obtained. Most within this group felt aggrieved about lack of access to a system they maintained had operated without fairness. Besides the candidates, a number of reporters and news executives in press and broadcast were clearly troubled that the California experience had exposed an area of substantial injustice for which no one had a remedy—that of adequate access to the air waves for numerous serious candidates.

Waldie, Hafif, Ward, and especially Roth complained bitterly that they did not get a fair share of news time. They also turned to the FCC. Roth, through attorney Michael Levett in Los Angeles, filed verbal complaint by telephone when he was not included in the KOVR primary-time debate limited to the top three Democrats, (Brown, it turned out, was a no-show.) Levett remarked that the FCC system for responding to such a mid-election protest seemed efficient, for after presenting the facts he received a return call within a few hours to advise him that it appeared, from a hearing officer's experience, that Roth would not get a favorable reply if he asked for a formal hearing because his protest lacked basis in law. This was because the KOVR program was a standing news-conference format and the station was free to select candidates for appearance on a news-judgment basis. Roth dropped the case.

Levett filed another FCC complaint charging a fairness violation in the marked disproportion of time being allotted Roth in comparison with those who topped the opinion polls. "Unfortunately, we got some figures before we made the call," Levett said. "It might have been better if we had gotten the FCC to run down the facts. We knew how little time Roth was getting on the major stations but, to tell the truth, when we began checking station records what really shocked us was how little time the whole race got." He told the FCC hearing officer on the phone that a hasty survey indicated the other candidates were being aired three or four times as much as Roth. He was informed that the commission yardstick was that fairness was violated when the disadvantage reached a 6 or 7 to 1 ratio.

Levett's visit to the studios to examine the records had one result: an immediate quickening of studio interest in Roth. The candidate chuckled. "We got this call from a Los Angeles station wanting to send a camera out to film what we were doing—right away. They said they were going to do a report on me, Waldie and Hafif. I suggested some better events another day but, no, they wanted to do it right then. We hadn't much to show except envelope stuffing on at headquarters, but they shot that. It was pretty obvious what prompted this sudden burst of interest."

When Roth, Hafif, Waldie and Ward were ignored in the big finale of the primary—the KNBC interview with Brown, Moretti and Alioto— Roth tried a different tactic: he bought an ad. He asked for 15 minutes reply time, then five. He finally took what KNBC would yield: one minute out of the hour designated for the Saturday "news conference." By all odds this was the most dramatic political spot of the year. It opened with Roth speaking straight into the camera, the most forceful and effective message he projected in any of his ads, and one he wrote virtually himself. "KNBC has graciously sold me one minute of time to answer the 59 minutes they donated to my three principal competitors," he began. "What did you think of the debates? Were real issues substantively discussed? There is one issue I would like to raise. The question of business and corporate contributions. All three of them have accepted hundreds of thousands of dollars. . . ."

The ad itself was not what embarrassed KNBC. It was what happened to the ad. Somebody pulled the plug. Through an accident, as everyone insisted and Roth came to believe, the ad was interrupted just as it got started. The rest of the minute ticked by, and there was no way to recapture the attention of that group of listeners who had been attentive to Roth's rivals.

Roth capitalized on his KNBC rejection as much as he could. He wheeled up to the curb directly in front of the studio in a mobile home placarded with his posters and equipped with television set and well-stocked bar. There he chatted with reporters on their way to the debate, played host genially to his competitors, and generally assumed a courtly manner in his ostracism. KNBC's chief competitor in the Los Angeles television market, KNXT (CBS), also made the most of Roth's ridicule of KNBC. It had a camera present showing Roth before the television set as his ad came on and the interruption occurred. At the time Roth's outrage was enormous. Recalling it, he managed to see the whole scene as humorous. "That final media thing in Los Angeles was actually great fun. CBS gave it very heavy play, what with the spot being cut off and my exploding 'Those --- bleep --- bleep guys' and everybody in the trailer starting to yell. And then the NBC program host Abernethy and another guy came running down and said 'Please don't blame us; it was a mistake.' I felt from the way they acted it really was a mistake.

"I didn't know quite what to do. I left for the airport. But at the studio, phone calls began flooding in, by the hundreds, they told me, objecting to what had happened. So the station desperately tried to reach me, and they got me just as I was getting on the plane. They invited me to appear on their late news show. My staff didn't want me to because they were going to negotiate for replacements for the spot, but I said, to hell with it, I'm going to get anything I can. So I went back. And I got the opening on the late KNBC news. Then, as I was going to sleep that night, I decided that I would sue them."

9

MERVIN THE MASTER

To the candidate, the most important news story is the publication of a public opinion poll. Poll results have a critical effect on campaigns—including strategy, the flow of funds, organization support, and the interrelationship between rivals. Do polls have an inordinately persuasive influence on voters? This question, while important, is not what most concerns candidates. In this campaign, the polls that worried politicians most seemed to be those published earliest, long before the public had bestirred itself to consider ballot decisions. The very early polls represented an initial line-up, and politicians seemed universally agreed that it is extraordinarily difficult to change that ranking. The assumption is that if a candidate were third, he pretty much stayed third; if fifth, he stayed there or fell lower. Maybe there could be a switch one step up but not much more. Most importantly, if a man were first, he stayed first.

In the governor's race, events did alter these early relationships, however, and opinion proved to be not as static as politicians' alarms would make it seem. In addition, tremendous efforts were made by campaign experts to shift the polls, and sometimes these efforts worked. The campaign was notable for the erroneous assumptions by candidates and media about public opinion. But it also was notable for the fact that all candidates, victor as well as vanquished, considered polls a key factor in the election system and that once published, the polls become a force themselves. Losers considered polls to be the most grievous disadvantage they faced. The opinion sampling related to the gubernatorial campaign may have provoked particularly sensitive reactions from the aspirants for several reasons: the large number of candidates, the lack of an incumbent, the Federal indictment that struck down the poll-leading Republican candidate, and an unusual climate of public indifference to the race.

No point is stressed more by the poll-taking professionals than that their rankings purport only to be the record of a representative sample when taken. But at the moment the polltaker asks a respondent, "Whom would you vote for today?" the count freezes that particular instant of response into statistics. Similarly, the reports seem straightforward and simple when published: "71 percent thus, 15 percent thus, 14 percent undecided." While pollsters insist upon the momentary validity of the response, virtually all who read the figures are unable to shake off the notion that the polls can be used to foretell the outcome. This is one problem attendant on the publication of opinion polls during an election, but it was not the central problem in 1974. What absorbed the candidates was the effect the polls had on their own campaign structures and in media news selection. The polls burst upon the election system with a volatility of their own. Next to money, polls were the most powerful force let loose, and they provoked massive reactions, sometimes of despair and sometimes of campaign cunning, aimed at changing the next opinion poll. What effect these reports have on the voting public has been closely examined and hotly debated elsewhere. The relationship between poll reports and the media proved fully as interesting.

Three kinds of public-opinion sampling were in evidence in the campaign: professional opinion pollsters hired by candidates for their own purposes; a highly respected opinion-research firm headed by Mervin Field, whose periodic political reports, the California Poll, reached the public through subscriber media; and private polls conducted by the media themselves, *The Los Angeles Times* undertaking the most substantial such effort. Each served candidates and the media differently. The first, designed exclusively to guide candidate strategy, was the least publicized and sometimes as close guarded from competitors as marketing reports. The newspapers, on the other hand, looked upon their opinion-sampling exercises as a legitimate news search. The California Poll was an exclusive to subscriber newspapers or broadcasters, but was widely circulated thereafter by the wire services. This poll, believed to have the greatest influence, provoked the most controversy.

The campaign illustrated the role of private polling exceptionally well because Brown was surrounded by media-attuned advisers committed to the use of polls over a long period. Brown himself was acutely sensitive to public moods discoverable through opinion-sampling techniques such as the revulsion against government spending and political venality; and he addressed himself to these matters. Most campaigns built opinion sampling into their budgets as frugally as possible, while those who were financially pinched depended on the California Poll. Brown's approach was unusual because polling was the underpinning of his success, but the cost was minimized by doing as much as possible within his staff. Some members had marketing-research know-how, especially Richard Maullin who had been an economic researcher with the Rand Corporation. Maullin hired a Los Angeles consultant, Dorothy Corey, to provide the actual interviewers but did the bulk of the preparation himself. Brown's advantage was akin to that of a field general whose intelligence service is superb; he was rarely taken by surprise.

As early as April, 1972, the Brown team had conducted a statewide survey that revealed the degree of public awareness Brown enjoyed, his identification as distinct from his father, and the number of Californians aware of his political-reform activity. They found, too, that they needed to broaden the issues with which he was politically identified. This does not necessarily mean that Brown derived his ideas from opinion sampling, but rather that he could test them against public response. The process of identifying what to emphasize and how to project his image for maximum public acceptance emerged from an extended familiarity with what the public was thinking. From this came the confidence with which he dwelt upon the promise of a "new spirit" keyed to efficient government and accompanied—paradoxically, the press thought at the time—with budget frugality.

Brown's use of opinion sampling differed markedly from the two or three measurements candidates ordinarily run on their own campaign progress. These, Brown did as well. In fact, in the final ten days of October he was sampling daily, so that the shift toward Flournoy was perceived by the Brown camp as soon as it was in Flournoy's, and perhaps sooner. In all respects, Brown's comprehension of what was currently on the public mind ran well ahead of that of any adversaries because polling was a tool he believed in and knew how to use.

Moretti's private polling firm, Hugh Schwartz of Public Response Company in San Francisco, was pulled out of its discreet anonymity on April 11 for an unusual press conference. At that point, Moretti exulted in the discovery that the Schwartz findings differed sufficiently from what Field had earlier disclosed to warrant major publicity, for it showed Moretti to have passed Alioto to become Brown's closest rival. Actually, Schwartz's report differed from Field mainly in its timing. A couple of weeks later, Field also confirmed Moretti in second place. But Schwartz's analysis drew considerable press attention and countered candidate complaints that their private polls were dismissed by the media as "propaganda." (In his story in *The Times,* George Skelton noted that the survey had cost Moretti $10,000.) Schwartz defined the support he found for Brown as "soft," and the same word was picked up in Field's April 24 report: "The very high level of initial support enjoyed by Brown appears to have been somewhat soft. Other candidates have chipped much of it away." Field never went as far as Schwartz, however, to claim that the race had narrowed to only the two, Brown and Moretti. Schwartz found a larger proportion of voters who had not yet made up their minds than Field identified, and it was this undecided element that gave both Moretti and Alioto hope. Later, Moretti's campaign manager, John FitzRandolph, spoke bitterly about the influence of polls. He felt that Moretti's rise was interrupted by news about the Zebra murders, which centered media attention on Alioto fortuitously close to a Field poll sampling.

Alioto had an abundant self-confidence and a political flair that helped draw him continuing coverage so that he could afford an indifference to polls. They were, he said in an interview May 19 with Richard Bergholz of *The Times,* "a kind of voodooism" that he did not need to practice. Despite the disclaimer, that same story noted that Alioto's staff had done enough sampling to be persuaded that Moretti lagged further behind Alioto than the California Poll showed. Originally, Alioto had discovered that his major obstacle was an unflattering image in southern California stemming largely from a *Look* magazine article that a court later found to be libelous. The difference in Alioto's image in the two parts of California was illustrated by a poll Alioto's team took after his wife, Angelina, had vanished and then returned home to protest, in part, the lot of a politician's wife. Her public exasperation tended to humanize the mayor for northern Californians, while in southern California people felt that Angelina's flight proved Alioto a tyrant in his own home and a "baloney artist" in public.

In the primary, neither Republican bothered with private polling. Flournoy stood at the bottom of everybody's list, and Reinecke towered at the top, but every informed political observer knew that these popularity measurements were meaningless in the face of Reinecke's pending prosecution. In the fall, in the run-off with Brown, Flournoy commissioned four private opinion samplings by Decision-Making Information, a national Republican polling firm located in Santa Ana. The first, which ran in mid-July, gave Flournoy and his supporters a very heartening picture: Brown 44 percent, Flournoy 40 percent, undecided 16 percent. The next test was scheduled for August 2-12. It was to be a disastrous period for Republicans: The Nixon tape admissions were followed August 8 by Nixon's resignation. Flournoy's stock plummeted. His private poll showed him down to 36 percent, Brown up to 53 percent. He struggled on; and at the end of August, with President Ford brightening the political picture with his candor and amiable demeanor, Flournoy's managers expected improvement in the sentiment. But mis-fortune hit again, for during the poll period, in early September, President Ford pardoned Nixon. It was a shaft right to the heart of Flournoy's effort to rally Republicans.

Despite vigorous campaigning, his standing slipped to 35 percent while Brown rose to 55 percent. Field later said that his efforts to measure sentiment at that period found Republicans so shattered by their national party disasters that his interviewers could not get the normal ratio of people to acknowledge that they were Republicans, and he had to expand his sample. Field's reports in August and October were not so discouraging as Flournoy's private count. Field showed a 14-point gap in late August, but by his next sampling time, September 28 to October 1, about three weeks after the Nixon pardon, Flournoy was only 11 points behind. The next private Flournoy count, October 25-27, showed only a seven-point gap, and at this point the Flournoy people felt that they could talk to the press about it. To the press, this narrowing was inconsequential, for Brown remained, as he had from the start, sub-stantially in the lead.

The Field staff argues that, since private polling is sure to be under-taken in a campaign, the public interest is served by an agency that will disclose the same kind of sampling data that the candidates sequester. Even Moretti's chief media consultant, Bob Squier, who joined in criti-cism of polls for their influence on the media and campaign support, nevertheless insisted that public access to this information was important. Since the candidates get it, the public should, he said. "A campaign is a transaction between three forces—the media, the candidate, and the polls," he said.

The data are made public in California through Field Research Corpo-ration, which since 1946 has issued the California Poll regularly in po-litical seasons. In 1974 it was subsidized by 11 newspapers and three television stations, each paying an annual fee for publication or broad-cast rights within their area. *The Times* reported paying $15,000 a year for the Field poll. Part of the cost of the poll is borne by Field as promo-tion for his commercial opinion sampling and marketing research. Field established his business at the end of World War II after training at Princeton with George Gallup's Opinion Research Corporation. It is today a national concern with a research and sampling staff, training program, computer center, print shop, and bindery. From the start, Field has strongly supported academic interest in public-opinion research, and he has encouraged scholarly access to his findings, lodging his data over the years with the political science department of the University of California at Berkeley. His significant position in California politics is paralled by that of similar agencies in Minnesota, Iowa and Texas; but because of the size of California and the reputation he has developed, Field's agency is often compared with Gallup and Harris polls. These polls are media-sponsored and their service is not for sale to individual candidates or for partisan purposes.

What the Field poll published about the governor's race was a series of 11 tabulations ranking Democrats and six on Republicans. After the primary, five more reports on Brown and Flournoy were issued. Field's information reached subscribers with explanatory material showing when the poll was taken, the size of the sampling, and how it was used. The final six were based on telephone interviews to cut time lag. Frequently, Field identified the composition of the cross-section sampled as to party affiliation, geography, age, sex, or socio-economic pattern, emphasizing, for instance, where Black sympathies lay. He usually asked in the interview, especially as the election neared, the probability of the respondent's voting; and he would sometimes separate from the large sample the responses of those likely to vote. He always included with his figures a form indicating sample tolerances for error plus or minus for the number of persons interviewed. An opinion report based upon 1,000 interviews (and Field's 1974 reports customarily included slightly more than 1,000) had a tolerance for error of 3.5 percent; a poll based on only 200 interviews, he indicated, might vary within a 7.7 percent range.

The top chart on page 185 summarizes the Field poll findings at various times before the primary election.

For Moretti, the February, 1974, poll was encouraging and showed results from his tremendous effort to get his name better known. But for Roth, Hafif, and especially Waldie, the February report was shattering. David Rogers, from the Waldie group, said, "We had just started to talk to our friends when the polls came out. We would start talking to people who had always supported Waldie in the past and immediately they would start talking about where he was in the polls. They'd say, 'Gee, it's just throwing money away. He can't win.' "

The critical word in a campaign is "movement." If a candidate isn't leading in an opinion poll, he must show that there is "movement," that he is challenging the leaders. *San Diego Union* reporter Otto Kreisher wrote about this on April 11: " 'Upward mobility' in the polls can inspire the committed workers, can attract other supporters . . . and can help attract contributors with which to buy name identification and more 'upward mobility.' " Statistical proof of this "upward mobility" is essential to a candidate, Kreisher wrote, "to keep supporters on the telephone and money in the coffers." And he quoted Waldie: " 'The polls are our primaries.' "

The effect of low poll standing is instantaneous. Contributions dry up. In the general election, when the August 22 Field poll showed Flournoy lagging by 14 points, Stu Spencer, his campaign consultant, said, "Contributions dried up like that!" He snapped his fingers. The August poll cost the campaign at least a half million dollars, Spencer estimated. That sum, spent in television ads, might have made the fast-finishing Flournoy the winner.

It could be, as Roth observed: "Polls are a self-fulfilling prophecy." Criticism seethed below the surface through the spring of 1974. The early polls, politicians contended, froze them into a status from which they could not escape. By May, the feelings of outrage among the trailing contestants over what they took to be the effect of these polls was almost explosive, and some of it spilled into political stories at the time. Although no reporter wrote a news story fully developing the subject then, *The Times* was sufficiently alerted to undertake a comprehensive story for the fall and another that winter on the relationship between opinion polls and political success. These stories criticized not the polling exercise but the impact the reporting of them had on the candidates' financial resources and organization morale, as well as on the media. Brown was the only Democratic candidate who did not inveigh against the polls. Among Republicans, Flournoy had no need to complain. After Reinecke's indictment, he stood 44 percent to Reinecke's 27 percent.

That polls respond to television advertising was taken as a matter of course. Brown once remarked that he was not worried about polls because he stood so many points ahead but that he expected to drop "when the others get their heavy advertising started." In April, when Brown had dropped from a February high of 46 percent to 29 percent, Douglas Faigin, Brown's press aide, was quoted in *The San Diego Tribune* as explaining such a decline had been anticipated. "Remember, that poll was taken right after heavy Moretti television advertising. We had no television in that period." The most explicit revelation of this cycle came from Roth and his ad consultant, Bud Arnold. Roth's saturation advertising campaign was designed to fall as near to the Field polling period as possible. "Everybody wants to be sure his television spots are running when the California Poll samplers are out there asking peo-

ple's preferences," Arnold said. "So you try to make an educated guess
as to which week or ten days you ought to hit the major media markets
with your TV ads." Field's samplers took to their telephones throughout
California on the evening of April 10, and Roth's ads on this occasion
were on the air the day before. That sampling showed Roth's first up-
turn, 3 percent. This type of deliberate effort to influence polls is rarely
described with such openness. Field himself was indifferent to it. His
general approach, he said, is that media messages to the voter are of
such small significance that it didn't matter much when ads were timed.
But if he shrugged off advertising's effect on the voters, he did concede
that the polls influence campaign organizations and fund-raising, a reality he felt that the election system has to live with. The benefits of
public awareness, he thinks, outweigh any harm.

Flournoy's aide, Spencer, said at one point, concerning fund-raising:
"There is Republican money and there is Democratic money and then
there is winner money. Right now Jerry has the Democratic money and
the winner money so he can outspend us." But in the primary there was
no party money. It was all money the candidates raised individually and
it was largely propelled by that "winner" psychology.

Equally clear to the candidates was the relationship of polls to news
attention. If advertising could bolster one's poll position, the improved
standing was then expected to generate more news coverage. The primary campaign produced so little news, apart from personal attacks by
the multitude of contenders, that the polls became significant news
events in themselves. In total, the number of poll stories was not large.
In the four newspapers coded in the primary, only 21 stories carried
headlines directly related to poll reports, some 3.4 percent of the total,
but "trends" reflected in polls were cited far more than the headline figure suggests. The most devastating thrust, the candidates felt, was the
reiteration of phrases like "trailing" or "lagging in the polls." In the
general election, polls similarly figured in only 3 percent of the headlines
but were discussed in 10 to 12 percent of the stories, and the impact
was illustrated by the fact that 48 times in the press stories Brown was
described as "leading" and 58 times Flournoy was described as "trailing."

Another aspect of the influence of the polls was media's reliance on
them as a means of classifying the candidates. According to their standing in the Field poll, the multitudinous Democratic candidates divided
into three tiers: major, minor, and inconsequential. The "majors" were
the top three, with Brown in the lead. The "minors" included all those
significant enough to have a place, however low, in the poll: Waldie,

Roth, Hafif, Ward. The rest of the 18 Democrats became "inconsequential." What rankled the campaigners most was that these rankings were imposed as early as 15 months before the election, as news editors used the poll reports to guide their attention. Ron Mires, news director of KGTV, San Diego, when asked what determined the classifications "major" and "minor," said, "The polls say so," and other broadcast editors said they acted on the same basis. Arthur Berman, assistant metropolitan editor of *The Times,* said he favored polls because "they are a tool for us to tell people what is going on." Harold Keen of KFMB-TV San Diego, said, "The polls establish who the front-runners are, so those are the most interesting to the public and the most important for television to cover." Sydney Kossen, political editor of *The San Francisco Examiner,* said, "The voter needs some indication of who the *serious* candidates are." To Roth's media consultant, Bud Arnold, "It was perfectly evident that the major newspapers had made a predetermination not to spend money covering candidates which the polls indicated had little or no chance to win. . . . They allocate manpower and space according to standing in the polls."

A remarkable parallel between news coverage given the candidates and their poll standings is evident in the second table on page 185 relating poll reports and final votes to two tallies of news coverage, headline mention, and total name use. This chart strongly suggests that patterns established early on the basis of "name recognition" fixed office seekers into a news category that reinforced the initial status, although many reporters contend these rankings were appropriate. Considering the fact that these four newspapers are the dominant daily publications in the state, there is a parallel here so strong as to warrant far more serious consideration of the effect polls have on news media and, thereby, on the campaign process than has been previously accorded. Some news editors—primarily those at *The Times*—voiced concern about the effect polls have on the election process. They talked of the impact on funds and supporters, but at no time did reporters or editors question whether their own news sense was influenced, even when they discussed polls as "handy" sorting devices.

Ken Reich, probably the most sensitive to opinion sampling among reporters because he managed *The Times* poll, felt that if there had been no polls, the allocation of space and attention would have been about the same. He thought the tumult over polls "nonsense." He viewed polls not as a stricture on the election dynamics but as an opening up of the system to newcomers. The novices, he felt, got more mention for getting some entry into Field's slate than if they had had to rely only on political reporting.

There were other views, though. Martin Smith, managing editor of *The Bee,* said he ordered his staff to avoid classifying candidates as "major" or "minor," a precaution that may have preceded or may have followed the paper's decision to endorse Roth in the primary. Bergholz of *The Times* said that Hafif had "a legitimate gripe" over the minimal coverage he received. "He busted his ass campaigning up and down the state and took more detailed positions on more issues than any other candidate," Bergholz said. "But he couldn't get anyone to cover him." Bergholz was critical of any policy that assumed Hafif, Waldie, or Roth were not serious competitors of Brown. "How do we determine who is minor?" he asked. "It's an arbitrary decision we should not make." His paper, he felt, gave ample coverage to those it considered "major" but scant attention to those defined as "minor." Reich conceded that Ward, the Los Angeles County Supervisor climbed to 6 percent in the polls but got such scant news coverage that his drive evaporated. "Ward had a genuine sort of rough populist appeal, which we probably cut off unfairly by giving him so little attention," Reich acknowledged. "That strikes me as the only case where we may have been unfair."

William Thomas, editor of *The Los Angeles Times,* saw no way to avoid polls. "Newspapers have always run them in one form or another, even if it was only man-in-the-street interviews," he said. "Outlawing polls because they affect the election would lead next," he said "to outlawing political reporters. Suppose that a reporter commented that a crowd is 'unenthusiastic' about a candidate's speech; that would have an effect on potential backers." Nevertheless, Thomas said that he sympathized with the candidate who stood low in the polls "because that more or less insures he will continue running behind."

Flournoy expressed irritation with *The Times* for failing to make an endorsement choice between himself and Brown in the final election. He noted that *The Times'* "hands-off" editorial of October 29 used a poll reference as its opening evaluation of Brown: "Whether it is Democrat Edmund Brown Jr., who holds a commanding lead in the polls, or Republican Houston Flournoy, we believe the state will be in able hands." The editorial appeared precisely when that "commanding lead" was melting, and Flournoy considered this to be proof that the media fall victim to their own assumption that polls properly allocate values. *The Times* editors were hypnotized by opinion samples based on name recognition, he believed.

What could be perceived in the election was a relationship between news coverage, advertising, campaign funding, and polls, and the polls seemed to be the pivotal center. All were intricately dependent upon one another. A candidate poured out his calculated best effort to get news coverage so that he registered as somebody, a "celebrity," a "name." The news stories could be shown then to contributors to verify candidate potential and to elicit money for television ads. The ads would increase name recognition and thereby provide a rise in opinion polls and, once moving upward in the polls, he got more news coverage. The modern campaign, at least as illustrated in this California experience, consists of this cyclical interplay.

Many criticisms of poll reports raised by the candidates received either direct affirmation or indirect support from Mervin Field. "The first goal of a candidate," he wrote in November, 1973, "is to achieve a high public visibility and do what he can to make that recognition favorable." In February, 1974, he noted, "The problem facing Waldie, Hafif and Roth is that they are generally not well known . . . Lesser known candidates always have the problem of getting what they call 'name registration,' but to be successful at the polls this usually is achieved over a matter of years. Beyond name registration, there is also the problem of providing the voter with some positive associations related to personality or previous performance. For lesser-known candidates to accomplish this in a race containing so many candidates is a very difficult task, particularly in a state like California." In other words, first impressions stick. Field disagreed, however, that this was solely the media's doing. He considered the media, in all forms, to be only one influence on a voter and less important than social factors such as family, party, organizations, associations, or friends. The 1974 election did not shake Field in his view, but he has conceded in some of his writing that forces at work within the election process are changing and that studies emphasizing the persuasive influence of social institutions were made a decade or two back. Today, he concedes, "social values are changing, party loyalty and standard liberal-conservative orientation [are] weakening. In such a situation, a growing proportion of voters may be open to influence by the media."

Field agreed with the candidates that the media tended to accept polls without sufficient analysis. "Observers ask, 'Where did the polls go wrong?' when an election outcome surprises them, instead of asking, 'Why did vote intentions shift?' I submit that this latter question is more interesting and more significant than the customary bear-baiting of polls." Field contended that whether they realized it or not, the media followed the public in accepting polls as predictions. Events in the final days of the primary appeared to confirm this observation. There were some efforts among the media to analyze the polls, but not with the depth Field invited. *The San Francisco Chronicle* on June 7, the primary out of the way, splashed across Page One pictures of Brown and Flournoy and Field's report on the fall contest with Brown 8 percentage points in the lead. Field promised the election "could be spirited." But on that same day, George Murphy interviewed Field—significant because he, not Field, had initiated it—to examine the "disheartening 47.4 percent turnout of voters." He quoted Field: "The electorate is tuning out the political process." In this story, Murphy called attention to the parallel between Field's last poll and the vote, but he did not reach back to note how close the first poll also had been to the vote. *The Sacramento Bee* also carried a story pondering what had happened in the election, especially the abandonment of interest among Republicans. In a June 2 column on the Editorial Page, political editor Richard Rodda called attention to some of the appurtenances of polls. "Name recognition as an advantage in politics rarely has demonstrated itself so clearly as it has in the 1974 primary election." And he ended his column: "It is somewhat of a travesty that politics is so much like the commercial world—the brand name, not the quality of the product, lures the customer."

When Labor Day came and the media reawakened to the campaign, a number of broadcast reports again set up the polls as reference points. Otis Turner at KCRA-TV Sacramento, in filming Brown at a Labor Day picnic, stressed that he had "the same kind of advantage he enjoyed in the Democratic primary . . . a 14 point lead over Republican Houston Flournoy." KFWB radio noted in its Labor Day news that, "The 44-year-old State Controller trails Brown in the public opinion polls." And KABC radio opened with a talk-show "poll" of phone-in listeners, anchorman Michael Jackson noting the station had tallied 63 percent of those phoning in for Brown, 35 percent for Flournoy, and 2 percent for minor-party candidates. Newspapers, however, did not dredge up old poll measurements much. They waited for Field's first fall report on October 8.

Polls were significant in media content throughout the fall. *The Chronicle* always played the California Poll on Page One. *The Times* usually carried it on Page Three, the principal political page. Its own polls started prominently on column one, Page One, a space reserved for exclusive reports. Since *The Sacramento Bee* was not a subscriber to the Field poll, it picked up the stories tardily from the wire services and played them inside, as did *The San Diego Union.*

In the general election, the media reacted in a strikingly different pattern. With two sides clearly established, any indication that newsworthiness was judged according to poll standing disappeared. There was no marked disparity in attention between the two. News space and news time were allocated with almost mathematical balance.

It is impossible to say how much reporters became hypnotized by the polls they had been recounting for more than a year, inevitably showing Brown in the lead. But there was the journalistic failure to discern the sharp change that was occurring in the public mind in the last ten days of October. The media as a whole seemed persuaded that the polls were prognostications.

A small indication of how this preconception worked came when Field lamented the time factor requiring him to telephone his last poll, on November 1, to *The Times,* rather than mail it. In discussing his findings with the rewrite man, Field thought he had put the focus on Flournoy's gain, but in *The Times* report this was relegated to the second paragraph and emphasis placed on Brown's "substantial lead." Field expressed disappointment in the way the poll had been reported and considered it "a good lesson" not to use the telephone again. *The Chronicle,* on the other hand, carried a prominent Page-One boxed story with a headline calling attention to the news below: "Flournoy Gains in State Poll." *The Chronicle,* in the same city as Field's office, received the copy as Field had written it, and their story emphasized Flournoy's rapid gain. *The Chronicle,* unlike *The Times,* had endorsed Flournoy.

The newspapers gave even less attention to Field's final release, which appeared on the last day of the campaign, Monday, November 4, and was stronger in its assertion of Flournoy's rise. It even carried admonitory paragraphs recalling the Harry Truman upset of Thomas Dewey in 1948 and emphasized the resurgence of Republican interest. It warned that "a strong late surge in the closing days could still produce a come-from-behind victory for Flournoy." Most subscribers to the poll had thought Friday's article had been the last and by Monday counted the event over. Attention now was turned to election day. Had editors read the Field report, they might have benefited by a psychological preparation for the events of election night.

Right up to election night, press reporters seemed universally agreed that Brown would have an easy and large victory, yet two television reporters who had traveled with Brown the day before said they sensed a change in his mood. "A new humility," one defined it, and the other felt the candidate "was facing within himself the possibility of defeat." Not newspaper reporters. They seemed assured that the polls were going to be confirmed by the vote. Only one press reporter, Brown's team later said, was intuitive enough to sense that "something was different" in election-eve attitudes among the Brown crew, Bergholz of *The Times*. He questioned Quinn closely during the cross-state flights, but Quinn scoffed at his alarms. Later Quinn acknowledged how difficult it had been during that last day, surrounded by media reporters, to maintain the ebullient anticipation of victory in the face of dismaying reports that were coming in at every stop from Brown's private polls. On election night *The Times* city room was stunned by early returns that showed Flournoy so strong. Editors and reporters were uncertain of a winner until nearly 11:00 p.m., and Bergholz, who wrote the main story, was too uneasy to sleep until he got next morning's confirmation of the narrow Brown victory.

The Los Angeles Times was more intrigued by polls, more genuinely concerned about learning from them and giving readers an insight from them than any other California medium. In each phase of the election, primary and general, *The Times* ran the largest total poll "mentions."

One article appeared on October 7 under the headline: "Polls: Mirrors or Makers of Public Opinion?" Written by Robert Shogan of the paper's Washington staff, it concerned polls then being undertaken for the 1976 presidential election, but it covered the national polling agencies, many national political figures and some academicians in its questions on the impact polls are thought to have on voters and political contributors. It warned that suggestions have been made that pollsters need official regulations. In another story, on January 3, 1975, "Political Polls: How to Avoid Distortions," the focus was on the criticism of the polls that welled up from the gubernatorial election; and the author, David Shaw, wrote that "many responsible critics" claim that the polls had prevented Flournoy's election. "There is a growing feeling among sophisticated poll-watchers . . . ," it said, "that newspaper polls on political races seriously distort and undermine the electoral process. The manner in which polls are now published can adversely affect fundraising, media coverage, staff morale, campaign strategy and voter turnout." The article dealt specifically with a number of "reform" proposals, such as prohibiting publication of polls more than three or four months before a campaign, or within ten days of an election.

The Los Angeles Times poll is one of a kind in California. It originated in 1972, and Ken Reich has been in virtual control of it since. It is based on concepts from some pioneering work on opinion sampling that Samuel Lubell described in 1948 in his book, *The Future of American Politics*. This plan assumes that shifts in opinion can be discerned by sampling precincts that were particularly representative of voter sentiment in an earlier, similar election. Reich chose precincts whose total vote in a previous model period coincided within a percentage point or two with the total state vote. He worked on the assumption that sentiment in areas earlier so representative of the whole state would be reasonably indicative of the current mood.

For the 1974 gubernatorial year, based on sentiment in previous Reagan races, he chose nine precincts, six to yield Democrat attitudes, three Republican. Approximately 100 persons were interviewed in each precinct. Reich designed the approach, chose the precincts, and directed the five or six reporters dispatched for the doorbell-ringing, with Mexican-American or Black staffers chosen for neighborhoods dominated by those minorities. Walking·a precinct usually took eight or nine hours, and Reich always polled at least one himself. In the 1974 general election he polled twice; in the primary, which he considered far more complex than the general election, he purposely began early and ran four polls, in January, late March, late April, and late May. In each case, his pollsters interviewed in the same key precincts, but made no attempt to catch precisely the same people.

The Times' commitment to this endeavor was indicated by the degree of staff time contributed to the poll and the Page-One attention each survey was accorded. Despite the great length to which his stories ran—long even by *The Times'* generous standards—Reich regretted that he was unable to get more than five or six quotes a precinct into the story. "The observations we pick up on interviews are blunter and more profane than newspaper stories usually provide," Reich said. The prime purpose of this kind of polling was to catch voter mood.

There were wide differences between Field's technique and Reich's in the selection of areas to poll and the make-up of the sample. Field's was done with greater resources and experience and a more complex formula to balance off socio-economic differences and voting habits. There was another major difference at the point of interrogation: Field often used a written slate of possible candidates that his interviewers showed to respondents in asking their preference. Reich never initiated a name or laid groundwork for a response but used open-ended questions and sought as many comments about the candidates as he could elicit. Reich counted only registered voters. In the primary he asked party affiliation, but in the general election he was careful not to, lest that shape the response. Reich found it difficult to draw out thoughtful explanations of why voters favor a candidate: not more than 10 percent, he figured, ventured a rational explanation for their preference, and very rarely in his polling had he discovered evidence that voters reach a decision because of something they read in a newspaper.

One advantage of *The Times* poll over Field's is the quickness with which it can move from precinct into print. This becomes particularly significant in the final poll immediately before the election. On Monday, June 1, Reich reported on interviews conducted in various sections of the state the four days before, including Sunday. It showed both Brown and Flournoy heading for "decisive victories" in their respective primaries, coinciding closely with Field's report. On Monday, November 4, the story similarly reflected opinions gathered over the prior weekend. In that last fall sampling, accompanying Reich in Culver City, John Shinn of the study staff discovered that a neighborhood indifferent toward the election on October 6 was by November 2 reasonably alerted to it and interested. At the same time there was a sharp increase in the articulation of support for either Flournoy or Brown. In October, the Culver City tally of "preferences" showed Brown 48, Flournoy 44, Undecided 50, and Declined to State 6. In the November 2 survey, the breakdown was Brown 56, Flournoy 52, Undecided 24, and Declined to State 12.

Shinn noted the strong impression both he and Reich received that Flournoy supporters were more emphatic than Brown's and seemed more committed to vote. In fact, Reich remarked that Flournoy could "take heart" from what was observed in this precinct and in another Reich had walked the day before in the distant mountain county of Amador. Reich said that the figures showed Brown ahead by a comfortable margin, but that comments indicated the election was likely to be closer than this margin would suggest. Brown's support, he said, was "softer" than Flournoy's. "Flournoy is not going to win," he concluded, "but the question is, how close he comes." In analyzing what he had compiled, he developed his lead around the figures: 354 in all the sampled precincts for Brown, 242 for Flournoy. Had he stuck to the voter "mood," he conceded he would have come out better, "but the figures weren't there to substantiate it." In sum, *The Times,* with more polls at its disposal than any other California paper, and more staff interest

and concern about polls, was as insensitive to the political news to be
found among the voters as the rest of the media. In fact, with Reich's
expectation of a Brown "commanding lead," it missed the boat somewhat more dramatically than most.

Reich, in mid-December, discussed what he acknowledged were er-
rors in his results. The Field poll, he thought, was more sensitive to the
transition taking place in public opinion than his had been, but he did
not quite know why. "There is no perfect way of doing this," he remarked, then added, "I'm not prepared to say it was all fallacious, but
the difference between my poll results and the close election does give
one pause." He felt, on looking back, that Flournoy was getting through
to the voters better than Brown, and, had the year been unmarred by
Watergate and by its burden of anti-Republicanism, Flournoy would
have won. Reich thought that his polling was too heavily concentrated
in the Los Angeles area and in working-class precincts. "If I had had
just one good upper-income precinct, he said, "I think I would have
caught the strong Flournoy movement in those last days." He was disappointed, but neither he nor *The Times* editors were deterred from
continuing their own polls. Reich decided that he would make his precinct selection with more expert assistance but he would also dwell less
on statistics and more on attitudes.

Intrigued by often-pungent remarks Reich was able to capture, another newspaper, *The Sacramento Bee,* tried to report opinions from
some haphazardly chosen local precincts. It was not a great success, but
it took *Bee* reporter Steve Duscha away from the campaign for a few
days. He had begun to find the campaign ritual "terribly unreal" and
wondered how much of its rhetoric registered with the citizenry. Ring-
ing doorbells, he found very little did. People were indifferent.

10

IMAGES AND ISSUES

In a modern television campaign, candidates talk less about large public questions and more about "image." In the California gubernatorial campaign, "image" went beyond personality, to political associations, political philosophies and political organizations. Ideology was conveyed by such code words as "fiscal responsibility," "compassion," "moderate," "bring unity." Party was used like a flag to stir familiar loyalties. Every press release issued by Brown's camp opened with the specific label "Democratic nominee for governor." Flournoy, attempting to woo Democrats, was chary of outright Republican identification and emphasized "independent."

The favorable image of the candidate was built through a succession of brief phrases and statements repeatedly injected into campaign remarks or press releases or staff interviews, and so introduced into news stories. Flournoy emphasized most his political experience, academic background, "maturity," and "trustworthiness." Brown projected a determination to change things and emphasized vigor, personal frugality, majority-party identity, and certain conservative tendencies which were labeled by the media as "tough on crime" or "fiscal conservative." Words like "action," "energy," and "change" often fell from Browns lips. Flournoy's speech, less crisp, contrasted Brown's "youth" and "inexperience" to the Republican's 14 years in elective office, subtly suggesting Flournoy's "maturity," "experience," and "reliability.'.

This kind of image differs from mere charisma. The smile, the stance, the voice, the manner of movement, all that the camera portrays was augmented by an array of formula messages intended to reinforce the televised reality and expand its dimensions. It became apparent that the brief, reiterated rhetoric used at public events represented a systematic effort to get a limited number of concepts across, as much to the media as to the immediate throng and that the repetition of these personality allusions was designed chiefly to suit the brief time span of television and radio. In other words, there appeared to be a set list of personal attributes, one favorable to self and one unfavorable to the rival, and it was possible to fit a large amount of what was reported about the campaign into this list of "positive image" and "negative image," whether the words were used in the press or on radio or television. The deliberate evocation of personal attributes through emblematic phrases is certainly not new in American political experience. Whether the shaping of so much content in this campaign to image slogans represents a significant enlargement cannot be determined since there are no past measurements. But this race seemed to rest heavily on a short roster of set phrases offered with little embellishment or amplification.

Reporters generally seemed to conclude that this concentration on image was stimulated by television's magnification of the person. Reporters talked a great deal about the growing popularity of personality stories about the candidates as people, rather than as power centers or party representatives or as effective leaders. Art Berman, *The Times* metropolitan editor who directed the paper's political coverage, dealt with the question of image when he spoke at a postelection meeting of Sigma Delta Chi:

"Jerry Brown wanted to be the man with the new spirit and Houston Flournoy wanted to be the man with the most experience, and to heck with the issues. That may be a little harsh, but the candidates certainly try to put their best foot forward and they don't really want to get too far into issues. They don't want to say things that might lose them a little support. They try to present a very general picture of themselves. I think our job was to go beyond that general picture and try to tell as much about these candidates as we could, where they stand on issues, where their campaign backing is coming from, where the millions pouring into the campaign came from. We started very intensively to do that sort of thing . . ."

How deliberate the Brown effort was to steer the campaign into these image areas was suggested by some remarks by Mary Jean Pew, a member of Brown's inner circle:

"I think the campaign aims to let the voter kind of garner his own impression. It's a perception that comes through the media in lots of ways: impression rather than specific knowledge. I'm not sure the electorate is that interested in issues. They want to know: 'Is this guy more likely to do what I like than the other guy?' A perception comes through better on TV than in print. Print can summarize Jerry's stand on something, but who's going to read it? TV lets the personality through. That's what people make up their minds on."

Insiders in both camps worked from this hypothesis. Kranwinkle

fort: "I think the people make their choice on
es problems, not on the specific problems them-
/'s problem-solving ability?" Some reporters saw
ray of personality news. Doug Willis of the AP
"turned on personality, just as every California
. Without a strong party, what else works?" Tom
eau chief in Sacramento, chided his colleagues for
the candidates down on issues: "Voters don't care
vote on whether they trust a guy . . ."

d the attention to personality among the media. He
t: "My personality is getting over. I'm getting known
across over a period of time. The differences between
and myself whatever they are—difference in character, dif-
s between the two parties—that will come through." But he also
aid, in an interview carried in *The Times* October 20: "I don't believe
in the politics of personality . . ." He disparaged the new fashion of reporters digging into the personal life of candidates. "Lincoln didn't have
a very satisfactory relationship with his wife," Brown observed, "but
he was a great President. Franklin Roosevelt seemed to have problems
with his family. Why is that relevant? He was a great President." He
thought such journalistic inquiries "a diversion from the central issues,
which are the political and economic questions—who gets what, when?"
That was a momentary lapse into Brown, the philosopher. Brown, the
candidate, was pragmatic in repeatedly stressing his "new spirit" to con-
jure up the image of "change."

→ The press was also absorbed in weighing Flournoy's conduct, mannerisms and charisma. The reporters often wondered whether his relaxed and comfortable air in television interviews—in contrast to
Brown's tenseness—might not win him votes. But on October 22, when
Flournoy had some reporters up for drinks in his hotel room after a day's
campaigning, he was asked why he didn't do more of the crowd-plunging
that cameras liked. One reporter puzzled over Flournoy's manner at
meetings. Asked a question from the crowd, he would frown, drop his
head, worry out the answer, but rarely look directly at his questioner.
Another noted that Flournoy did not take his hands out of his pockets
when going through a crowd in Watts, a largely Black area of Los
Angeles. And still another remarked that Flournoy had not stopped to
talk with a single patient while visiting a clinic when the cameras were
present. Flournoy laughed. It just wasn't his way, he said. In the clinic,
he felt that it would have been an intrusion had he stopped to talk with

a patient: "Those were sick people," he said. "I had no right to disturb them." These reporters noted Brown's increasing poise during crowd encounters. He had learned to make the gestures the cameras found symbolic of human warmth. Lacking the central excitement of an issue-difference, the image differences emerged as significant.

For whatever reason, "psyching" Brown became a preoccupation of the traveling press. Watching Brown before the cameras, newspaper reporters began to reflect in their stories the emphasis on the personal figure. They discussed appearance, mannerisms, attire; key words about the campaign became personality-oriented: "warm," "cool," "aloof," "approachable." Flournoy's strategists were delighted at the narrowing of media attention to image, for their whole campaign was designed to display Flournoy's experience in contrast to Brown's inexperience, maturity versus youth, relaxed amiability versus taut intensity. But Flournoy's chief problem was to establish his identity. As late as October 20, he was saying to Richard Bergholz of *The Times*: "Visual identification is the hardest part to get in a campaign, and it comes from cumulative exposure on television."

Bergholz was more troubled by Flournoy's failure to fix an identity in policy than in pictures. He noted that Flournoy was trapped between his past reputation as a progressive, even a liberal, Republican when he had served as a legislator and his dependence now upon such ultraconservatives as Reagan and Reagan's finance men. It became difficult for voters to get a solid clue to his political philosophy. "In the real world of politics," Bergholz wrote, "Flournoy comes off as an indistinct blurred image in the eyes of the majority of Californians."

The youth of both candidates, their intellectual level, their individual but differing attractiveness were so remote from the cliche politician that reporters enjoyed writing about personality. They concluded that Flournoy was more predictable, and some thought him "more honest" or "less a demagogue." They did not like Brown's persistent twinning of Flournoy with Reagan because they knew these two Republicans had had little to do with each other, although they recognized the political effectiveness of this tactic. On the other hand, they felt that Brown scored a valid point when he criticized Flournoy as being less assertive than himself. They quoted him saying such things as, "The whole issue of this campaign is: Do you want a passive, weak-kneed, sleepy administrator . . . or an aggressive advocate protecting the public treasury and representing all the people?" Near its close, the campaign settled into a series of personal exchanges. At the UPI editors' meeting, one editor challenged Flournoy: "Your opponent calls you a Mr. Milquetoast and says you lack leadership . . ." Flournoy replied that Brown's aim was less to criticize Flournoy than to emphasize "how aggressive he is," and added: "This boils down to a difference in temperament between us."

Television assignment editors, denouncing issues as "dull" and disparaging "talking heads," favored profile stories. Bob Rollen of KNXT told a Sigma Delta Chi meeting after the election that his station had assigned reporters to spend time with each candidate, "to get to know him, to be able to describe him in some way—not his press releases, not just how he is pressing the flesh—but have something real to say about him . . . The best stuff we did on Jerry Brown was at his home—you know, he has those stark white walls, plastic palm trees, he keeps his tie on and, when the crew arrived, the pool cleaner was there. He said, 'God, don't show that—don't show that I've got a guy who comes to clean my pool! . . .' At Flournoy's house, he didn't know we were there. We got in before he arrived, and nobody told Hugh we were waiting. He walked in and said, 'Hi! Pardon me, I gotta get a beer,' opened up the refrigerator and popped a can of beer . . ."

Brown doesn't have plastic palm trees, and there may be other exaggerations in Rollen's remarks, but they demonstrate a belief about which candidate cared most for his public appearance.

The preoccupation with this "humanism," as one *Times* reporter called it, would seem to narrow the interpretation of "image" merely to "personality." But "personality" was only one aspect of the total "image" this study attempted to analyze. This one part was isolated, however, and attention paid it was measured. Under the label "lifestyle," news media references to the individual candidate's appearance, style, family, tastes and friends were collected. The press, traveling with the' candidates and more constantly subject to impressions of their personality, were most absorbed in this kind of material. (See the count of "mentions" shown in the bottom table on page 185).

Some television attention escaped this count. The profiles various stations developed about the candidates stressed personality, family, home setting, personal tastes; and such were usually carried at times other than newscasts. These lifestyle references were classified as "positive image" factors since the reporters' references were invariably cast in flattering or favorable terms.

In the 24 percent of references to image, the total of 1,931 mentions could be catalogued into 31 separate categories. Devising this list was a rough, experimental effort. It aimed to draw attention to this evolution in campaign tactics, and to identify in campaign rhetoric related by the media, the whole range of communication pertaining to the man himself, not programs or issues. The roster turned out to have nine "positive image" factors for Flournoy, seven for Brown; seven "negative image" factors for Flournoy, eight for Brown. The categories differed for each candidate, both positive mentions and negative, and they tended not to balance off (though Brown's "inexperienced/youthful" disadvantage was often contrasted with Flournoy's "mature/experienced" positive category). They were not, it must be emphasized, invented. They were specific concepts, frequently repeated in the media, concepts so clear that coders could pick them out.

The difficulty in pinpointing this elusive quality of image was suggested when Flournoy commented in some annoyance after the campaign on the frequency with which the word "low-key" had been used to describe him. This term did not seem derogatory as reporters used it. It was identified as a "positive image" factor for Flournoy because it seemed often to be used as a favorable contrast to what was sometimes suggested as a stridency in Brown's vigorous approach. At any rate, the term "low-key," as a favorable "image" element for Flournoy turned up in 5 percent of the press stories; in 8 percent of the television stories; and 2 percent of the radio stories. References that had "negative" connotations in this area were collected under "dull/professorial" or "inactive."

The difficulty in defining image as "positive" or "negative" can also be illustrated with a point concerning Brown, whose earliest asset was name. Flournoy would assert, "If your name were Green, you would not be here contesting with me for this post," and Brown took to acknowledging this in his own speeches. The favorable aspects of his name got very little media attention in the campaign, and never from Brown, but the unfavorable implications—the suggestion that he was riding his father's coattail—became a persistent criticism. It became so frequent that it was recorded as a "negative image" element under the code phrase "shadow of his father." To voters appraising young Brown, it may well have been the candidate's most attractive point, but what appeared in the media during the campaign was Flournoy's persistence in pressing this for its unfavorable implications and Brown's attempt to diminish attention to it.

Classifications identified in the concept of "image" shown in tables on pages 186-87.

Political ads are a well-recognized part of image-building. The image thus projected may be more direct, more forceful and more controlled than what makes its way into news. But the degree of purposeful propaganda that campaign managers were able to convey through the news was astonishing. If issues continue to diminish in importance and candidates successfully back away from state problems in dealing with the electorate, then reporters from all the media, seeking substance for political stories, may have to rely increasingly on image content.

News carrying positive or negative references tagged to the two men was remarkably consistent in all the media. There was a general spread of "image" mentions unfavorable to Brown and favorable to Flournoy, which may have arisen in part because two more positive factors were tabulated for Flournoy and one additional negative factor for Brown. On the other hand, reporters were transmitting what originated from campaign headquarters more than what they defined for themselves, so it would appear that they were responding more to the vehemence of Flournoy's charges against Brown's own claims for image advantage. As a rule attack is favored by news media since it makes livelier political content. But it also seemed that the Brown team, purposely moderating its attacks against Flournoy in an effort to avoid changing a political climate in which Brown had the lead, did not swing as hard as did the underdog. What occurred is evident in table at top of page 187.

The spread, in short, was unfavorable to Brown, favorable to Flournoy. In each case, Brown's negative image factors were carried in media accounts more frequently than his positive factors, while Flournoy's positive image factors received more newspaper and broadcast mentions. But there is a marked difference between each medium in how each was handled. The political world tended to explain Brown's last-minute slippage in terms of the image Flournoy conveyed in his ads. It would appear that image in news content may also be a factor worth weighing.

It is interesting to compare what reporters actually put into their stories in relation to replies they gave to a questionnaire submitted to 100 of the news people on all levels in all media in the campaign. One section of this questionnaire asked for rankings according to the respondent's opinion as to what the voter most needed to know to vote wisely. The choice was among seven kinds of political news. The points and the highlights from the 35 replies follow.

To vote wisely, the voter most needs to know the candidate's:

1—Personal history, achievements, etc.
51% thought this rated first or second in value.

2—Personality, appearance, family, charisma.
75% thought this last in importance.
3—Associates, supporters, fund donors.
48% named this as first or second.
4—Stands on issues, priorities among public problems.
74% named this first, and another 26% thought it rated second or third.
5—Popularity (poll standing).
53% put this last.
6—Ability to "win" over rivals in debate.
78% put it among the last three.
7—Campaign activities, meetings, press conferences.
62% ranked it fourth and fifth in importance.

A second question asked: Which among those seven news categories did your own medium emphasize?

• No respondent named personality factors first; in fact, 45 percent named this last, seventh or sixth in ranking, and 25 percent pegged it at fourth or fifth.

• A majority, 58 percent, said their medium had stressed issues most; and another 24 percent said they had stressed issues second to something else.

• And 34 percent noted that they thought campaign activities (No. 7) such as meetings and press conferences had received the most emphasis in their medium. This category did get the most attention among campaign functions, next to attack. Although 48 percent considered it critical for voters to know a candidate's associates, supporters and donors, only 6 percent claimed that their medium had given this first priority in attention, and 39 percent said it had been second or third. None thought poll-standing got much emphasis, a view that ran counter to what candidates themselves thought, and what this study confirmed. On debates, no reply suggested that this rated first, second or third in attention. It fell, in relation to what voters needed to know, into fifth or sixth place in 63 percent of the replies. But in discussing what their medium had done in news reporting, 4 percent said that theirs had given the debates most attention; 7 percent thought they got second place; the majority, 54 percent, thought they ranked about where their own views of its value pegged it—fifth or sixth place.

When the same respondents were asked what they thought most persuaded voters, the emphasis scale shifted drastically. No. 1 selection for 75 percent of the journalists was "personality, appearance, etc."; 13 percent issues, and 37 percent more placed this in second place with the rest tending to put it in third, fourth or fifth place and none last; 9 percent felt that personal history and achievements were most persuasive, and 25 percent felt they rated second place. Nobody thought that the debates mattered much to the voters; nor poll standing; nor even campaign activities.

The emphasis on issues, which this reflected—with a high standing in each of the three questions—was consistent and coincided with the persistent concern of reporters about issues. As for the importance these media people thought personality, or image, had for the voter, there was overwhelming unanimity: It matters most. But equally unanimous was their own appraisal that in the list of factors most needed for a wise vote, it mattered least.

Reporters traveling with Brown expressed frustration that they could not "chink the kid's armor," that they could not translate the "new spirit" he spoke of for their readers. Reporters for two months had sought specifics on Brown's program and got primarily an assurance that the key to Brown's new administration would be new people and a change in tone of government, but rarely details about policy. Promised position papers on tax shifts, job programs and education never materialized. "I gotta give my readers some idea what you're gonna do, Jerry," Murphy of *The Chronicle* said on more than one occasion. He never got it. No reporter got it. All they could do was report that Brown gave no details. Most of them were experienced enough to be aware of all the reasons a candidate has for resisting campaign commitments, but none had ever encountered such a degree of resistance as in Brown's campaign.

The reporters argued endlessly over the value and purpose of issues in campaigns in contrast to the increasing attention to charisma, or image. None of the reporters assumed that issues, coldly intellectual, lay at the core of the voter's interest, and they sought issues that might stimulate their readers and create a sense of excitement in the campaign. But in their pursuit of Flournoy and Brown, and particularly of Brown, the reporters sought some engagement with the compelling problems of state government.

No other level of candidate-media interaction had such intimacy as that of the traveling press. At no other place were issues taken so seriously. Yet, the reporters were subjected as well to the candidate's personality. They faced the risk of an excessive focus on personality, although much of the reporters' conversation dwelt upon the candidate as a person; the grist for their mill was factual statement, commitment to a program—in short, issues.

Issues, however dull, serve a purpose in a campaign. They act as signposts to a candidate's priorities and general approach to the day's dominant public questions. Obligated to report 60 days of campaigning, and needing content for those daily stories, the newspaper reporter inevitably latches onto key state problems. Reporters for broadcast also crave issues, but only as short-cuts to a quick interview.

The candidate, however, has his own approach to issues. Strategy is keyed to certain priority points. Much of the campaign consists of a contest between the candidate's effort to harp on his priorities and the news media's effort to assess him on issues reporters think significant to the public. Often they work at cross purposes. Each may be struggling to focus the campaign on quite separate areas. Conflict lies at even so crude a level as getting each other's attention. When both concur in the discussion of some point, they may differ over what should be emphasized about it. At the reporter-candidate level, issues are the quickening that comes when substance can be discerned in the flow of rhetoric. What was actually said? What was new? What did it disclose? This is where newspaper reporters grub for stories; this is where they serve the public.

Kenneth Reich said early in the year: "If the press is really critical, it could affect the course of the campaign." It didn't work out that way. Some have suggested that the California press was not sufficiently persistent. Flournoy remarked that he understood the eastern press to be more merciless in interrogation. He wished the reporters had pierced Brown's armor more successfully.

State spending was the issue mentioned more often than any other, even inflation, in press accounts of the campaign. It drew 16 percent of all mentions in stories on both candidates. The reporters were tenacious. Broadcasters, however, were less concerned. Television gave inflation top attention and accorded political reform more notice than fiscal policy. Radio gave Flournoy's record as Controller its most frequent mention, followed by political reform, with state fiscal matters figuring only moderately in radio news.

It was not, of course, an issueless campaign. It was possible to identify in the various media reports 23 specific issues. Fifteen of them were in fields of broad public interest such as education, energy, consumer interests, environment, and law enforcement. In addition eight special issues arose or were peculiar to that moment in history. Watergate/Nixon was one of these, even though it had no direct relationship to this election. Two other matters of public concern—the death penalty and drugs —started off promising to be lively issues, for there were differences in the two men's views. Brown opposed the death penalty but said he would adhere to a law imposing it, if it were held constitutional, which he doubted; and Flournoy supported the death penalty for specific cases. These two areas never became central in media interest, however, and by the end of the campaign had become very minor. A controversial November ballot issue dealing with building a dam (Proposition 17) drew more attention than the death penalty. The $1.3 million Governor's Mansion being built in a Sacramento suburb to house the new governor was a significant issue, for Brown chose to use it symbolically to convey the frugality in personal lifestyle that he wanted to emphasize, along with conservative public spending. (If elected, he said, he would not live in it. Familyman Flournoy said he would be happy to.)

The five most frequently mentioned general issues reflect a slightly varying emphasis in each medium, although the list of leading issues reported in each emerged as very similar. (See table on page 187.)

Despite all the identifiable issues that were reported, it seemed to the media an issueless campaign because the newspaper reporters failed to find substance in the candidates' positions, and neither they nor their broadcast colleagues could generate excitement about them. Several factors contributed to this situation: the purposely blurred discussion by the candidates, their refusal to indulge in specifics, and the relative similarity of most of their views.

Los Angeles Times editor William Thomas warned, however, that the strong-stand-on-issues candidate, who may make good copy because of vehement position-taking, may also turn out to be an irresponsible officeholder. Forceful positions are not necessarily better than guarded ones. Thomas indicated some sympathy for a candidate who may not want to commit himself, but noted: "*The Times* will keep right on pressing them about issues, though, because we think it's important." But Flournoy was not badgered by the press as much as Brown. He was, for one thing, more open, more easy to talk with, and more interested in exploring ideas with reporters, who also knew him better. Essentially, however, they went after Flournoy less aggressively because they did not expect him to win.

And Brown's gift for eluding press inquiry became a standing joke. It chanced on October 23, when Brown was doing his "media event" of greeting people at Grand Central Market in Los Angeles, that UPI was shifting personnel, and Bob Sweet arrived with suitcase and typewriter to join the Brown camp. He stopped to chat with his rival, Evans Witt of The Associated Press, to get a line on where things stood. Sweet remarked, by way of greeting, "I understand you had a big news day with

Brown yesterday." "Oh yes," Witt replied. "It was the greatest fiction-writing day in the history of the AP. 'Jerry Brown says something.' "

The effort to avoid confronting issues did sometimes include brevity of contact with reporters, and there were complaints, but persistence could usually wangle interview time. Brown, despite allusions to his being "aloof," was available to the major press and was pleasant and informal in such circumstances, even if given to asking more questions than he received.

There was the combination of the political climate, the shifting relationship of the media to the electoral process and certain contemporary distracting circumstances, all of which inhibited the press in coming to grips with substance in the campaign. Clearly, the most important of the circumstances was the strategy of the Brown campaign to maintain a dull, dull campaign because of Brown's large lead in the polls.

This deliberate strategy was apparent in many of Brown's comments. Early in the fall he was talking with the traveling press about his aim to bring conflicting sides together on various issues. When he was asked if this mediation process had enough drama to quicken public interest, he flared: "Drama! Why all the demand for drama! Drama for drama's sake! Can't we have a nice, quiet election with some serious attention to problems?"

Preparing for election night, *The Times* assigned its Sacramento bureau chief, Tom Goff, to write advance stories on each candidate, disclosing after the winner was known the kind of goals he had set for his administration. Goff was disappointed in the interviews he obtained. "Neither one," he said, "had really thought very concretely about what he would start at the morning after election." Of the two men, however, he said that Flournoy had the more definite plans.

Brown stymied efforts to bring him to a commitment, and this elusiveness continued even after he was hailed as the victor. When a reporter asked him the morning after, "What are you going to do first?" Brown quipped: "I'm going to get an airplane for Sacramento."

11

29 ANIMALS IN THE ZOO

"We tried to orchestrate it, and it didn't work. We called this press conference, and we had a decent release and a decent statement, we thought—something direct we wanted to get said. Well, they took it right out of our hands." Kenneth Drake, the young Santa Monica newspaper reporter who was Flournoy's press secretary in the primary campaign, was recalling his initiation in press relations. "This was my first try, and I just thought, 'My God, this is the turning point'! I had this gut feeling that the whole campaign would hinge upon this failure. I was sick. I was beside myself. I agonized." And the candidate? "Hugh was sweating. Visibly. It was a very uncomfortable 45 minutes."

Drake's recollection of reporters running away with the news conference was more than an illustration of the usual dynamics of reporters vying for control. It was particularly representative of the climate in which the 1974 gubernatorial race was conducted and of the media's overwhelming preference for news that lay outside the campaign.

The reporters had assembled at Flournoy's summons. However, they were not interested in him as a candidate but in a fragment of news linked to the developing crisis around Richard Nixon that he might provide. A question had arisen—prompted by a Democrat on a state tax board—concerning the speed with which California was pressing its investigation of the possibility that Nixon had an additional state tax liability. The Democrat had suggested that Flournoy, as a Republican and a member of the State Franchise Tax Board, might "whitewash" such an inquiry. Flournoy was outraged that publicity had been given to the board's investigation, which he insisted was confidential. Drake figured that in this furor the media might turn out for a Flournoy comment. He was right. This was even exciting enough for television. Flournoy intended to rebuke the Democrat for leaking the investigation and to assure the public that California tax investigations of anyone—private citizen or President—were confidential. "They turned it completely around," Drake said. "None of Hugh's comments even got used. Hugh got up and laid it out, and the reporters then took off in a totally different direction. All they cared about was President Nixon, not how Hugh felt."

The parrying and ducking that followed made for one of the most frustrating news conferences in a primary noted for candidate frustration. "It was a real lesson," Drake said. "I had misjudged the basic media interest. We set it up wrong."

But this was not an isolated instance. In news conference after news conference in the primary, candidates found themselves pressured to talk about some aspect of the Watergate-Nixon situation, or about Patty Hearst and the Symbionese Liberation Army, or about the spate of random killings in San Francisco, not about their own proposals for California's future or their own leadership. The candidates found reporters interested only in comments that could be linked to extraneous events already recognized as news.

A tendency to appraise events in terms of their bearing upon what is already considered news was demonstrated throughout the campaign, but it was most characteristic of the primary. Events outside dominated media interests and made the contest a struggle for media attention rather than a test among the candidates, and by doing so, it threw into focus some news selection standards that usually escape notice.

Just as the media favored news connected to existing major stories, so did they tend to find news in people already in the news. Reinecke, tangled in the web of Watergate, suffered most. And the reverse—media inattention—had driven George Moscone out of the race before the primary (in 1975 he was elected Mayor of San Francisco). The media's proclivity for the already popular worked to Alioto's advantage, for he was frequently tossed into the midst of "outside" news—his wife's escapade, his city workers' strike, the Zebra murders. It also worked to Moretti's advantage as Speaker of the California Assembly but not as much as he expected. Most of all, it aided Jerry Brown and reinforced his lead.

Indeed, Brown's strategy in the primary was devised around the news entree provided by his name over the four previous years. In the primary, he could coast. He did not plead for attention. He did not join in the protests of other candidates that the media were ignoring the campaign. He was, at this point, indifferent to the media. He had a lead only mischance could erode, and his aim was to avoid mischance.

Most candidates did all they could to lure the media. The Peace and Freedom Party's candidate, Elizabeth Keathley, went so far as to campaign nude on a nude beach. She was rewarded by having her slightly blurred figure on most television newscasts and displayed in most newspapers. In less sensational style, all the candidates sought attention. Moretti, for instance, when he wanted to spell out his antismog program, held his news conference at a gasoline station to provide a visual background for his message. No television cameras attended. Roth chose a pharmacy as setting for his attack on high drug prices for the elderly. Nobody came. These weren't the only instances of neglect, but, as a rule, only one or two newspaper reporters showed up for such events, and television almost never.

Alioto invited the media on a junket intended to dramatize the modern style of vote-stumping by a one-day leap from Los Angeles, the largest vote center, to the remote ghost town of Bodie, where there were three Democrats, to emphasize that every vote counted. It made colorful copy though Alioto was appalled that George Skelton of *The Times* began his story: "When a candidate comes to Bodie, you figure he is in trouble." In *The Sacramento Bee,* which carried a map to show where Bodie was and a one-column cartoon of Alioto addressing an attentive cow, Lee Fremstad reported the event with "High Noon" hyperbole: "Dust dulled the gleam of the Italian Gucci loafers and left its mark on the blue custom-tailored suit. . . ." But no television. Roth developed a scheme to illustrate his criticism of property-tax exemptions for insurance companies that allowed them to build headquarters free of local tax. He called a news conference atop a hillside in Griffith Park with a map drawing attention to the pertinent towers jutting from the Los Angeles landscape below. For this, television responded. Unfortunately, the smog was so dense photographers could barely see the candidate, let alone the valley. As a media event, it failed. Television's evaluation of the campaign, Roth felt, was demonstrated when one San Francisco station's camera crew, en route to cover him, was diverted instead to a news conference by an 18-year-old girl friend of actor Richard Burton at a northern California movie-making location.

Brown was as unsuccessful in drawing television as the others when he had to act the candidate. For instance, he rode a commuter train one morning into San Francisco, as an appropriate base for comments on the state's need for rapid transit. Along trudged his staff with an outsized sketch of modern trains and statistics on highway costs versus rail costs. The visuals were set up. He was ready to orate. The date, it turned out, was one of the more dramatic episodes in the Zebra case. One or two reporters darted in, took quick notes and were off. No cameras. Brown got no television response either for his major primary-campaign effort at political theater. For this, he invited the media on a bus trip through the historic Mother Lode gold-mining towns, topped by a raft ride down a stretch of Stanislaus River rapids. When The Los Angeles *Times* reporter phoned his office, he didn't even try to dictate: That was the night of the SLA shoot-out. And there had been no television coverage, despite the spectacular setting.

The campaign disclosed the disadvantage newcomers face in the initial stages of an election, when their advancement depends so heavily upon prevailing news standards. Not only did the broadcast media diminish primary coverage, but newspapers also were erratic in their attention. Only the ubiquitous *Los Angeles Times* made an effort to sum up the whole field and give continuity to reporting on the large number of contenders. *The Bee* reported on them when they came into Sacramento. Newcomer-candidates felt, however, that even *The Times* handled the news in a way to deprive them, automatically, of serious consideration. Most other newspapers singled out one candidate at a time for the conventional "profile," or feature, ran stories about "a day in the life of . . ." or wrap-up accounts tracking a candidate's appearances. What rarely emerged was a sense of continuous coverage of an unfolding event.

The usual clusters of volunteers within each of the major parties—the peripheral but essential party organizations—were in disarray. Republican groups were dispirited by the Watergate entanglement of Reinecke, and Democrats were split among the party rivals. Political parties, choosing their leadership figures through an open-election process, were subject to the whim of an uninterested and easily distracted media. No other mechanism was available to link candidates and public, so control over the campaign apparatus was clearly in the hands of the news media, and their power was used to constrict a choice rather than open it.

This was ironic, for there had been a shift in recent years in how candidates are chosen. No longer did initial selection remain the domain of special interests, party bosses, or a handful of businessmen and editors. A far freer selection was now opened to the voter through the primaries. But for this process to work, some kind of communication link must exist between candidate and the public, and the candidate looks to the news media to provide it. The 1974 primary was notable, above all else, for side-tracking of the political communication system when it becomes clogged with other distracting news, faces a great abundance of candidates, and when the news selection in broadcast is aimed primarily at maximizing advertising revenue for the stations, while the FCC's "equal time" rule is used as justification for skirting an event deemed to be dull.

One difference between the primary and general election campaigns was in the apportionment of coverage among the candidates. In the latter, the two major candidates received very even-handed treatment.

In the four newspapers monitored, Brown's name appeared 3,993 times and Flournoy's 3,621 times: Brown had 52 percent of the references; Flournoy had 48 percent of the references.

In television, the total television newscast time monitored was 257 hours 23 minutes. In this, the total allotted to the campaign was six hours. Within this, Brown spoke 57 minutes 44 seconds, 51 percent of direct time; Flournoy spoke 55 minutes 14 seconds, 49 percent of direct time. Radio, far more dependent on what was fed to it and less on what it sought out, had a rather different pattern. With radio, in the fall campaign, Flournoy made the greater effort. On the monitored radio stations, out of 4 hours 21 minutes allocated to the campaign, the apportionment of direct access was: Flournoy spoke 7 minutes 31 seconds, or 61 percent of the direct access; Brown spoke 4 minutes 46 seconds, or 38 percent of the direct access.

But for the primary, reporting differed greatly. The even distribution of attention in the general election was not evident here. The difference could be observed most clearly in newspapers, the only medium whose output was collected all through the primary. News clips showed that among Democrats, Brown received almost one-third of the name menions; among Republicans, Reinecke received twice those of Flournoy. Through the primary, from April 1 through June 3, the four newspapers used the names of the candidates in the ratio shown in the table on bottom of page 187.

The frequency-of-mention paralleled the poll standings of the respective candidates, and it also showed a remarkable similarity to the ultimate election totals for the Democrats.

An interesting aspect of newspaper coverage in the primary is that of 7,881 name-occurrences, Reinecke received 24 percent. Reinecke had a rare news "legitimacy" because of his Watergate embroilment. Similarly, Mayor Alioto got into the news often with "law-and order" problems in San Francisco, and received 15 percent of the name-mentions. Waldie, although able to campaign only on weekends, was often in the news because of his outspoken role on the House Judiciary Committee, then deep in the Nixon impeachment inquiry. He received 5 percent. In other words, 44 percent of the attention went to candidates who were interesting to the media over that two-month period more for their provocative relationship to news outside the campaign than for the campaign itself. Waldie often found the press interested in what he had to say about Washington affairs, but his campaign would land in the last paragraph or the last few seconds of a broadcast, if mentioned at all.

In his struggle to get some media focus during the primary, Flournoy had far worse problems than the Democrats. Long before Reinecke was indicted, the shadow of the ITT financial pledge for the proposed San Diego Republican National Convention of 1972 and Reinecke's role in the arrangements threatened his political life. Flournoy refused to discuss this issue. He decided to campaign with no reference at all to his beleaguered opponent. His tack, instead, was to talk state problems. "It's our belief that Hugh can win if he can get the campaign to involve California talk, not Washington talk." So he tried rapid transit, consumer needs, new housing starts, land-use planning. He failed.

The chief characteristic of the primary was frustration. On each side, news media and candidate, the expectation of what ought to occur was at odds with what did occur. The media expected interest-provoking news; the candidates expected attention. Neither was forthcoming. Both sides were consequently aggrieved.

Looking back after the primary, campaign professionals and party activists, as well as many reporters, could not recall when media interest in political news had been at a lower level. Among reporters there was a constant undercurrent of anxiety, even among *Los Angeles Times* reporters, over whether anybody read their stories. Yet, political reporting two decades ago had been the top news job on a newspaper. By the 1960's though, other specialized reporting became significant—science, education and finance—and political stories lost their former primacy.

The diversion of candidate attention to television contributed to the erosion of interest in politics in the press. Roger Kent, a former Democratic Party state chairman in the postwar period, noted another change. "Media experts have a totally new importance in the campaign," he commented. "Advertising dominates strategy. What happens in the news isn't the key to campaign success anymore." Stuart Spencer, the Flournoy campaign manager who was deeply involved in the successful Reagan gubernatorial campaigns and the other Republican races in the 1960's, said: "It has never been like this year. I've never seen so many outside distractions affect the media and so little coverage of a campaign. . . . Maybe I'm in left field, but the television news format seems to be more show-biz than news. Solid political news seems on the wane."

It has been popular to describe contrivance for television's benefit as a "pseudo-event," and most television news or assignment editors used this term derogatorily in voicing distaste for news conferences.

This was particularly striking during the primary. They were openly scornful of news conferences as "selling" sessions that represented unreasonable demands on the busy news crews. The universal disparagement of these conferences by the broadcast media seemed inappropriate, however, in the absence of an alternative means for a candidate to reach the voters. And it seemed especially inappropriate coming from the television world, which contrives film to appear as on-the-scene footage when it is shot in advance of the event or after it. A large proportion of television coverage of the campaign, including some so-called coverage of debates and speeches, consisted of a quick question and answer about the core of forthcoming remarks before a candidate ever ascended the platform. It ill became the industry to raise the question of who was being "pseudo."

A more advisable term for efforts designed to create visual interest in a campaign, or to endow some public appearance such as a news conference with an air of importance might be "political theater." Dramatization for a political point is useful and can be educational, as it often is in a courtroom or classroom. There are, of course, some valid dramatizations and some that are gimmicks or frauds. But there seemed to be a dangerous denigration of the political process in classifying as inherently false or "pseudo" all efforts to capture the attention of the news media or to so describe news conferences that set forth a candidate's position on the issues. The most successful efforts at "political theater" involved the candidate in contact with everyday citizens in colorful settings, and these occurred mainly in the general election.

In mid-May, with primary election day approaching, Ethan Wagner, Moretti's assistant, noted, "'Up to this point coverage on television has been very, very miniscule. We sometimes feel we have been more successful getting on than others, but that's not the test. The test is getting out there on issues Moretti really knows about. They don't cover that." The special poignancy of the Moretti complaint was that he felt confident in discussing serious state issues. As Speaker of the Legislature's lower house, he had been at the center of action on these problems. The news crew at KABC radio in Los Angeles was the most responsive to Moretti's complaints, but other responses were more representative. KABC news producer Randy Roach said: "Bob Moretti has been criticizing the media for not covering the campaign. Well, that's because this has been a really boring campaign. If it's interesting, we cover it.

If it isn't, we don't." And, he added, as so many others in his position
had: "It is up to the candidates to make themselves interesting and to
do something newsworthy. It is not media's responsibility to go after
them and draw them out." Roach added: "I hate to say it, but we're after
sensationalism. We search for sensationalism."

Manipulation of news conferences was not necessarily all one way, it
should be noted. The candidates could be adroit in using them to hide
something from the media. For instance, during the primary when the
first financial statements were to be filed with the state and made public,
Flournoy's strategists decided to defuse news value in the sizable loan
he had taken from David Packard, the California electronics manufac-
turer who had been Under Secretary of Defense. They would announce
it themselves, first. They chose Fresno, in the middle of California's main
agricultural region, for this disclosure. Plane schedules made it an awk-
ward place to reach. *The Los Angeles Times,* a few other reporters and
local television were present for this news conference, but the major
broadcast audience was blocked. "Say it in Fresno" came to signify a
calculated way to avoid media attention.

If political news conferences were disdained, so were news statements
by people without recognizable status beyond that of candidate. Roth
discovered a conscious distinction as to news value of candidates if
one already held public office and the other did not. In March he issued
a set of proposals for a state tax reform. It was not carried by *The Times,*
the paper he had expected to be most interested. A month later, when
Moretti issued his views on tax reform along similar lines, *The Times*
carried them. Roth made a statement about the state regulations of milk
prices. No news. Moretti came out with an identical set of comments on
milk prices and got a good play in *The Times. The Times'* Richard
Bergholz was assigned to Roth at the time, and the candidate asked him
about the difference in handling the two stories. Obligingly, Bergholz
asked his editors what happened. The reply: "Moretti is Speaker of the
House."

In such a climate, it was understandable that candidates often found
they had to say something two, three or four times to have it picked up
by the media, even when it involved a personal attack. Flournoy's camp
decided to mount a heavy attack on Brown for accepting campaign contributions from multiple committees, especially from an oil company
whose name in the official filing had somehow lost the word "oil," a fact
actually uncovered by workers for one of Brown's rivals, Herb Hafif.
Hafif got very little media recognition from this coup; Brown simply said

that a mistake had been made in identifying this firm, with which his father had connections. Flournoy had little better luck than Hafif, until *The Times* finally picked it up after several tries by Flournoy to lodge a charge of "political hypocrisy" on Brown's part. "It didn't catch on," Drake said in an interview. "We decided to try again. We had another forum, and this time we used a new phrase: Hugh called Brown "a political streaker.' That's when *The Times* did carry it. The tag did it. Because *The Times* used it, it was picked up by others. In a sense *The Times* validates a lot of what goes on in this state journalistically."

Waldie, too, found it necessary to float stories repeatedly before "connecting." He issued a news release disclosing his personal income and his income-tax return very early in the campaign—one of the first members of Congress to do so. In California, however, the story got back-of-the-paper play. On the other hand, Brown later won considerable media flurry over disclosing his finances. Waldie decided "for the heck of it" to float his story a second time, and he issued a new release without reference to the earlier announcement. This time it got very good play all over the state.

Repetition may not have been as necessary in the general election, when the press was alert and more interested—and faced with fewer candidates—but it did occur. For instance, in the general election Brown purposely talked first with *The Times* about his pledge of no new taxes in the first year as governor. On a midsummer flight to Los Angeles accompanied by *Times* reporter Bergholz, Brown casually mentioned this —which at the time seemed to his strategists to be a very important statement. But Bergholz was on a special assignment, trying to get some specifics about what the candidate might do in relation to the state Supreme Court's *Serrano* school-finance decision that mandated equal funding for each pupil in the state. Brown did not want to discuss it. And Bergholz, his attention riveted to the story he was pursuing, ignored the no-tax remark—and possibly didn't hear it.

The Times did try to deal with issues in the primary and draw out the candidates. Even the long, sober smog plans and the transit proposals received column after column of attention. "Position papers" were reported. Mark Murphy, *The Times* metropolitan editor, said later that the paper probably overcovered the primary. "We inundated the reader," he said. "We gave even our best readers more than they could digest." *The Times'* principal fault, he suggested, was failure to "decide what the issues were and force the candidates to face up to them."

Throughout the primary Brown had one principal issue, political reform, that could and did generate news attention. He had identified political reform as his target as early as 1971, and this was fortuitously keyed to the overriding public interest in Watergate. He dwelt on the need to curb lobby expenditures in Sacramento, to open records on campaign spending, and to limit the sums that could be spent in campaigns. He phrased his views pungently. For instance, in his Fresno meeting with Moretti, Brown said: "He's talking about needing more laws. We don't need them. We need to revitalize the executive branch. This is the age of John Mitchell, Dick Nixon, Spiro Agnew. We need political reform. That's why I've laid such heavy emphasis on clean government."

In his KNBC debate at the end of the campaign, Brown said: "State reports show that lobbyists are spending $6,785 a day wining and dining government officials . . . , almost a million dollars a year. I don't think that's right because it's a form of political payola. Why should the representatives get free meals, many of them gourmet feeds, and the rest of the people who pay taxes don't?" Asked if he was charging the Legislature with being corrupted, Brown replied: "The whole Sacramento scene has been corrupted. . . . It's a gravy train they're riding on." And asked what difference there was between such lobby spending and his own campaign contributions, he replied: "The contributions are publicly reported. Those lunches and dinners are going on in secret. . . ."

By and large, few reporters made serious efforts to analyze the various campaign strategies or to examine the campaign in relation to those who managed and financed it. The major papers used a feature-story approach to Brown's campaign crew, drawn by its youth and previous media experience. Columnists commented on Alioto's organizational problems. The most significant story probing into campaign management was in *The Times*. Bergholz disclosed on May 21 Flournoy's meeting in San Francisco with conservative Republicans in January when Flournoy "made his peace with the big money backers of Governor Reagan" and promised, if elected, not to "undo" Reagan's achievements. There was another *Times* story, on May 27, by Kenneth Reich about the political disenchantment of the four "dark-horse" Democrats who had expected the Watergate atmosphere to give them a chance, a story picked up in its entirety by *The Sacramento Bee*. Bill Boyarsky did some extensive interpretive pieces for *The Times*: a 44-inch story about political reform forcing "reality" on the season's television ads, and another running 59 inches about Brown's campaign style—"traditional politics dressed up for the '70's." In the latter he pointed out the media background of the Brown crew and their canny persistence in getting Brown's name projected the four years past, especially on radio.

Other stories lurked in such areas but remained uncovered—stories about campaign objectives, campaign tactics, campaign personnel apart from the candidate himself, stories about pressures shaping the relationships of the candidates to one another. If interest had not been so narrowly confined, some interesting news might have come to light.

One such incident came unexpectedly to the attention of participants in this study five months after the election. Disclosures of this sort are not easily uncovered in the tensions of a campaign, of course, but the example suggests what was available behind the scenes:

It was apparent to the Democratic participants in the primary that Brown's strategy was to diminish news attention. His staff leaders conceded that if Brown had not been leading in the polls, "this primary would have been an exciting race . . . , a tough, hard-fought primary." Not only was Brown's staff able to impose an aura of dullness over their campaign; they also felt that they could extend it by reining in his chief opponents as well. Two of Brown's principal strategists disclosed that they had dug into the private lives and business operations of Moretti and Alioto six months before the campaign and then told them what had been uncovered, with the suggestion that disclosure might come if the race were to veer from a "gentlemanly" course. The discoveries were not criminal, the Brown staffers insisted; they had a lawyer advise them on that. No, they said, the material was just the kind that would interest the public, the kind of news that television would like, material that Brown's aides thought would discredit his rivals, should they invite its revelation by attacking Brown.

Brown's aides disclosed this in the context of making it clear how effectively the Brown crew had controlled the primary. Brown strategists interpreted the media's indifference to the campaign as a result of their efforts. They had manipulated media response in this fashion, they said, and had carefully contrived the "dullness" as a highly successful tactic aided by muting Alioto and Moretti. (Both Alioto and Moretti later denied having had such midcampaign approaches.)

The disclosure of this tactic came in a discussion of the campaign before the staff of this study and its advisory committee, which included participants from the East Coast, a number of university consultants and several people experienced in other campaigns—about 30 people in all, invited in March, 1975, to a conference in San Francisco to review the campaign. Tom Quinn, who had directed the Brown organization, had refused, unlike the other campaign leaders and candidates, to discuss campaign strategy or objectives during the campaign itself. He did attend the March conference, however, and arrived with David Epstein, a campaign associate. The long-delayed revelations about how Brown had won came with many people present, including Roth, Peter Kaye, Flournoy's press secretary; and the Roth and Flournoy media consultants, Ken Sullet and Bud Arnold. Quinn made his remarks knowing that these men heard them. The proceedings were tape-recorded, but Quinn had come with an understanding that his remarks might be used but without attribution. Still, within two weeks of the conference, *The Los Angeles Times* had a story headlined, "Political Blackmail Tactic Denied by Aide to Brown." The story purported to cover the revelations at the conference and carried Quinn's denial of showing the material to Moretti or Alioto. Robert Fairbanks' story related that "Quinn told *The Times* that the Brown organization investigated their [Moretti and Alioto] backgrounds and developed reports on each as is done in most political campaigns. However, he declared there was never any intention to present the material to them and warn them of its possible use."

The Sacramento Bee carried a story the same day, leading with the statement that Brown's campaign had gathered "politically embarrassing dossiers on his major Democratic opponents" to be used "were Brown personally attacked during the 1974 campaign." In *The Bee's* story, by Martin Smith, Quinn was quoted as saying that there was nothing sinister about the collection of files on Brown's rivals. *The Bee's* account continued: " 'The material in the Moretti file,' said Quinn this week, 'appeared only to indicate that there might be problems in the campaign-spending reports which the former Speaker had filed.' But Quinn told *The Bee* he met personally with Moretti and one of Moretti's aides for their explanation of them. Quinn said the explanations were convincing and as a result the Brown forces refused to make a campaign issue of them."

The Sacramento Union talked the next day with Governor Brown about the incident and quoted him as describing his campaign as "one of the cleanest ever conducted." He said, "Both sides met regularly to keep it that way. Both in the primary and the general, we struck pretty much to the issues and I'm proud of it."

In *The Chronicle,* Quinn was quoted as saying that no approach had been made to Alioto about any report on him. Alioto's staff confirmed this. *The Times* story also made this point.

The propriety of such efforts to restrain political contention or limit one's adversaries may be argued, as they have been in the California press. It may also be questioned whether the expansiveness of this boast of control over the political climate within the primary may have outrun the facts, as the denials by Brown, Alioto and Moretti seem to indicate. But two points emerge from this incident that cannot be evaded: First, the media did not probe seriously into the internal workings of campaigns; had they done so, they might have produced some stories of importance to the public. Secondly, these remarks reinforce previously gathered evidence showing a purposeful deflection of the campaign process away from the exposition of issues and ideas. What happened here was a sophisticated manipulation of the news climate that successfully dampened media and public interest for the benefit of one candidate. Such a practice, if unchallenged by vigorous political reporting, would be far more harmful to the democratic system in the long run than squeeze plays against adversaries.

12

THE NOTHING-HAPPENED ELECTION

No amount of computer tabulations, no study of media output can quite convey the fundamental change in the relations between newspaper reporters and candidates that occurred in the general election period. Instead of being reluctant, harassed, too busy and distracted with other news, the press had its political experts dogging every step of the campaign, eager for every word, demanding press releases, taping every chance speech so they could run it and rerun it in search of some new inflection. A reversal of expectations occurred. In the primary the candidates felt rejected. As the general election progressed, it was the news media that became disappointed and thwarted. The press looked for more in the way of lively stories than the candidates produced. Reporters wanted some development, either the disclosure of policies to draw sharp differences between the men, a focus on some key issue, or a marked change in the relationship of the candidates. None of these took place.

The most evident change in coverage was the close day-in, day-out scrutiny the candidates received from a handful of press reporters assigned to follow them, seeking the kind of intimate insights that might reveal clues to their character and potential political leadership. This group provided the stories that gave the campaign a continuity, and it came to have a life through their observations.

Most broadcast editors, on the other hand, were not so interested. Television and radio paid this phase of the campaign more attention than the primary, but broadcast reports were on a very different level from those of the four major newspapers and the wire services.

In the general election, as in the primary, the priorities of the news media had to be recognized. Media standards for news necessitated a great deal of "activity." Media taste for conflict encouraged biting personal "attack." Events had to be staged in settings that made good "visuals" for television; since only KNBC consistently followed the candidates, the candidates had to move from city to city to reach into the separate media-markets. They had to time news announcements for weekdays, not weekends, since local television newscasts run weekdays. They had to set time aside daily to make routine telephone calls to radio stations and make sure that tape excerpts from their speeches—"actualities" —reached the smaller stations. They had to accept the enforced companionship of reporters from the state's major newspapers and subject themselves to daily wrangling over the day's news release or each speech's innuendo. They needed always to be attuned to what might be recognized as news by the media and lob their remarks into that restricted field.

All these requirements, as well as the need for money to buy television ads, underlay the functioning of the campaign process. But within these constraints, and equipped with staff to cope with them, the two candidates could rather effectively shape the news. Flournoy chose the usually slack summer period to issue "position papers," to make a conscientious circuit of the editors of small newspapers throughout the state and to reassure Republicans who had hitherto ignored him. He made 29 speeches before organizations during August, usually the least politically astir period of the year. But the most significant media move Flournoy made was to hire as his new press secretary Peter Kaye, who had experience both in broadcasting and newspapers. Brown used the summer for less visible activity. He met with groups representing opposing views on some of the hottest issues in the state: the right of public employees to strike, the farm workers' demand for elected union representation; public health questions, education, finance. These meetings exposed him to areas of conflict that would have to be solved politically but they did not change his campaign tactics; he did not venture into specific discussion of these problems.

The summer was notable politically for the Watergate-related events in Washington that were leading to President Nixon's resignation. Brown managed to keep himself in the news somewhat with comments on the scandal, while Flournoy steered clear of any reference to the Republican President. With Gerald Ford elevated to the Presidency, Flournoy expected his situation to improve. Then came Ford's early pardoning of Nixon, which pulled the bottom out of Flournoy's improving position in the polls. But Flournoy made an aggressive impact with his summertime talk to the Broadcasters' Association. He followed this in the fall with another, this time to a conference of small-newspaper editors before whom he criticized the wire services for insufficient continuity in their coverage. Peter Kaye said that he noted an immediate response on the part of The Associated Press and an eventual increase in United Press

International's coverage, but the bureau chiefs of both wire services denied that Flournoy's remarks had any effect on their operations.

Labor Day, the traditional opening of the campaign season, jogged all the media—broadcast and print—into a momentary interest in politics. The candidates each held labor meetings in Southern California, Flournoy at a steelworkers' picnic in Cucamonga, where former international president David J. McDonald introduced him, and Brown at a Los Angeles breakfast accompanied by the California Labor Federation's executive secretary, John F. Henning.

Both campaign starts were well covered by television, with several stations venturing as far as a hundred miles that week to pick up live footage, while both candidates traversed all major media markets to provide some colorful local activity. Such attention created a new kind of problem for both camps—helping TV crews get their film out in time for the evening news. Brown's scheduling secretary on Labor Day finally found someone to handcarry film to Los Angeles by commercial plane from a Bay Area picnic Brown had attended. The KNBC crew with Flournoy had to use a small plane to get its film out of a distant mountain town visited by the candidate because it happened to bear his family name. From that date on, each campaign staff had daily problems meshing their events with television's deadlines and film-processing needs.

Three levels of campaign coverage developed. The first contained a core of 26 people, all newspaper or wire-service reporters, who were in virtually continuous attendance in alternating sets of eight or nine at a time, shifting from one candidate to the other every week or so, and in most cases getting a week's vacation. Most were the well known political writers of the state's major newspapers, although a few were covering their first political campaign. This generally constant crew consisted of *The Associated Press:* Bill Stall, capital bureau chief and principal political writer (later Governor Brown's first press secretary); Douglas Willis and Susan Sward of his staff; sometimes Steve Lawrence. *United Press International:* Carl Ingram, capital bureau chief and principal political writer, with his staff members Bob Sweet, George Frank, John Balzar. *The Sacramento Bee:* Richard Rodda, Lee Fremstad, Steve Duscha. *The San Francisco Chronicle:* George Murphy, Michael Harris and, sometimes, Peter Weisser. *The San Diego Union:* Otto Kreisher and Mike Davis. *The San Diego Tribune:* John Kern and George Dissinger. *The Los Angeles Times*: Richard Bergholz, Bill Boyarsky and Kenneth Reich, the first line, followed by Tom Goff, Sacramento bureau chief, and capital bureau staffers Jerry Gillam, William Endicott, Robert Fairbanks and George Skelton.

The second group consisted of reporters diligent in coverage of the candidates when they appeared locally, and who also occasionally traveled with the campaign. This included reporters who were experienced political writers but who represented newspapers unwilling or unable to fund extensive or continuous travel, such as Sydney Kossen or Dennis Opatrny of *The San Francisco Examiner;* Bill Martin or Gayle Montgomery of *The Oakland Tribune;* Harry Farrell of *The San Jose Mercury.* It also included several television reporters who were knowledgeable and interested but assigned only when the candidates were in their area. The more prominent were Warren Olney of KNXT Los Angeles (CBS) or Howard Gingold, KNXT's Sacramento correspondent; Leo McElroy of KABC Los Angeles; John Beatty of KGTV San Diego; and Harold Keen of KFMB-TV San Diego. It also included two radio reporters from KFWB in Los Angeles, Tom Woods and Charles Sergis, who accompanied the candidates frequently in the last 10 days of the campaign, the only radio personnel to travel, although an occasional radio reporter covered in Los Angeles or San Francisco areas.

It is difficult to classify KNBC, which gave far more coverage than those generally in the second level but not as much as those in the first level. KNBC's two reporters on the campaign were Saul Halpert and Heidi Schulman, with Sacramento reporter Vic Biondi doing additional reporting. KGO-TV's Ric Davis and Valerie Coleman, who covered more than most television reporters but not as much as the KNBC team, also fell into a special class.

The third level of coverage represents the one-shot visitors, often representing smaller California publications and stations, but often, too, eminent names in journalism from out of state, representing *The Washington Post, The Wall Street Journal, The Christian Science Monitor, The New York Times, Time, Newsweek, Village Voice, Rolling Stone,* and the national networks. ABC television sent Frank Reynolds with a camera crew to California for about four days, two with each candidate, to film a network report. CBS sent Leslie Stahl who met with both camps and prepared network material. Peter Kaye, discussing the campaign at a meeting of the Sigma Delta Chi journalism fraternity on November 26, 1974, described his impression of what the NBC network had done in preparing a night news report: "They managed to accomplish the whole thing without a reporter. They used Jack Perkins' voice, which I presume was connected to Jack Perkins, but he never saw me.

He never talked to Hugh. As far as I know he never talked to Jerry. I wrote a letter to Dick Wald and said, 'You people have achieved an electronic breakthrough. You have scooped CBS and ABC. You've managed to cover a campaign without a reporter! It's marvelous!' "

There was also a fourth level of coverage—the television or radio interviewers or talk-show hosts and commentators who aired the candidates on scheduled appearances. These interviews could be by people very informed and concerned about politics, as were Bob Abernethy and Jess Marlow on KNBC. There were the editorial writers and editors too, who met the candidates as they made their rounds in pursuit of newspaper attention.

The principal campaign action took place, of course, between the small group of persistent followers and the candidates. The Brown and Flournoy staffs sought to hold this group's interest and meet its logistical needs. Normally, Flournoy's media following was slightly smaller than that of Brown whose name was better known to the Eastern press and whose representatives he excited more as a national figure who also looked like a winner.

A difference in the two campaigns showed up mainly in relation to the smaller fry. When stray freelancers, college newspaper reporters or representatives of inconspicuous radio stations showed up, Brown's office usually refused to let them ride the press bus. As front-runner, Brown could be firm about keeping his media companions to a manageable and significant group. Flournoy, as is customary with the underdog, was likely to be more polite to less consequential news representatives. For instance, Gari Dill, a polished young woman with a weekly talk program on Los Angeles UHF station KVST wanted to interview both candidates for a show on "leadership qualities." Brown's staff firmly declined, but Flournoy welcomed her, and the interview was videotaped as the campaign bus threaded its way through Los Angeles freeways.

The interest symbolized by the presence of various news people was not always correctly interpreted at headquarters. On Labor Day, Brown's chief press secretary, Douglas Faigin, was exulting at the good portents he saw in the bus full of media people at the Pleasanton picnic. "A great start! An absolutely marvelous start!" What made Faigin so cheery? The Sacramento bureau chiefs of both AP and UPI had elected to be with Brown rather than Flournoy. As it happened, however, this came about not out of preference for news about Brown but from personal and professional convenience—illness in the family, a staff shortage. Neither reporter had given any thought to his own presence as signaling a media priority. This kind of interpretation—or misinterpretation—of the comings and goings of people in the small campaign world is part of the speculation that thrives in politics. Everyone is absorbed in drawing conclusions from surface events. When Peter Kaye was absent from Flournoy's entourage for three days at one period, for instance, rumors spread that he had been fired for a remark that had appeared in a *Wall Street Journal* article suggesting "gloom" in the Flournoy ranks. Although unattributed, the remark was assumed to have been made by Kaye. The press was mildly surprised when he showed up again, as peppery and forthright as ever. Later, he acknowledged having been reprimanded for the indiscretion—"deservedly", he said—but his absence had been occasioned by a stint of speech-writing.

With the candidates, the news media's struggle was to find something fresh in the candidate's manner, since the events and even the remarks varied little, and this might come from a chance interview conducted out of hearing of the other reporters or from the unexpected reply generated by an unexpected question. What *The Times* reporters enjoyed—especially Boyarsky—was pulling together out of the personality revelations of the day one cohesive story that established a mood or gave insight into either candidate as a human being. Reich, on the other hand, wanted to press on the issues, and Bergholz was after the "why" more than the "what" of political positions. Murphy of *The Chronicle* enjoyed he succinct, pithy phrase that set a tone, something said by chance that made an intriguing lead or encouraged a bit of arch writing. Otto Kreisher, reined tight by his *San Diego Union* editor to stick with hard facts, was often the most restless at not getting something solid. John Kern of *The San Diego Tribune* had a lot of company in his search for a "pattern " under the superficial activities and the drum-beat of the stock phrases and routine jokes. But the single most astonishing thing about the two-month campaign was that nothing happened in it. At least nothing observable. Clearly something did change because the election results did not follow early poll ratings. Brown dropped, Flournoy rose.

As the campaign progressed, the candidates became better at speaking and at meeting crowds. They perfected their remarks and grew comfortable with them. The campaigns seemed to be one-directional communications—all outward, all part of some preordained plan undeterred by any events of the campaign itself. This was most apparent in the Brown camp, which held tighter control over its operation, but both were far more concerned with projecting their own images than with responding to events or attacks. The campaign, from the close view of it obtained by reporters, was more a personal projection than an encounter session. When Brown visited Redding, for example, he paused at the local television station for an interview before heading for the newspaper office. A broadcast reporter there talked with him a few minutes before the camera was ready, urging upon him some of the data showing that unemployment in the timber trades was far higher than in the state or nation as a whole, and stressing that remarks directed to housing starts, the job climate and tax relief would all be welcomed locally. But when the camera came on, Brown gave his usual "new spirit" talk: about bringing change in government. He didn't refer to the local situation.

Although "nothing happened," some issues did arise that involved the media and the candidates significantly, but without affecting the course of the campaign or the relations between the two candidates. Three issues can be said to have reached major proportions—and they are identified as "banks," "pensions," and "Larry Lawrence."

Brown developed the banks question out of a dispute simmering between Flournoy as controller and legislative Democrats. California law had long asserted state ownership of abandoned or forgotten savings accounts and their accrued interest, which amounted to about $1 million a year. But banks had been collecting fees for processing this transaction. The fees were the center of the controversy. Some legislators considered them far too large. Estimates of their accrued total ranged from $1 million to "tens of millions." The dispute antedated Flournoy's term in office but his modest efforts to curb fees ran into political charges by Democrats that he wasn't reducing them enough. As the fall campaign picked up, two "taxpayers" filed a $100 million suit representing an effort to capture those excessive fees for the state, a case handled by a San Francisco attorney, Gary J. Near, who identified himself to *The Los Angeles Times* October 26 as an attorney for Edmund G. Brown Jr. Although this issue came to sharp focus in the campaign, the tangle of banking regulations and the allegations in the lawsuit enabled Brown to make repeated platform criticisms of Flournoy, suggesting he had deprived the state of "millions of dollars of rightful revenue." It was a strong attack and it kept Flournoy on the defensive, but it never became an effective thrust because it required too much explanation to interest broadcasters. For newspaper reporters familiar with state politics, a bank largess that had been enjoyed long before Flournoy's term as controller hardly constituted a fatal flaw.

The newspapers, especially *The Times,* carried lengthy discussions of the situation. In the monitored press there were 52 references to it, primarily involving Flournoy. Television mentioned it 8 times, radio 6. Radio's reports were remarkable, however, for 2 carried on KFWB. That station's political reporter, Tom Woods, demonstrated that even so complicated a question can be reported clearly and informatively in less than two minutes. Woods noted the existence of lawsuits as early as 1961, made clear the state's long debate over limiting the bank charges and added that current inquiries by Flournoy's office into bank practices concerned "only small organizations." "Since Brown raised the issue," Woods added, "Flournoy says he'll impose a 12 percent maximum."

The second issue, pensions, was significant because it was raised by the media and the candidates entered it reluctantly. Pensions for California legislators, considered among the most handsome, had been subject to press criticism for decades. Each year the lawmakers had to appropriate large sums to compensate for the inadequate contributions they made from their own state pay, but an extra clause was added in 1965 when the "one-man, one-vote" opinion forced redistricting. This cost a number of members their jobs. To ease the blow, an "instant bonus" was provided for men who retired early from redistricted seats, and they could start drawing money immediately, whatever their age. An AP reporter in the Sacramento bureau, Evans Witt, made clear the significance of this provision in its 1974 application by digging out the exact "bonus pension" that would be drawn by those quitting the Legislature that year, several of whom aspired to higher office, including Moretti who, at age 38 would be entitled to draw more than $8,000 a year. Others in their forties would be entitled to $10,000 or $12,000 a year. This quick pension would have totaled a million dollars above the ordinarily generous pension.

The Los Angeles Times, so rich in by-line staff, does not ordinarily run a wire service story on front page, but it accorded Witt's pension article that recognition in July. Witt himself modestly conceded that he was no lone trumpeter; *California Journal* had identified the questionable bonanza in 1971, and other reporters were putting fragments of the pension plum together for public comprehension, UPI having done a series on the subject and *The Sacramento Union* having printed articles displayed with a gold-colored drawing of the Capitol dome spewing out treasure. The press exploded on the subject, once it recognized the number of relatively young men automatically eligible for the bonus. Letters from constituents inundated the lawmakers. Anthony Day, editor of *The Times'* editorial pages, observed that the paper's editorials on the subject were among the strongest that it had ever printed: "Rip-off in the Legislature" (September 6); "A Legislative Raid on the People" (September 19); and "The Public Is Angry" (September 22). As editorials poured out, so did further news stories, *The Chronicle, The Bee, The Union* and most papers of the state joining in.

Before Brown's early September press conference in Los Angeles, the first in the fall drive staged to have Moretti present as witness to party harmony, Quinn had some misgivings lest Moretti's presence trigger the pension question. *Times* reporter Reich said he had not thought of pensions as a campaign issue until on his way to this press meeting. Pondering Moretti's future, however, he got in some punishing, persistent questions on the subject to both Brown and Moretti. Brown conceded that he did not approve of the pension bonus in principle but wouldn't want to deprive Moretti of his good luck. Anyway, he added, the law was on the books. Thereafter the issue kept floating at the edges of the campaign. Flournoy had been in the legislature in 1965 and had voted for the bonus then, and, while not a beneficiary, he had Republican friends who were. Flournoy was reluctant to get into the question. But interest grew. Finally Flournoy proposed a "special session" to revoke the pension, but he muffed the dramatics that any media-minded politician would have managed over such a step. First, he couldn't reach Reagan in advance, and Reagan was openly belittling any "revoke-the-pension" try. Then a Republican legislator, Assemblyman Robert McLennan, who had earlier opposed the bonus, beat Flournoy to the headlines with a forceful demand that the Governor intervene and call a "revoke" session. When the Governor finally issued his call, the Democratic legislative leadership countered the move by reassembling on their own initiative. The pension was revoked, but Flournoy failed to make capital of it or to shame Brown for his do-nothing position.

The pensions issue was an exceptionally clear-cut example of the difference in political reporting between the broadcasters and the written press. It never would have surfaced without newspaper initiative and follow-through. There were, all in all, 68 stories tying pensions to the campaign in the four newspapers monitored, in addition to "mentions." Yet, the subject drew almost no attention from the broadcast media. Television carried 6 references, 5 of them "bare mentions." Radio carried 2 "bare mentions."

"Larry Lawrence," the third issue, was of interest for illustrating a style of candidate-media interaction not often used in this campaign— the leak. Brown's press aide, Llew Werner, and campaign assistant David Epstein drew Reich and Kreisher aside to pass on a confidential tip. The

Brown aides had a fistfull of legal documents referring to 1961 litigation between the state and owners of the Del Coronado Hotel in San Diego, concerning a shoreline boundary dispute, and they suggested that the reporters might like to investigate the issue. "Remember," Kreisher recalled Werner saying, "we're making no charges, we are just presenting you with these documents."

The question of just where hotel ownership reached in the tidelands was provoked initially when the Del Coronado's owner wanted to build some extensions and challenged the state's claim to a stretch of the shoreline. In 1961, a jury found in the hotelman's favor. There were further differences that culminated in 1966 in a three-way agreement among the City of San Diego, the state and the hotel. The question was revived in 1971, however, and ultimately came before the state Lands Commission, of which Flournoy was a member as Controller. Questioned then as to what move to make, the state attorney general recommended against reviving the question, although one member of the commission's staff had urged taking the matter to court. This latter recommendation was among the documents shown to Reich and Kreisher. The two reporters immediately understood the implication that the Brown camp felt might be drawn: that there must be some link between Flournoy and the present owner of the Del Coronado, Larry Lawrence.

A wealthy, self-confident, prickly Democrat, Larry Lawrence had backed Moretti in the primary, did not like Jerry Brown and let that fact be known. Flournoy's campaign manager, Stu Spencer, telephoned Lawrence to invite him to meet Flournoy. Lawrence accepted, and Spencer and Flournoy flew to San Diego, where they signed up Lawrence as chairman of "Democrats for Flournoy." Some immensely effective television and radio spots resulted for Flournoy's benefit. "The ability to govern isn't inherited," said one ad. "Flournoy has judgment and maturity . . . . We can't afford Jerry Brown's inexperience and immaturity," stated another. Brown acknowledged to the press at one point that those ads infuriated him. The documents slipped to the two reporters constituted retaliation. It was a rather unusual type of media-candidate interaction; the candidate responded with a news leak.

Documents in hand, the reporters went off to investigate. Lawrence, of course, got phone calls. He was outraged. He claimed that relatives were being pumped for background about his activities, even people who knew him 25 years before in Chicago. He called this a "plumber style" inquiry, alluding to the discredited White House probes. He was so angry that he telephoned The San Diego Union's publisher, seeking to get the reaction into print. As it happened, the Brown camp's tip had come on a Friday and Kreisher, his investigation not complete, left town with his editor's permission on weekend reserve military duty. He returned Sunday night, October 22, to find on Page One of his paper, a story by reporter Ruby Sexton containing all of Lawrence's allegations including the "plumber squad" quote, with no background on the litigation and no comments from either campaign staff.

Once the story was printed in *The Union,* however, Flournoy picked it up as a charge against Brown for hounding Lawrence. The tidelands boundary issue was finished and fixed in law, he said, before Lawrence ever bought the hotel. State attorneys were satisfied the case should not be reopened. Nor had Flournoy ever dealt with Lawrence about it. Kreisher wrote a backgrounder for Tuesday's paper, and *The Times* ran very much the same thing after a longer inquiry. The incident never persuaded any reporter to question—either personally or in print—Flournoy's integrity over the link with Lawrence, but it provided Brown with the opportunity to make frequent unfriendly allusions to Lawrence and Flournoy. (Lawrence got so much publicity out of it that local television used news about him—with a reference to his role in supporting Flournoy —when he had an emergency appendectomy during the campaign.)

The localism of this dispute intrigued that city's two television stations. On September 23 KFMB carried a 3 minute 12 second news item —the longest of the campaign—outlining the contretemps and carrying several Flournoy quotes on it, including the candidate's explicit: "I was not on the state Lands Commission when the decision with regard to that boundary was made." On the Larry Lawrence issue, the monitored television stations carried 20 references. No other state issue drew so much television attention. For television, it had the advantage of sharp personal antagonism that could be expressed in angry quotes, without going into background detail.

But if some Brown maneuvers aimed at using the media misfired, so did some of Flournoy's. One of the most amusing concerned a publicity stunt that went mildly awry. In September, Los Angeles was afflicted with a transit strike whose chief victims were those dependent on public transportation—the poor and the elderly. Flournoy headquarters got a call one day from an ad hoc agency calling itself Transit Victims seeking drivers to help people who had grave transportation needs. After checking out the legitimacy of the request, Flournoy's staff decided to offer a campaign bus for medical visits and hit upon holding a press conference at the bus's initial trip so that Flournoy could talk about the transit strike and transportation needs. Drake called local television. KNBC was interested and had a crew on hand next day when the Flournoy bus picked up some women designated by Transit Victims, drove them to a medical clinic and there had the planned press conference. It drew considerable attendance: Radio News West, Channel 13, KFWB, *The Los Angeles Herald-Examiner*, *The San Diego Union*, *The Wall Street Journal* and *The Washington Star*, as well as *The Times*. That done, Flournoy drove off to a campaign lunch.

KNBC reporter Warren Wilson was just shooting some concluding footage when a couple of nurses came running out to claim the whole thing was a fake: The women brought to the clinic had not seen a doctor. Intrigued, Wilson tracked Flournoy down at the political luncheon and got on film a reply that he had entered into the transportation stand-by plan in good faith and would continue to offer his bus, if genuine need arose. (The bus was actually used for over ten days.) Wilson used the entire episode in his film, from Flournoy's initial statement to the nurses' outrage and Flournoy's reply, and was happy because the station used nearly four minutes of it at six o'clock and again on the 11:00 p.m. show. But Drake, who had dispatched the Flournoy bus for what he thought were genuine patients, protested: "I go around talking to television news directors and they say, 'We want to see him doing something, we don't want head shots.' They almost say, 'Give us a carnival.' Then when we do a number for them, they come down on us for staging it."

Despite such episodes, there was no evolution in the campaign. At one point Kern said that his tapes on either man "sound exactly like the ones I got on Labor Day. They are saying precisely the same thing." On election eve, Quinn confided to Dick Bergholz of *The Times* that, "just to see if anyone would notice," the Brown team had prepared for the last day a press release couched in terms almost identical with the opening release issued on Labor Day. Nobody noticed.

What was the media reporting? Through the use of the computer, it was possible to build a composite from all media "mentions," compressing every point touched upon in the news stories into a single, simple chart. This disclosed exactly what most frequently drew the attention of reporters. What was most arresting about the composite was the strong impact of "attack" as a story topic. All media accorded "attack" stories 10 percent of their total points mentioned, more than any other category among campaign activities.

Given the year, it seemed remarkable that so much attention was paid to "party." In California for 50 years, party has been of relatively minor importance; politics has been largely personal, built around an individual's capacity to draw voters across party lines. And after Watergate, party declined nationally in voter esteem, study after study showed. Yet, surprisingly, in this contest, "party" was the fifth most emphasized factor in the election. This thrust of party references into political reporting reflected the strategy of both candidates. Each had a special reason for making repeated appeals to his party. Flournoy aimed to muster the disillusioned and disheartened Republicans, without whom he could not win. Brown, who had never figured in his party affairs, was bent on assuring the Democrats he was genuinely committed to the party's base.

As the campaign went on, close coverage of the two men was reduced to *The Times, The Bee, The San Diego Union, The San Diego Tribune,* and occasionally *The Chronicle.* The wire services, although not present every day, settled in more permanently than any group other than *The Times,* and covered consistently through October to November. The press crew with Brown became irritated as time went on because the candidate was not always as accessible as in the opening week. He had taken to traveling often in a separate car, making a scheduled appearance and vanishing. There was never any question where Flournoy was. His openness and his staff's obliging style kept the media informed.

On October 20, *Time* appeared with Brown's face on its cover—alone. The story virtually assumed his victory. California reporters were unanimous in their indignation at what seemed to them journalistic intervention in the political system. How much effect this publication had, with its newsstand display, was hotly argued by news reporters. Brown confined himself to remarking, "Obviously *Time* feels something interesting is happening in California. . . ." There were many other magazine articles exclusively on Brown, including pieces in *Esquire, San Francisco* and *Los Angeles Magazine,* but perhaps the most provocative aspect of the *Time* article was the radio plug the magazine used all that week with a voice far more rhapsodic than any political ad dared use, exalting "a young idealist out of the West emerging into prominence in politics." It sounded like a Brown ad until the tag line. Flournoy did not let his disappointment show, but he added a quip to his standard speech about the big exclusive *Newsweek* was going to have November 5.

In their association with each other, the candidates and the reporters who tagged after them often seemed to be functioning on different levels, aiming at such totally different goals that they were not in effective communication. This was most evident with Brown. The press understood Flournoy's political constraints that dictated general statements to placate ultraconservative, monied Republicans to keep money flowing into his campaign. Even under that pressure, however, Flournoy got out more precise details about state questions than did Brown. Steve Duscha of *The Bee* wrote on October 20 about Brown's joking with reporters about the value of "positive vagueness," and Duscha added: "'Although said in jest, the phrase reveals a lot about the tone of Brown's campaign."

Arriving at Sacramento late one night near the end of the campaign, Brown loitered in a motel lobby with the reporters, chatting. To allay the criticism that they did not have enough opportunity to talk with him, he would at times purposely create an opportunity for mingling. The dimly lit, drape-hung artificiality of the motel lounge was the nearest to hearth the group had shared in the past two months. Kreisher asked, "You know what you are, Jerry? A 'tabula rasa.' We don't know what's going to be written on you. We don't know what's been erased. We don't know anything specific about a Brown administration." Brown answered as he often did, in a torrent of words, very earnestly, his heavy dark brows drawn together, his lean face serious, his voice rising and thinning a little. He said a candidate for office can't know what he is going to do until he gets into office and studies the problems with the information then at his command. He said the circumstances shift. He said the present economy was uncertain and made planning difficult. He said over and over that he thought he made plain the kind of administration he wanted. Then he said, "Do you know whose phrase that is, 'tabula rasa?' It's Hume. David Hume." And he admonished the reporters, "You ought to read him. He's interesting." Then lightly, in a good-night summary before he walked out to the car, he said, "I'm getting through. The voters are getting to know my personality, my philosophy." One of the reporters remarked, "Brown has a lot of that academic flotsam and jetsam floating around in his mind and he uses esoteric quotations as conversation fillers." He added, "It isn't an easy mind for the other people to link up with."

One particular evening produced the sharpest illustration that candidate and press reporters moved on different planes. Brown clearly felt he was being frank and forthcoming about his candidacy; the traveling press felt he was more "on camera" than "on the record." This evening followed a taxing day. For about 15 hours the press bus had tagged the candidate's auto for repeated stops, parking-lot meetings, student gatherings, two noisy Democratic dinner-rallies in different towns, and over and over the same "new spirit" speech. By 11:30 P.M. the entourage stopped at a drab motel in the small city of Marysville. Llew Werner had asked some local Democrats to have cheese and crackers ready, and he brought out the liquor. The "press room" was a utility room under the motel stairs, makeshift tables along two sides, a bare plank on saw-horses in the center, and ten temporarily installed telephones. Bill Boy-arsky of *The Los Angeles Times* had been talking on the bus about what he called the surprising vehemence of Brown's attack on Flournoy in the candidates' most recent debate. As the reporters drifted into the improvised press room, Boyarsky picked up the theme. "Jerry seemed more personal in his cracks. Maybe this is a new turn in the campaign. There is a growing climate of animosity between those two." Someone speculated that maybe this was the one real thing happening in the cam-paign: The candidates were getting damned mad at each other. Brown strolled in with Werner, opened a beer and sat down across from *The Chronicle's* Murphy. He had heard the comments about his sharp at-tacks representing "a turn in the campaign." Someone pressed him on whether this was a shift? "No," he answered. "The campaign is over. Nothing is going to change. Flournoy is trapped by circumstances. Both of us are riding circumstances. There is a certain amount of preordina-tion in all this. Things outside our own control. Fate."

Abruptly, Murphy of *The Chronicle* became solemn. "Jerry," he be-gan, "there are 21 million people in this state. Not voters, people. What you do will affect them. . . ." Brown shot back: "You can't quantify people. You can't talk about them in terms of 21 million. Each person is an individual. . . ." John Kern interrupted: "The question I get asked most frequently—you may think it odd, but it really is: 'Are your side-burns naturally gray?'" Brown brushed this aside: "I never heard of anybody deliberately making his hair gray." Murphy was still digging in. "Twenty one million people in California. And a billion dollar budget. . . ." Brown corrected him: "Ten billion. . . ." "Okay, So it's big, see. . . ." Murphy was tired, as was everyone. Another quip was on the candidate's lips, but Werner, straddling a chair nearby, restrained his boss: "No, no . . , he means it. He's serious."

"I've got four kids," Murphy began. "There are big problems in this state. Real problems. People are going hungry. They are jobless. What are you going to *do* for them, Jerry?" Brown matched Murphy's air of sincerity. "Listen to my speeches," he said. "I'm telling what I'll do. I'll bring divergent ideas together. I'll bring in different people who can work together. I'll find new approaches to those problems." Murphy began to tick off the names of particularly contentious legislators: "Can you work with him . . .? And with him . . .?" "I think so," said Brown.

"We can communicate. . . ."Murphy pressed on: "It's a big job, Jerry. It's a frightening responsibility. What are you going to *do?*"

Very low, almost to himself, as though he were standing apart from the scene and in a monologue, Brown began talking about his youth. "I'm not one of the pampered rich," he said. "My father didn't give me any endowment. He didn't even give me a car when I was in the university and that made me pretty sore at the time. I didn't move in select social circles. I had to toe the line. When I was a kid if you walked on Mrs. So-and-So's lawn going home from school, she called the school and you heard about it the next day. If you swiped somebody's ball, you heard about it. I learned from that experience. I believe in responsibility. We were taught to be responsible for our own actions. That's what I want to get across. . . ."

Somebody asked, *"Can* you? Can you make today's Americans be responsible? That's not exactly the prevailing attitude. . . ." Brown replied, "That's what I want to do," then paused before continuing. "How do you bring them all together, blacks, whites, South of Market, Potrero Hill, Marina [divergent San Francisco neighborhoods] into one way of thinking so they can solve common problems? I'm trying to do that."

Someone mentioned the Burton brothers, the two liberal congressmen from San Francisco who have spoken traditionally for the very poor. "They live too close to the edge," Brown said. "They speak for a small number, a slice of the community, not the consensus. I'm seeking that middle area. I want to address all, in terms they all can understand and support. . . ." He spread his hands wide over the table. "They have this map of the United States, and every Census time they figure out the place somewhere in the Middle West that is the exact center of the population, and they run stories about that town, that point which represents the middle of population distribution, you know? Well, I want to *be* that place, in my person. I want to express what Middle America thinks, by finding what they can agree on."

This may well have been Brown's most explicit revelation of the campaign. He was dealing in the specifics he deemed important: His words reached to the core of his own attitudes. Someone asked: "Don't you believe in movement forward, in change, in pushing ahead of the masses to lead?" "Yes," he said, "but first there's got to be some consensus. That's what the country needs most. A common ground. . . ."

They had all been listening, hushed, completely attentive. But Murphy wouldn't give up. "I still want to know: What are you going to *do?*"

13

CONCLUSIONS

Has television so trivialized politics that it represents just one more seasonal spectator sport, and the selection of our leaders is not nearly so important a public issue as the selection of announcers to join Howard Cosell on Monday Night Football?

The turnout at the polls, confirmed by public opinion sampling, shows that the prevailing attitude toward politics in America today is apathy. Broken faith on the part of politicians is one of the causes, but television —the medium through which most Americans get their news—must assume a major share of the responsibility for this indifference.

By the immediacy of its presentation and by its immense reach to the public, television has a great potential to make self-government more effective. Yet the first and most far-reaching conclusion from this study of the 1974 California governor's campaign is:

1. *Television served to erode rather than support the democratic process, and it distorted the political campaign.*

 Television intruded its own program priorities, its entertainment standards, its cult of excitement, its economic pressures and its merchandising formulae upon the election process. The result was apparent in the quantity and in the quality of the political communication between candidate and voter, both in news and in advertising.

The distortion and the disservice to the democratic process came about through: (a) forcing campaign news to conform to standards considered appropriate to the camera; (b) management attitudes which disparaged politicians; (c) entertainment goals rather than informational goals; (d) news selection scaled to popular interest out of "rating" rivalry; (e) imposing on political advertising the same formula in message duration and in cost that serves commercial merchandising.

News reports in broadcast were so limited that over the final two months on six major television stations, reports on this important election represented only 2.3 percent of television's news time and 2.1 percent of radio's. If the KNBC share in that coverage were subtracted, since it represented a third of the total and was the only effort in California

broadcast media to report the race as a continuing event, then the remaining five television stations gave only 1.5 percent of their total news
time, and much of that in superficial reports running one minute or less.

Nothing more forcefully disclosed the absence of journalistic concern
than the cheerful acquiescence by all broadcasters in the agreement that
fixed extremely narrow limits on coverage that would be permitted of the
six debates between the two main contenders. This restriction drew no
protest from any source, citizen or media. Not only did the stations accept the restriction against reproducing the debates, they failed even to
report to their viewers as news what was said on most of them and, apart
from KNBC and KGTV, made no consistent effort to sum up these exchanges even in "normal" news reports of up to 2½ minutes.

Another harmful aspect to television's standards: The competing elements in a political campaign, whether economic, social, individual or
organizational, do not lend themselves to facile screen exposition in 30
to 90 seconds. They are not easily explained under any circumstances
and only with consummate skill can they be depicted. Major public
questions need time and need talk. But with a news-selection standard
that is basically visual, not intellectual, action-oriented and entertain-
ment-focused, not informational, what television reports in its newscasts
is frequently unimportant. This superficiality has been emphasized by
the deliberate withdrawal of political specialists from television newsrooms. Television executives thus fulfill their expectations that "politics is
dull" by rendering it dull through the unimaginative triviality of their
medium's reporting.

⇒ Equally perverse is the intrusion of the television industry's own economic objectives. Commercial television programming is dependent on
advertising. The station's primary goal thus becomes building ever-larger
audiences to enhance its program ratings so that advertising yield in-
creases. This puts a premium on news with maximum audience interest
and photographic excitement to be found in violence, natural disasters,
human interest stories, weather, and sports. With popularity the measure of news value, political news sifts to the bottom of the scale.

⁃ In advertising, television also imposes its own framework, suitable for
its own economic advantage, over the access candidates could buy. This
mode of communication is highly prized by candidates because it is the
only television appearance they can control. But the industry effectively
forces political advertising to conform to the same time span found
suitable for commercial advertising—the 30-second spot. Although the
law compels stations to sell time to candidates at their lowest commercial

rate, that rate is still so high that 30 seconds before a prime-time Los Angeles audience cost as much as $3,200 in 1974.

The conclusion considered next in importance:

*2. *Television dominated the candidate's entire campaign effort.*

The purpose of the campaign became that of attracting media, rather than communicating with voters. So desirable is the access to television's immense prime-time audience that television's preference in news shaped the campaign conduct and necessarily affected all news the candidate developed. Pursuit of television became the central campaign focus. This was expressed in two ways:

(a) The effort to lure television cameras for news coverage ("free media") was the chief purpose behind the staff selection, behind campaign strategy, behind the scheduling of events even to the choice of weekdays rather than weekends for campaigning; it lay behind the constant travel and dictated the content of speeches and remarks to reporters; it influenced the very phraseology of the campaign.

(b) All other campaign effort went to raising money in order to purchase television advertising ("paid media").

3. *Opinion polls were pivotal to a candidate's access to the media.*

Poll standing has a close relationship to a candidate's ability to raise campaign funds, and therefore to the advertising he can buy; but his place in the polls also affects his news coverage. News attention occupies a key position in the domino-system springing from the impact public-opinion polls have on a campaign, and all media tended to adopt poll standings as a measure of candidate importance. Coverage was tailored to poll status. This meant the candidate with an early lead in opinion polls tended to get that lead reinforced by the news attention he drew. The candidate lagging in the polls got scant news coverage, and this inattention made it even more difficult for him to raise money for advertising.

The curious link in the cycle was the press. Newspaper stories became evidence to potential contributors of a candidate's significance. But a candidate's news value depended upon his poll standing, which depended upon his television spots, which depended upon his fund-raising, which depended upon his getting into the newspapers . . . and *that* depended on his poll standing. When there was upward mobility, the cycle worked advantageously. Once the candidate fell in the polls, the whole communication system he depended on to reach voters began to disintegrate.

4. *Television advertising represented the single largest cost factor in political campaigning; it was access to the public through licensed air-*

waves considered to belong to the public that made political campaigning so expensive.

Half of the total campaign cost in the governor's race was the price of advertising, virtually all of it the buying of television time. Overall, primary and general, $3,467,797 was spent on media advertising, only a fragment of it for newspaper ads.

Certain conditions magnified the importance of television advertising, and the most significant was the inadequacy of broadcast news coverage. Candidates who had expected newscasts to help alert the public to their presence and message and provide access to the voters discovered in the primary that they were virtually barred from television, and in the general election, coverage was so small it could hardly be described as access to the electorate except on KNBC and to some degree on KGO-TV. Advertising access became critical. Money-raising, always a burden to a candidate and sometimes demeaning, became the absorbing preoccupation in order to buy television time.

5. *There was a dramatic difference between press and broadcast agencies in the commitment to conveying campaign information.*

The largest newspapers in California made significant financial commitments to campaign coverage in an attempt to provide readers with adequate data about the candidates on which to form their decision.

Broadcast abandoned political specialists, provided no observable extra time for politics, did no advance planning for coverage of the campaign (apart from KNBC and to a lesser extent KGO-TV), and undertook (with those two exceptions) little or no travel and no extra expense for coverage. They did, however, pour money, time, planning, staff effort, and fundings into election-night reports, when the campaign was over. Radio made the least commitment of any medium, reporting on it mainly through wire-service news or from communications the candidates would volunteer to them through phone calls or through forums taped when the candidates came to the studios. Radio reporters (with the exception of KFWB) made the least effort to go out to the campaign and did the least analyzing or interpreting.

6. *A marked interrelationship existed between the three communication channels—radio, television and the press—the most significant being broadcast's dependence on the press.*

The media comprise far more of an interrelated system than the public recognizes. Newspapers are prized by broadcast newsmen for the depth and detail of their reports, especially in political news. Broadcast news staffs recognized that newspapers were superior sources for political information and almost unanimously said that voters could not learn enough through television or radio to make wise judgments on how to vote, but needed the insight newspapers provided.

In another direction, however, it was observable that the press was beginning to "cover" political appearances on television as news. Newspaper political writers were beginning to appraise the candidate's strength in part by his television advertising, by his effectiveness on television, and by his ability to "make" news by what he said on television.

7. *Quite apart from such interdependence, newspaper political reports were heavily influenced by television.* This was revealed by:

(a) The growing press concern with candidate personality and "image," and what was acknowledged to be increasing news attention to a candidate's lifestyle and domestic values.

(b) A surprisingly close parallel in story emphasis across the three media. The extraordinary amount of press attention to the visual aspects of the campaign was the result of television's dominance over the campaign and its determination of priorities.

(c) Most significantly newspaper editors' strong concern about response to the intrusion of broadcast into the news field. Television, by the rapid increase of its news programming, has thrust the newspaper world into a re-examination of it own reporting capabilities, suggesting far more emphasis on interpretive and investigative reporting and less concern for immediacy. No similar sensitivity over how to improve performance was expressed in broadcast.

8. *A "media" campaign diminished involvement of the public in the election process and deflected leadership selection and policy formulation away from voter participation.* This was shown in three ways:

(a) Organized volunteer activity, whether by party or by grassroots district effort, seemed wasteful of time and money when arrayed against the larger impact possible by purchase of television ads. The number of people involved in a volunteer rallying of local support across a huge state becomes inconsequential in comparison with television's audience. The campaign exhibited a virtual abandonment of volunteer participation among Democrats except as they were needed for television crowd scenes, and very little organized get-out-the-vote effort. Republicans attempted more organization but for them television advertising also took precedence.

(b) The variety of appeals to bloc interests such as labor, women, teachers, etc., all lost importance in contrast to the opportunity for one, single communication to all voters as television viewers. As a result, clarification of positions important to these individual groups diminished. and the response of these interest groups to the candidate became less important. Endorsements either by organizations or by individual leaders withered in significance and declined in number. Even editorial support by newspapers became less critical than it had been in the past; and *The Los Angeles Times,* once the most influential Republican voice in the state, in 1974 terminated its editorial endorsements in major races. Alternate types of advertising appeal such as newspaper ads, bumper strips, buttons, and billboards were virtually eliminated.

It would appear that the campaign which becomes purposely media-oriented abandons the intricate pattern of group consensus and association-interests formerly involved in the dynamic process of candidate comparison. Instead, the campaign is directed toward the voter as an individual alone with his television set, and it reaches him primarily through 30-second interruptions in prime-time programs, when he is most bent on recreation and on seeking an escape from life's burdens.

(c) Television mandates such simplification of the candidate's message that it gets reduced to a kind of shorthand replete with personal image and vague as to program specifics. The thrust of political campaigning thus becomes personality rather than substance. Accountability is lost since commitment to program is blurred. Broadcast cannot be blamed for the politician's notorious tendency to generalize in order maximize appeal to all segments of voters. But the brevity television imposed on political communication enouraged this trait.

A campaign style based on personality leaves the citizen out of decision-making. Specifics about policy, about priorities in handling problems, about the hard decisions on spending, all get removed from the campaign's verbiage. The two candidates tended, by their style of communication, to support the contention often heard among broadcast newsmen (but never among press reporters) that today's governmental problems are too complex for the electorate. When candidates avoid discussion of governmental problems facing the prospective winner, the voter cannot share in making decisions about the future.

9. *Broadcast stations were so affected by the federal requirements for "equal opportunity" that they applied precise measurements to the allocation of time for candidates even in exempt newscasts.*

Despite the specific exemption from "equal time" for bona fide news reports, news interviews, news documentaries and on-the-scene coverage, it was discovered that broadcast stations kept careful logs of the total seconds accorded rival candidates on newscasts and balanced their coverage to minimize protests from the public or from the FCC, even though they would be within the law in exercising news judgment. When a large number of candidates was involved, as in the primary, stations largely elected to avoid "'equal time" problems by failing to cover the campaign, except for one or two stories related to such news as poll publications. This compressed all candidates but the top three or four into an equality of *no* opportunity.

10. *The responsibilities Congress imposed on broadcast concerning political campaigns were based on assumptions about news interest in politics that current conditions in the industry have invalidated.*

Congress explicitly exempted bona fide news to insure freedom in its production, but this was based on an expectation that political campaigns would constitute attractive, lively, inviting news for television and would get generous or at least adequate coverage. The "fairness" doctrine assumed that political debate and controversy would make its way into television so naturally that the government's chief concern must be to assure a chance for all sides to be aired. What appears omitted in the law's careful balance of equities is some response to outright news disinterest such as was experienced in California. So audacious a limitation of the public's opportunity to see and hear campaign debate certainly was not foreseen, nor was the industry's acquiescence.

Although individual aggrieved candidates and proponents of some viewpoint barred from the air can lodge protests with the FCC, no mechanism exists by which the vitality of the campaign itself can be insured.

Without a complete turnabout by broadcasters, that vitality can only be attained by so bold an innovation as "free time" for candidates — some formula devised by Congress for frequent, brief, unpaid access to television for candidates at all levels that will permit this communication medium to support, rather than erode, the democratic process. "Free time" raises problems. It needs to be patterned thoughtfully. Only the emergence of concerned citizen groups, dedicated to revitalizing the process of leadership-selection in this country can rescue the election system from the current demeaning formula of 30-second shots of packaged politicians.

Appendix 1

ACKNOWLEDGMENTS

The study on which this book is based was sponsored by the California Center for Research and Education in Government, a nonprofit agency that seven years ago pioneered in publishing *The California Journal,* a monthly analysis of state government and politics that has spurred similar ventures in New York and Illinois. The center also sponsors academic intern studies and issues such government-related publications as an almanac of California's government, a roster of public officials, an annual for students, and booklets on ballot measures. The project was funded by grants from the John and Mary Markle Foundation and The Ford Foundation.

The project staff consisted chiefly of journalists experienced in political reporting. The project director, Mary Ellen Leary, has been a political reporter in California since 1944, mostly with the Scripps-Howard newspaper, *The San Francisco News,* on which she was political editor and associate editor. She was a Nieman Fellow at Harvard University and has been a freelance writer for journals of opinion and public affairs in this country and in Britain. The project associate director was Ann W. Johnson, who had done research work with the Speaker of the California Assembly and with ACTION in Washington, D.C. Three key members serving as catalysts, overseers and editors through the project were the three principals in the California Center: Thomas R. Hoeber, president and publisher of *The California Journal,* with previous experience in legislative research and administration and in teaching government at Sacramento State University; Ed Salzman, since 1973 editor of *The California Journal,* with 20 years of prior experience as news reporter in print and radio, half that time as Capitol bureau chief for *The Oakland Tribune;* and Bruce Keppel, managing editor of *The California Journal,* with extensive prior newspaper reporting experience in Milwaukee, Minneapolis and at *The Sacramento Bee.*

Staff members who participated in the project on a continuous, though part-time basis: In Los Angeles: Kathleen Neumeyer, former United Press International reporter; the late John Shinn, former McGraw-Hill bureau chief; and George Mostroianni, professor of journalism, Fullerton State University. In San Francisco: Barbara Erickson, freelance journalist; James Benet, education editor for Newsroom on San Francisco public television KQED; and Patricia Moran of *The California State Bar Journal*. In San Diego: James Buckalew, professor of journalism, San Diego State University. In Sacramento: Vonnie J. Madigan, journalism graduate, Fresno State University; and Julie Thompson. Others who undertook briefer assignments on the staff: Joe Konte, San Francisco newspaper reporter; and William Slater, Stanford University.

Four university professors in political science and in communication fields gave the study direction, technical guidance, encouragement and continuing assistance: William L. Rivers, Department of Communications, and Richard Brody, Institute of Political Studies, Stanford University; Edwin Bayley, dean, School of Journalism, and Eugene C. Lee, director, Institute of Governmental Studies, University of California, Berkeley. A helpful consultant in the television field was Andrew Stern, senior lecturer, U. C. School of Journalism. A consultant in computer analysis who worked over a long period with the project, under Dr. Brody's guidance developing data from the media output, was Louise Comfort, political science professor, San Jose State University. Others whose occasional advice was generously given: David W. Jones Jr., teacher and lecturer in communications, Stanford University; Rollin Post, political reporter, public television station KQED; Walter Gieber, professor of journalism, San Francisco State College; Dr. Peter Sperlich, U. C. Berkeley Political Science Department; Richard Reinhart, U. C. School of Journalism; Dr. Merrill Shanks, director, Research Survey Center, U. C. Berkeley; and Stephen Barnett, professor of law in the communications field, U. C. Berkeley.

Sage counsel, encouragement and guidance were received also from Robert Goldmann of The Ford Foundation and Forrest Chisman of the Markle Foundation.

In addition, the foundations supporting this study drew together an Advisory Committee on Media and the Political Process that consulted with the staff on two occasions: Richard Reeves, former political writer on *The New York Times* and a contributing editor to *New York Magazine;* George Will, national syndicated columnist; Stephen Hess, Brookings Institution; Richard Neustadt, Harvard University government professor; and James David Barber, Duke University.

We hope that the study will quicken interest in improvement of the election process and will encourage the media to more vigorous and substantial political reporting.

Appendix 2

METHODOLOGY

An election hinges on communication between voter and candidate. The middleman is the media. What occurs at the nexus is critical to the conduct of self-government in this country.

To identify what does take place at this point was the purpose of the study that underlay this book. The 1974 election was not a random choice. The contest for governor seemed likely to be predictive of trends developing in other urbanized states.

The contest that put Jerry Brown into office as Governor of California was particularly attuned to the media, and admirably suited to the study. It was not necessary, nor would it have been feasible, to devote detailed attention to all 29 candidates for governor and to the state's 500 newspapers, 350 radio and 50 television stations. Based on the expertise of *The California Journal* staff and in consultation with political scientists and media scholars, a limited number of candidates, newspapers, and television and radio stations was selected for detailed study.

Eight candidates, six Democrats and two Republicans, were chosen. They were the eight for whom the "California Poll" identified a measurable public awareness, and in the June primary they were to receive 93.9 percent of the two-party vote and 93.5 percent of the total vote for governor.

The research method combined the normal approach of fact-gathering, comparison, analysis, and evaluation with the journalists' techniques of first-hand observation and interview. The number of staff sharing in the project observation made possible corroboration or challenge of various findings in the study process. It was particularly helpful that there were opportunities for periodic interviews with the same subjects. The quotations selected for this report are, unless otherwise noted, representative of a large number of others.

Information was gathered in part by observation of the campaign by the project staff, by traveling with the candidates and reporters; in part by extensive interviewing of candidates and campaign staff and editors and reporters—more than 20 media editors and executives; 64 reporters,

179

21 from the print media, 16 from radio, and 27 from television. Within campaigns, 48 persons were interviewed, some six times.

All candidates were interviewed often; their headquarters and campaign operations observed; speeches, publicity, public appearances followed; their staff management, press aides and advertising directors all were interviewed while the campaign was in progress.

Candidates have been sufficiently identified in the text. Media identification for 1974 is more fully stated below.

The print media:

The Sacramento Bee, family-owned evening newspaper dominant in the capital, published by McClatchy Newspapers, Inc.; Eleanor McClatchy, publisher; C. K. McClatchy, editor; circulation, 166,000.

The San Francisco Chronicle, family-owned morning newspaper; Charles DeYoung Thieriot, president - publisher; circulation, 470,000.

The Los Angeles Times, family-owned morning newspaper published by the Times-Mirror Company; Otis Chandler, publisher; William F. Thomas, editor; circulation, 905,000.

The San Diego Union, morning newspaper owned by the Copley family, Copley Press Inc.; Mrs. James S. Copley, publisher; Lt. Gen. Victor Krulak (Marine Corps, ret.), president; circulation, 175,000.

In addition, the two statewide wire services, The Associated Press and United Press International, and in the Los Angeles area, City News Service, and its subsidiary Radio News West, were observed and their staffs interviewed.

Six television stations were selected:

Los Angeles: KNBC-TV, Channel 4, NBC-owned and operated. Newscast monitored: 5:00-7:00 P.M. weekdays; rating at time of study 10.6 leading other early news programs in its area and reaching 403,000 households and over 500,000 adults. The market area included Los Angeles County, Orange County, and parts of Santa Barbara, Ventura, Kern, San Bernardino, Riverside, and San Diego counties.

KTLA, Channel 5, independent, with a small news operation. Newscast monitored: 10:00-11:00 P.M. with a considerable audience.

San Francisco: KGO-TV, Channel 7, ABC-owned and operated. Two newscast periods were selected, both strong in the market area, the late-night program dominating the region in audience and considered one of the strongest in relation to market area in the country: 5:00-7:00 P.M. and 11:00-11:30 P.M.

San Diego: The two stations chosen divide most of the audience in that market area almost evenly.

KGTV, Channel 10, NBC affiliate, 6:00-7:00 P.M.

KMFB-TV, Channel 8, CBS affiliate, 5:30-6:30 P.M. News rating in 1974 of 13 (ARB) reaching 69,000 homes, 103,000 adults.

Sacramento: KCRA-TV, Channel 3, NBC affiliate; 6:30-7:30 P.M. newscasts.

Five radio stations were selected:

Los Angeles: KFWB, Westinghouse affiliate, all-news station. Newscasts monitored: 7:30-8:30 A.M. and 5:30-6:30 P.M.

KABC, ABC network station, primarily talk-show format and phone interviews. Small news staff, heavily dependent on wire services. Newscasts monitored: 9:00-10:00 A.M. and 11:00-12:00 P.M.

San Francisco:KCBS, CBS network, all-news station. Newscasts monitored: 7:30-8:30 A.M. and 5:30-6:30 P.M.

KSAN, independent progressive-rock station, with five-minute newscasts at four intervals: two 15-minute news programs at 12:00 noon and 5:45 P.M. Newscasts monitored: 5:45-6:00 P.M.

There was a pronounced difference in the hospitality with which the study was greeted by newspapers and the arms-length caution and, in some cases, suspicion the electronic media initially showed. One television station first selected as a study subject, KNXT, a CBS-owned-and-operated station in Los Angeles, refused to cooperate. The Los Angeles focus was therefore shifted to KNBC. Television executives and news personnel were somewhat wary but became cooperative as they came to understand the study. Radio executives and editors were generally open and responsive but operated under such time pressure it was difficult for them to turn contemplative about their roles. The press, however, was in all cases enthusiastic, interested, open and responsive. Of course, newspapers risked little from research intrusion, while broadcast had licenses at stake.

All the television and radio stations were monitored the last ten weekdays of the primary (May 21 to June 3) and every weekday from September 2 until the election on November 5. In sum, the project monitored over 600 hours of broadcast news (more than half of it television), from which news on the campaign was extracted for analysis.

These elements were included in the approach:

1. Analysis of the structure of campaign organizations in operation; analysis of media structure, news control, news selection, reporter assignment and area of initiative in the press, radio and television.

2. Identification of what the media and candidate discerned to be

their respective performance missions; what assisted and what hindered in accomplishing them; how successfully either segment felt it achieved its objectives and how well others considered they had done;

3. The definition of responsibility the various media felt toward the voter and toward the political process and the degree and kind of responsibility the candidates expected the media to fulfill;

4. Analysis of the several areas of conflict in goals between candidates and the media.

The one research area where method did not follow well-established lines was in the effort to create a computerized system for analysis of news content more revealing about media techniques and media commitment to political coverage than in conventional content studies. For instance, an effort was made to identify through internal evidence whether a camera staff was sent to cover the event reported or whether a newspaper reporter was on the scene. The content analysis was far more detailed in its classification of story content and emphasis. Having available a total of 1,467 newspaper stories, 204 television stories, and 180 radio stories, a code was developed (with small variation for each medium in those areas pertinent to its function) that was extremely ambitious in its detail and that made it possible to go beyond headlines and leads to tally the frequency with which certain factors in the campaign experience were mentioned by reporters in the body of all the stories. The aim was to identify what drew reporter interest and what received primary focus in the news accounts. For this purpose, a total of 8,143 references were identified and tabulated, in three general groupings, and subsequently subjected to computer analysis.

The information collected has by no means been exhausted in the data developed for this book.

TELEVISION BROADCASTING TIMES, GENERAL ELECTION
September to November 1974

Television Station News Program	Total Time Monitored	Total News Time (ads subtracted)	Gubernatorial Time	% Gubernatorial Time to Total News Time
KCRA-TV, Channel 3 Sacramento 6:30 - 7:30 PM	42 Hrs.	32 Hrs. 9 Mins. 56 Secs.	35 Mins. 27 Secs.	1.8
KGO-TV, Channel 7 San Francisco 5 - 7 PM	72 Hrs. 28 Mins.	63 Hrs. 41 Mins. 43 Secs.	1 Hr. 47 Mins. 33 Secs.	2.8
KGO-TV, Channel 7 San Francisco 11 - 11:30 PM	22 Hrs.	17 Hrs. 23 Mins. 30 Secs.	6 Mins. 7 Secs.	0.6
KGTV, Channel 10 San Diego 6 - 7 PM	43 Hrs.	31 Hrs. 36 Mins. 57 Secs.	39 Mins. 11 Secs.	2.1
KFMB-TV, Channel 8 San Diego 5:30 - 6:30 PM	44 Hrs. 30 Mins.	34 Hrs. 6 Mins. 29 Secs.	25 Mins. 26 Secs.	1.2
KTLA, Channel 5 Los Angeles 10 - 11 PM	35 Hrs. 7 Mins.	27 Hrs. 26 Mins. 7 Secs.	20 Mins. 35 Secs.	1.3
KNBC, Channel 4 Los Angeles 5 - 7 PM	66 Hrs.	50 Hrs. 58 Mins. 35 Secs.	121 Mins. 6 Secs.	4.0
TOTALS	331 Hrs. 5 Mins.	257 Hrs. 23 Mins.	6 Hrs.	2.3

RADIO BROADCASTING TIMES, GENERAL ELECTION
September to November 1974

Radio	Total Time Monitored	Total News Time	Gubernatorial Time	% Gubernatorial Time to Total News Time
KABC Los Angeles 9 - 10 AM	41 Hrs. 55 Mins.	30 Hrs. 59 Mins. 38 Secs.	1 Hr. 35 Secs.	3.3%
KABC Los Angeles 11 - 12 M	41 Hrs.	31 Hrs. 49 Mins. 8 Secs.	1 Hr. 30 Secs.	4.3%
KFWB Los Angeles 7:30 - 8:30 AM	46 Hrs.	34 Hrs. 4 Mins. 6 Secs.	 36 Mins. 4 Secs.	1.8%
KFWB Los Angeles 5:30 - 6:30 PM	43 Hrs. 55 Mins.	33 Hrs. 14 Mins. 59 Secs.	 34 Mins.	1.7%
KCBS San Francisco 7:30 - 8:30 AM	43 Hrs. 55 Mins.	31 Hrs. 11 Mins. 31 Secs.	 14 Mins. 35 Secs.	.8%
KCBS San Francisco 5:30 - 6:30 PM	36 Hrs.	23 Hrs. 8 Mins. 20 Secs.	 17 Mins. 8 Secs.	1.2%
KSAN San Francisco 5:45 - 6 PM	10 Hrs. 12 Mins. 30 Secs.	10 Hrs. 7 Mins. 9 Secs.	 11 Mins. 27 Secs.	1.9%
KRAK Sacramento 7:55 - 8:00 AM	3 Hrs. 45 Mins.	3 Hrs. 3 Mins. 29 Secs.	 1 Min. 57 Secs.	1.1%
KRAK Sacramento 11:55 - 12:05 PM	7 Hrs. 30 Mins.	5 Hrs. 44 Mins. 53 Secs.	 4 Mins. 20 Secs.	1.3%
KRAK Sacramento 5:55 - 6:00 PM	3 Hrs. 40 Mins.	2 Hrs. 55 Mins. 55 Secs.	 5 Secs.	.05%
TOTALS	227 Hrs. 52 Mins. 30 Secs.	206 Hrs. 19 Mins. 8 Secs.	4 Hrs. 21 Mins. 30 Secs.	2.1%
GRAND TOTALS Radio and Television	608 Hrs. 57 Mins.	463 Hrs. 42 Mins.	10 Hrs. 26 Mins.	2.2%

CALIFORNIA POLL 1973 - 1974

	August 1973	Feb. 1974	Apr. 10	May 1	May 27
Edmund G. Brown Jr.	42%	46%	29%	36%	34%
Bob Moretti	9%	14%	16%	18%	14%
Joseph Alioto	22%	20%	15%	16%	16%
Jerome Waldie	6%	5%	5%	5%	7%
Wm. Matson Roth	1%	1%	3%	6%	6%
Herb Hafif	—	2%	1%	3%	2%

1974 PRIMARY: DEMOCRATS

	Field Polls 2/74	5/74	Newspaper Headline Totals	Head %	Newspaper Name Totals	Name %	Vote Totals	Vote %
Brown	46%	34%	99	31%	1465	32%	1,085,752	39%
Alioto	20%	16%	82	26%	1138	25%	544,007	19%
Moretti	14%	14%	79	25%	1016	22%	478,469	17%
Roth	1%	6%	34	11%	489	11%	293,686	11%
Waldie	5%	7%	24	7%	362	8%	227,489	8%
Ward	0%	3%	—	—	—	—	79,745	3%
Hafif	2%	2%	—	—	157	3.4%	77,505	3%

LIFESTYLE (total mentions)

	Press	Television	Radio
Brown:	45 (8%) (with 10 stories half or fully devoted to this.)	13 (8%) (No story fully devoted to it; 1 gave half the story.)	3 (2%) (No story half or fully devoted to it.)
Flournoy:	20 (4%) (No story fully devoted to it; 2 were half.)	17 (8%) (No story half or fully on it.)	7 (4%) (One story totally devoted to it.)

(Percent relates to the number of stories within each medium.)

BROWN: POSITIVE IMAGE
(Times mentioned and percentages of stories carrying mention)

Image Factor	Press		Television		Radio	
New Spirit	87	(16%)	32	(16%)	17	(10%)
Demo. Identification	51	(9%)	23	(11%)	11	(6%)
Pledge to Unify Demos.	15	(3%)	7	(3%)	4	(2%)
Tough on Crime	21	(4%)	10	(5%)	2	(1%)
Fiscal Moderate	24	(4%)	16	(8%)	5	(3%)
Lifestyle	45	(8%)	13	(6%)	3	(2%)
Simpler Life Advocate	23	(4%)	19	(9%)	5	(3%)
Other	22	(4%)	14	(7%)	6	(3%)

BROWN: NEGATIVE IMAGE

Image Factor	Press		Television		Radio	
Publicity Seeker	48	(9%)	14	(7%)	10	(6%)
Lacks Credibility	112	(21%)	45	(22%)	21	(12%)
Arrogant/Shrill	29	(5%)	6	(3%)	7	(4%)
Inaccessible	24	(4%)	10	(5%)	7	(4%)
Inexperienced/Youthful	44	(8%)	13	(6%)	8	(4%)
Big Spender	25	(5%)	15	(7%)	10	(9%)
In his Father's Shadow	32	(6%)	20	(10%)	12	(7%)
Incompetent	25	(5%)	13	(6%)	6	(3%)
Other	25	(5%)	11	(5%)	4	(2%)

FLOURNOY: POSITIVE IMAGE
(Times mentioned and percentages of stories carrying mention)

Image Factor	Press		Television		Radio	
Experienced	40	(7%)	23	(11%)	14	(8%)
Academically Qualified	23	(4%)	11	(5%)	4	(2%)
Politically Independent	47	(9%)	25	(12%)	9	(5%)
Political Moderate	32	(5%)	14	(7%)	2	(1%)
Credible	23	(4%)	8	(4%)	2	(1%)
Mature/Reliable	34	(6%)	9	(4%)	9	(5%)
Likeable/Accessible	20	(4%)	7	(3%)	4	(2%)
Lowkey/calm	28	(5%)	16	(8%)	4	(2%)
Lifestyle	20	(4%)	17	(8%)	7	(4%)
Other	7	(1%)	9	(4%)	2	(1%)

FLOURNOY: NEGATIVE IMAGE

Image Factor	Press		Television		Radio	
Inactive	41	(8%)	22	(11%)	13	(7%)
Dull/professorial	14	(3%)	2	(1%)	2	(1%)
Recycled Reaganism	60	(11%)	25	(12%)	12	(7%)
Dependent on Conservatives	15	(3%)	4	(2%)	1	(.1%)
Allied to Old GOP	50	(9%)	20	(10%)	16	(9%)
Tool of Special Interests	23	(4%)	9	(4%)	6	(3%)
Incompetent	25	(5%)	4	(2%)	3	(2%)
Other	8	(1%)	9	(4%)	3	(2%)

IMAGE MENTIONS (% of total)

Press	*Positive*		*Negative*	
Brown	288	(44%)	364	(56%)
Flournoy	274	(54%)	236	(45%)
Television				
Brown	134	(48%)	147	(52%)
Flournoy	139	(59%)	98	(41%)
Radio				
Brown	53	(38%)	85	(62%)
Flournoy	57	(50.4%)	56	(49.6%)

COVERAGE OF FIVE ISSUES

ISSUE	PRESS		TELEVISION		RADIO	
	Brown	*Flournoy*	*Brown*	*Flournoy*	*Brown*	*Flournoy*
Fiscal Policy	84 (16%)	86 (16%)	22 (11%)	27 (13%)	11 (6%)	16 (9%)
Inflation	73 (14%)	73 (14%)	28 (14%)	25 (12%)	9 (5%)	16 (9%)
Candidate's Record	61 (11%)	94 (18%)	26 (13%)	47 (23%)	14 (8%)	23 (13%)
Political Reform	57 (11%)	34 (6%)	30 (15%)	19 (9%)	18 (10%)	9 (5%)
Education	49 (9%)	43 (8%)	19 (9%)	18 (9%)	10 (6%)	9 (5%)

(% = % of each medium's stories)

FOUR-NEWSPAPER COVERAGE: PRIMARY 1974

Democrats	*Name-Mentions*	*% of total*	*Republicans*	*Name-Mentions*	*% of total*
Brown	1,552	31%	Flournoy	986	35%
Alioto	1,214	24%	Reinecke	1,870	65%
Moretti	1,058	21%	Total	2,856	100%
Roth	487	10%			
Waldie	381	7%			
Hafif	157	3%			
Other	176	4%			
Total	5,025	100%			

INDEX